NELSON'S RIGHT HAND MAN

THE LIFE AND TIMES OF
VICE ADMIRAL SIR THOMAS FREMANTLE

E.J. HOUNSLOW

The History Press

First published 2016

The History Press
The Mill, Brimscombe Port
Stroud, Gloucestershire, GL5 2QG
www.thehistorypress.co.uk

British Library Cataloguing in Publication Data.
A catalogue record for this book is available from the British Library.

ISBN 978 0 7509 6504 0

Typesetting and origination by The History Press
Printed and bound in Malta by Melita Press

CONTENTS

FOREWORD

By Lord Cottesloe, Great-Great-Great-Grandson of Admiral Sir Thomas Fremantle

It is my privilege to write a few words for Mr Hounslow's book regarding my forebear.

He was one of that 'splendid band of brothers' of Nelson's captains who lived when Britannia ruled the waves and the British Empire was at its height and arguably a force for order. He was present at Santa Cruz, Copenhagen and Trafalgar.

There were four Fremantle admirals with the Knight Grand Cross (GCB) of the Most Honourable Order of the Bath in four generations, the last one being Sidney Fremantle, who was Vice Chief of Naval Staff during the First World War and commander-in-chief at Portsmouth during the post-war years. So he had positions of power and influence at a time when the British Empire was at its most powerful and the world was arguably a better place for it.

Admiral Sir Thomas Fremantle did not only start our family's tradition of naval service but, in buying The Old House in Swanbourne, he unwittingly started our family's relationship with this beautiful Buckinghamshire village that has lasted some 220 years through to the present day. Later, his son Charles, the second of the four Fremantle admirals, was to carry the family name to Australia when he commanded the first British naval expedition to Western Australia that resulted in the Australian city of Fremantle.

ACKNOWLEDGEMENTS

The production of this book was made possible by a number of people, all of whom have contributed in various ways. I owe them all a debt of thanks.

Firstly, the team at The History Press; they have been incredibly kind and helpful and have contributed their professional expertise to ensure a high standard to the final product. Equally important has been the contribution made by Tina Gossage, whose meticulous checking and corrections ensured my manuscript reached the publishers in a legible state. Her patience and enthusiasm were invaluable.

Fundamental to the whole project was the kindness and co-operation of Lord Cottesloe, who graciously gave his blessing to this work, and also his daughter, Mrs Duncan Smith, who helped both with the illustrations used in the book and with permissions to quote from the family records. Cdr Charles Fremantle's expertise on the history of the Fremantle family has been vital and, together with Caroline's kind hospitality, have made this task so much easier and more pleasant than might have been the case.

Professor Elaine Chalus's advice and her insights into the eighteenth-century mind have helped me enormously and I am greatly indebted to her for the time she has spent helping me.

Many of the illustrations have been provided by Mr Andrew Tibbets, who is the great-great-great-grandson of Admiral Sir Andrew Green. I feel privileged to have seen the mementoes left by his ancestor, who was such a close friend of Admiral Thomas Fremantle.

Thanks are also due to Will Atkins for the maps, and while I am conscious that many others, not specifically named above, have also helped me, hopefully they will accept my assurances that I am extremely grateful.

1

INTRODUCTION

By the end of the eighteenth century Britain had one of the most dominant fighting forces the world had seen since the eclipse of the Roman legions. The Royal Navy ruled supreme over the world's oceans, exerting control, protecting the empire's trade and demonstrating Britain's power such that this small maritime nation was able to build, and retain, one of the world's largest empires. The Royal Navy possessed no 'secret weapon', nor any significant technological advantage unknown to other navies. What it relied upon was the quality of the crews and officers manning the ships. Their offensive spirit gave them self-confidence and a belief that, man for man, they could out-sail and out-fight any opposition.

Other nations might covet the size of the markets and the riches the British derived from their empire, but until they could defeat them at sea, there appeared to be little possibility of changing the status quo. The Royal Navy had such influence on Britain's defensive strategy that even 100 years later, the then First Lord of the Admiralty, Jacky Fisher, was able to boast, 'The Empire floats on the Royal Navy.'[1] At the beginning of the nineteenth century, however, a challenge was to emerge. Napoleon Bonaparte had gathered his fearsome Armée de l'Angleterre along the northern coast of France. Numerically superior to anything Britain could muster and already master of the vast majority of Continental Europe, Napoleon boasted, 'Let us be masters of the Channel for six hours and we are masters of the world.'[2] He would have undoubtedly needed more than six hours but it was no idle boast. He had already divided and beaten the land-based coalitions that British subsidies had cobbled together and were he to gain control of the Channel, albeit for a limited period and if the weather was suitable, the vast armadas of invasion barges stored in Boulogne and along the northern coast of France could have transported the troops, artillery and supplies such that a successful occupation of the British Isles appeared a serious threat.

Britain's main credible defence against invasion was sea power, not just to police the Channel but to actively blockade the enemy fleets in their home ports, to attack French interests throughout the Mediterranean and the Caribbean and, where possible, to intercept and prevent trading vessels reaching France and assisting their war effort. That they were able to carry out these tasks successfully was mainly due to the skill and efforts of men such as Thomas Francis Fremantle. The experienced, battle-hardened officers commanding the Royal Navy vessels and fleets were at the peak of their profession and at the apex of this group was Nelson's 'band of brothers'. They were a small number of tough, aggressive sea captains who were both his professional colleagues of choice and, in many cases, his close, personal friends. Among this latter group was Fremantle.

A mark of the confidence that ran through the Royal Navy was contained in a letter that Admiral John Jervis, 1st Earl of St Vincent, wrote to the Board of the Admiralty in 1801 stating, 'I do not say they [the French] cannot come, I only say they cannot come by sea.'[3] How the British navy achieved and then exercised this dominance is intertwined closely with the story of Fremantle for, from the age of 11 until his untimely death at the age of 54, the Royal Navy was central to his life. It was not to be the whole story, for Fremantle was also a family man and his life was influenced strongly by his wife, Elizabeth Wynne, usually known as Betsey. The Royal Navy was instrumental in bringing them together but her strength of character and her ability to build a home for the family in rural Buckinghamshire provided another narrative thread running through this story. It is also through her inveterate diary-keeping that we are able to get a glimpse of her husband, the private man behind the uniform.

How was Britain able to ensure that naval standards remained so high? The eighteenth and nineteenth centuries were hardly known as periods when merit automatically met with career advancement. Rather, it was an age of vested interest, family networks and, in many cases, blatant nepotism. This, after all, was the age when army commissions were often bought and sold like any other commercial product, and promotions during peacetime frequently went to those rich enough to purchase them. Although the Royal Navy had no comparable system, the chances of naval officers making their way in the service without mentors in positions of influence were remarkably slim. Fremantle was not immune from this system and he needed to operate within the complex rules and norms that governed advancement in the navy, both in public life and in society generally. Indeed, this was not just an eighteenth-century phenomenon. In the early part of the twentieth century Fremantle's grandson, Sir Edmund Fremantle, a distinguished and very senior admiral, wrote:[4]

A distinguished naval officer, has I think said that success in the navy is one third interest and two-thirds luck. This is a paradoxical view which I entirely deny. There is interest, of course, and thirty or forty years ago there was much more, and there always must be some. Luck also comes in, and there is some wisdom in speaking of the 'bark which carried Caesar and his fortunes;' but I should be inclined to put at least half down to pure merit, which is certain to be recognised in the Navy.

To judge Fremantle's progress through the naval hierarchy by twenty-first-century mores is therefore irrelevant. The concepts of open competition and equal opportunities were simply non-existent. The parts played by such figures as Admiral Sir Hyde Parker, Admiral Lord Nelson, the Marquess of Buckingham and, indeed, Fremantle's own younger brother, Sir William Fremantle, are essential to the understanding of this remarkable man's life. It was not simply a case of preference or privilege smoothing an inevitable path to advancement, for both the mentor and the pupil had something to gain from the relationship. No senior officer would lavish patronage on someone who they felt would be unworthy of their attentions; the relationship was seen as a two-way street, beneficial to both the donor and the recipient.

In short, the more successful an officer, the more patronage he could expect to receive, and the possibility of serious riches through the system of prize money added further fuel to this system. Flag officers could expect to receive a share of the value for every ship and cargo captured in their area of command, which was 'condemned' by the High Court of the Admiralty. Therefore, a strong financial incentive existed for admirals to push for young, aggressive frigate captains to be included within their command. It was the roving, fast sailing frigates that were most likely to snap up vessels with valuable cargos and it was the smaller ships that were usually commanded by the most junior captains. It was rumoured that Sir Hyde Parker made some £200,000 from prize money while in command of the lucrative West Indies fleet.[5] Despite its obvious imperfections, somehow the system generally succeeded in ensuring the best did reach the most important positions of command.

Fremantle and his naval colleagues were lucky. They were joining a navy that had already been significantly reformed during the years immediately preceding their careers. For this they had Admiral Sir George Anson to thank. He had joined the Royal Navy as a boy volunteer in February 1712, aged 15. He was from a distinguished family. George's father was William Anson of Shugborough Hall in Staffordshire and his mother was Isabella Carrier, who was the sister-in-law of Thomas Parker, 1st Earl of Macclesfield, the Lord Chancellor. This relationship was to prove very useful to the future admiral, who was destined to be one of Britain's greatest admirals, immortalised for his circumnavigation of the globe between 1740 and 1744. On his return to England, the prizes he had taken made certain that the rest of his life was to be one of considerable wealth.

What distinguished Anson's subsequent career was not that he was a gifted naval officer, which he most certainly was, but that he adjusted to and manipulated the political aspects of his career so successfully, a talent given to few sailors. On his return to the UK he became an MP. At this stage of his career the Royal Navy was at the nadir of its fortunes with aged admirals who in battle displayed indecision, sclerotic thinking and, in some cases, blatant cowardice.

Anson was to prove an honourable exception to this malaise. In May 1747, he commanded the fleet that defeated the French Admiral de la Jonquière at the First Battle of Cape Finisterre, capturing four ships of the line, two frigates and seven merchantmen. This victory, together with his heroic circumnavigation that had brought so much treasure back to the exchequer, made Anson a national hero. His fame, coupled to his excellent political contacts, meant he became the man the navy and the government looked to to turn its fortunes around.

He was promoted to rear and then vice admiral and elevated to the peerage as Lord Anson, Baron of Soberton, in the County of Southampton. However, it was in June 1751 when he was appointed to the Admiralty that his career as a naval administrator took off and he introduced a series of reforms that were to change the navy forever, placing it in a position where it would dominate the world's oceans. He ensured the navy was equipped with both the ships and structures from which Lord Nelson and the other captains such as Fremantle would benefit. His tenure at the Admiralty was to continue until his death in June 1762, just three years before the birth of Fremantle.

As First Lord of the Admiralty, Anson served throughout the Seven Years War and, along with Pitt the Elder (Lord Chatham) as Secretary of State for War, he was able to provide an efficient naval service, enabling the simultaneous protection of the Channel, attacks on France's Atlantic coast, blockading of the main French seaports and support for the army's efforts in recapturing Québec and the Canadian provinces. It was the ultimate proof of Anson's reforms and the Royal Navy did not let him down.

His reforms were varied and touched most aspects of naval life. They included the transfer of the marines from army to navy authority and proper uniforms for commissioned officers. With the creation of the temporary rank of commodore, he at last gave admirals a chance to promote young, effective, forceful post-captains above their time-serving older and more senior colleagues. He reputedly stated that in his opinion 'a person entrusted with command may and ought to exceed his orders and dispense with the common rules of proceeding when extraordinary occasions require'.[6]

He ensured that those officers who were too old, or incompetent, retired on half-pay and placed revised Articles of War before Parliament that tightened discipline throughout the navy. Two of his most important reforms were instigating the systems that allowed both close and open blockades of enemy ports and overseeing reforms of the shipbuilding programme to ensure that far more third-rate seventy-four-gun two-deckers were built. These were ships that were eventually to prove invaluable in the wars with France.

Thanks to his supply-side reforms, Britain was able to keep ships on station, blockading French and Spanish ports for months on end without unacceptable losses to scurvy and illness. He appointed businessmen to the Victualling Board and ensured that fresh produce got regularly to ships on patrol, lessening the illnesses that had inevitably occurred on ships stocked only with salted goods.

Thus, Fremantle was joining a military force that had been improved out of all recognition. It was a navy made more professional with a greater war readiness and backed by a vast industry on shore. More importantly, it had captured both the imagination and the love of the British public to a degree the army never had. Despite these reforms, Fremantle would also require one other important ingredient: opportunity. A naval officer's career in the Georgian age needed this as much as talent and courage, for without opportunity even the most promising of careers could be stillborn. Only wars could provide a plentiful source of opportunities for promotion. In war, new ships would be commissioned and only in times of war would early deaths and injuries among senior officers result in increased opportunities for young, ambitious naval officers. Indeed, the traditional toast of the navy was 'A Bloody War or a Sickly Season' (and a quick promotion!). When Fremantle joined the navy in 1777 there was undoubtedly a relatively elderly 'blockage' of senior officers holding up promotion for younger men. Sixteen years later, in 1793, the two key commanders-in-chief of the Mediterranean and the Channel were Hood and Howe, 69 and 67 respectively. However, just a few short years later in 1798 the average age of Royal Navy post-captains and above had fallen by an average of ten years.[7]

During peacetime the Royal Navy relied on a system whereby ships were laid up in estuaries and anchorages around Britain known as 'in ordinary'. Ships in such a condition would receive minimum maintenance, be stripped of rigging, supplies and such like, and be left in a condition whereby, should war threaten, they could easily be brought back into a seaworthy, fighting condition with the least possible expense and delay. The system suited the exchequer but for young officers, especially those with little influence in Admiralty circles, peace was the death knell to career prospects.

There had been a few, albeit short, periods of peace in the years preceding Fremantle's birth but, as already stated, the Seven Years War (1756–63) had involved most European powers, in particular Britain, France, Prussia and Austria, and had served in building up both the quantity and quality of British warships.

For the main two protagonists, France and Britain, it had been a lengthy and expensive slogging match primarily fought over who should control the colonies of America. The conflict had raised the British national debt by a staggering 80 per cent. Now the Treasury was keen that the colonies, which had been the subject of the conflict, should contribute their share to the national finances. So, in 1765, the Whig administration of George Grenville introduced the infamous Stamp Act. The Grenville family was to have a lasting impact on the fate of Fremantle. Both George Grenville and his second son, who subsequently became the 1st Marquess of Buckingham, became great friends and mentors to the Fremantle family. It was ironic that a Grenville administration lit the first match leading to the American War of Independence and unwittingly providing young Fremantle with his first experience of war.

The Stamp Act required the American colonies to pay taxes on all paper used for legal documents, newspapers, etc. The revenue was collected in British currency, not in colonial paper money, and proved to be extremely unpopular. Of course, any new tax is likely to be unpopular but the Stamp Act proved to be extraordinarily so and united the people of the east coast states of America, making it impossible to collect the monies due. Although the following Whig administration of Lord Rockingham repealed the act rapidly, the damage had already been done. The nascent states of America had experienced the heady feeling of power and inexorably the path to revolution and independence was opening up. It would not be long before the Royal Navy would be needed again. By the time Fremantle was almost 10 years old, and just two years before the youngster went to sea for the first time, Britain was at war again. The war was being waged some 3,000 miles from Britain and the Royal Navy would play a key role.

Ships began to be taken out of 'ordinary' and new ships lain down in the shipyards dotted around the south coast of Britain. It would not be long before France and Spain would ally themselves with the rebellious states of America, seeing the ideal opportunity to both embarrass and possibly seize British colonies in the West Indies and, for Spain, the chance to take back Gibraltar. From the outbreak of the American Wars in 1775 until Napoleon's abdication in 1815, no British government had any real option other than to keep a strong navy.

Fremantle's forty-two-year career was to coincide with Britain's greatest period of need for naval power, as the following table shows. Only in 1817, two years before his death, was there a significant downturn in Royal Navy ship numbers. His career coincided with, and was made possible by, this growth and constant need for a strong navy.

ROYAL NAVY SHIPS 1797–1817

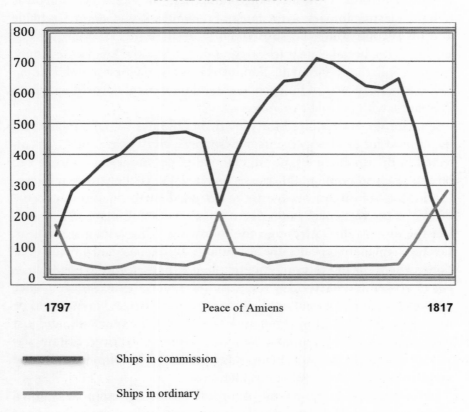

Ships in commission

Ships in ordinary

2

EARLY DAYS, 1765–1787

The Fremantle family's origins are not clear but the most likely origin is that the founders of this remarkable dynasty came over with William the Conqueror. There is a village named Fromantel in Normandy some 35 miles south of Caen, and another named St Jean-Frommantel between Orleans and Le Mans, either of which could have been the origin of the family name. Hampshire county records from the thirteenth century show several references to 'de Fremantle' with differing spellings of the last name.[1] This would indicate French origins and there are several place names in and around Southampton and Bournemouth that possibly indicate the Fremantles had come over as part of the Norman invasion force and acquired land during the immediate aftermath of William's successful takeover of the English throne.

A further clue to the family's origins is supplied by John Fremantle, father of Thomas, who applied for a Grant of Arms in 1761. He received back from Garter and Clarenceux King at Arms a grant that confirmed him as 'John Fremantle of St Paul's, Covent Garden, son of John Fremantle, late of the City of London and grandson of John Fremantle of the County of Hampshire descended from the ancient Fremantles of Fremantle Park and hath always borne a Coat of Arms and Crest as from his ancestors of whom honourable mention is made in sundry books in print and manuscript'.[2]

The very fact that John Fremantle had gone to the trouble of making such an application indicates here was a man determined to better himself and to assert his place in society.

By the seventeenth century the Fremantle family were well established in and around Southampton. In 1660 one of the family moved to Northamptonshire in order to take up the post of land agent for Lord Crewe. He had considerable estates in and around the small Northamptonshire village of Brackley centred on Steane Park, a magnificent country residence, approximately 1 mile north of Brackley. John Fremantle moved to Moreton Pinkney, a small village a further 6 miles north of Steane Park, where he and his wife Bridget Howes had four children between 1665 and 1673: Thomas the eldest, John, Samuel and Walgrave.[3]

Thomas studied at Lincoln College, Oxford, before joining the Church and subsequently becoming rector of Hinton-in-the-Hedges, near Aynho, also in Northamptonshire. With its geographical proximity to Steane Park it was almost certainly a rectorship that was within the gift of Lord Crewe, hence it was likely that he also owed his livelihood to the Crewe family.

The second son, John, seemed to be of a more independent mindset. After marrying Catherine Carter he embarked on a career as a merchant in Lisbon. Precisely what type of trade he was in was not documented but it is likely, from British interests in Lisbon at the time, that it was either shipping or the wine trade that provided the family income. The couple's first child was a girl (Maria) but their second was a boy also named John, who grew up in Portugal but subsequently crossed over the border to Spain to become secretary of the British Legation at Madrid. There he met and married a Spanish girl, Maria Teresa de Castro.

In her diaries,[4] Betsey Wynne describes Maria Teresa as being, according to Fremantle family legend, a mere schoolgirl when she married and also of 'extreme ugliness'. Whatever the truth was concerning her looks she certainly passed on the Mediterranean characteristics of dark hair and eyes that seemed to have been passed down in the family for at least a couple of generations as people who met her grandson, Thomas, frequently commented on the darkness of his eyes.

After his marriage, John Fremantle and his wife moved back to Britain to take up a senior post of Secretary to the Board of Customs. The couple lived in the City of London close to John's place of work and had seven children, of which only four survived into adulthood. The eldest child, also christened John, was to be Thomas's father.

John was born in 1737 and while still a young man, according to family legend, he eloped from a ball with a young girl and subsequently married her. The young girl in question, Frances Edwards, was the daughter of a rich Bristol merchant. Whether the story regarding the unorthodox courtship is true or apocryphal, he certainly married Frances Edwards, who proved a valuable addition to the Fremantle fortunes. Whatever the truth was as to the start of their marriage it did not seem to alienate the Edwards family[5] as they were still living in close proximity to the newly-weds by the time Thomas Francis was born and subsequently christened in Hampstead Parish Church.[6]

Thomas Francis was the couple's third son and was born at 9 a.m. on 20 November 1765.[7] Soon after his birth, the Fremantle family moved from Hampstead to Astons Abbotts, beginning a family relationship with the county of Buckinghamshire that has lasted to this day. Thomas's father bought a house in Aston Abbotts probably with the dowry provided by his wife's family as he did not appear to have a significant source of income of his own.

More importantly for Thomas's future career, by moving to Aston Abbotts the Fremantle family were brought into the nearby Grenville-Temple family's circle. Their country house at Stowe was just outside the town of Buckingham, less than 20 miles from Aston Abbotts. John Fremantle was already active in Whig politics when he moved to Buckinghamshire so nothing could have been more natural than that he should become known to the local Whig grandees, the Temple-Grenville family.

As one of the most prominent Whig families in the country, it was entirely possible that the Temple-Grenvilles first met the Fremantles because of their geographical proximity and their shared politics. When the Fremantles first moved to Aston Abbotts the incumbent of Stowe House was Richard Grenville-Temple, the second Earl Temple. His sister, Hester, married William Pitt (later the Earl of Chatham) and his younger brother George Grenville was Prime Minister from 1763 to 1765. Luckily for the Fremantles, Earl Temple died in September 1779 for he was renowned as one of the most argumentative persons of his age. He reputedly libelled many who opposed his views, was said to love faction and had the money to pursue his feuds. He died without leaving a direct heir and the title was inherited by his nephew, the son of his younger brother, George. George Nugent-Temple-Grenville became the third Earl Temple and proved to be a staunch friend to the Fremantles. Had John Fremantle planned it, he could not have come up with better patrons than the rich, politically minded Grenville-Temple family.

Wherever and however the first meeting was contrived between these two families, it was Thomas's younger brother William who was to tie them together in a relationship that initially spanned across quite a wide social divide but eventually became one of friendship and mutual dependence. Such is the importance of the relationship between the Grenville-Temple family and the Fremantles that it is worth diverting from the story of Thomas Fremantle for an instant to cover that of his brother, William, and his relationship with the George Nugent-Temple-Grenville, who was to become the 1st Marquess of Buckingham – two individuals who would be pivotal in Thomas's life.

William Henry Fremantle was born on 28 December 1766, making him just over a year and a month younger than Thomas. When he was 16 he was bought a commission in the army in the 66th (Berkshire) Regiment of Foot. Of far greater importance to the family fortunes was that he was appointed to the office of Earl Temple (later 1st Marquess of Buckingham) in July 1782 during the earl's first period as Lord Lieutenant of Ireland. The relationship obviously worked well and was to last throughout Earl Temple's political career.

In February 1789, when Buckingham was again in Dublin as viceroy, William Fremantle sold his army commission as a captain and bought an interest in the office of Irish Secretary, albeit resident in London. While living and working in Dublin William became a friend of Arthur Wellesley and the two of them were arrested and fined £10 each by magistrates for assault. This family friendship between the Fremantles and Wellesley was to pay further dividends when Wellesley, as the Duke of Wellington, would appoint Thomas Fremantle's nephew, John, as his senior aide-de-camp (ADC) at the Battle of Waterloo.

William was subsequently prepared, if Buckingham agreed, to return to Ireland as private secretary to his successor, Lord Westmorland, with the offices of black rod and first secretary, 'relinquishing all profits and emoluments from the latter'. Nothing materialised from this idea and instead Buckingham managed to find him an appointment as deputy teller of the Exchequer.

William Fremantle's various Irish sinecures were abolished under the 1801 Act of Union that created the United Kingdom by the incorporation of the Kingdom of Ireland into that of Great Britain. He became very dissatisfied with the compensation he received and, once again, it was the (by now) Marquess of Buckingham who led William's appeal for better terms from the Addington government. The outcome was a pension of £1,027, and Selina Hervey, whom he had married in September 1797, received £722 as 'keeper of the late parliament house'.*

William was extremely adept at forming influential connections and by 1800 he started to become a favourite of King George III. Living near Windsor allowed him easy access to the royal family and in April 1802 he wrote to the King soliciting a royal household appointment in lieu of his deputy tellership. His close association with the Grenville family told against him for the King had a particular dislike of all Whigs. Despite William's protestations that he differed markedly from the marquess in his political thinking, the post was never offered to him. He remained on good terms with King George, somehow steering the difficult course between the royal household and his Whig friends and remaining in harmony with both sides. He thereby demonstrated a degree of subtlety and subterfuge that Thomas would never have been able to emulate.

The death of William Pitt in January 1806 led to Lord Grenville's formation of a new administration and naturally William expected a post somewhere in government. Despite Grenville's attempts to find him a post in the Treasury his hands were tied by the close links with the Prince of Wales, who regarded Grenville's Whig administration as his particular supporters and it would be his nominees who had to take precedent.

William was disappointed and, although the Marquess of Buckingham continued to press his case, it was not until July 1806 that he was eventually found a post as patronage secretary to the Treasury. It was to be during this administration that William's elder brother, Thomas, had his one and only flirtation with political power.

---

*   Mrs Selina Felton Hervey was the widow of the Hon. Felton Hervey, who was the grandson of the 1st Earl of Bristol. He had committed suicide. Selina was the daughter of Sir John Elwell Bt, so she had brought with her to the marriage with William not just money but links to two of Britain's powerful families. Her son from her first marriage was also influential in military circles when, as Sir F.E. Hervey-Bathurst Bt., he served as assistant quartermaster-general during the Waterloo campaign and ADC to Wellington during the subsequent occupation of France.

William continued his career in politics after Thomas's rapid departure from the Admiralty and continued to play an influential and advisory role even when Thomas was an admiral. William's access to the highest reaches of British political society and his subtle manipulation of both royal and Buckingham influences played key roles in Thomas's career advancement. There are numerous examples of letters written by the Grenvilles to assure the smooth passage of Fremantle's naval career. Although it would be overstating the case to say Thomas owed his career to William and the Marquess of Buckingham's influence, it was certainly extremely helpful to have such mentors.

The young Fremantle was fulfilling the role of so many well-to-do family sons by taking up a post in the navy. The eldest, John, had gone to the army, William had initially had a commission in the army before taking up his career in politics and, although there is little information about the early years of Thomas's life, we do know that on 24 July 1777 at the age of 11 he joined the navy. He went to sea on HMS *Hussar* initially as a captain's servant, subsequently as a midshipman. He must have already received adequate schooling because, although the navy provided education, it did expect its young recruits to have a basic grounding in arithmetic, reading and writing. From that base of knowledge, the navy was content to take over all subsequent education in trigonometry, celestial navigation and all the other essential skills expected of an eighteenth-century naval officer.

Midshipmen were officer cadets and for many the rank of midshipman represented the first step to becoming an officer in the Royal Navy. Midshipmen were taken on personally by seagoing captains and it was important the family had influence either with an existing seagoing captain in order to get a berth or with the Admiralty itself, who could order a captain to take on a midshipman. Such was the reality of Royal Navy recruitment in late eighteenth-century Britain.

Midshipmen were accounted for as part of the ship's complement. Numbers on board ran from a full complement of twenty-four on a first rate man-of-war to six on a frigate and, possibly, only two on a sloop. The idea was that they would learn the principles of seamanship and naval command in a practical environment so that after six years they would be in a position to take their lieutenant's examination. The reality was that many were mature men who had failed their examination consistently. Indeed, there was one character, Billy Culmer, who boasted he was the oldest midshipman in the navy and, as he was not promoted to lieutenant until he was 57, he was probably correct.[8]

Midshipmen were expected to stand a watch on the ship, learn navigation, seamanship, mathematics and other accomplishments considered essential to young naval gentlemen. These included how to eat properly at formal mess occasions, how to handle their drink and generally the rudiments of commanding the crew of a man-of-war. They would also be expected to be familiar with rigging sails, watchkeeping and supervising a gun battery. Midshipmen kept detailed navigational logs, which would be shown regularly to the captain so he could keep an eye on their progress. Indeed, a good captain would institute a regular system of education for his midshipmen that closely resembled a school at sea. Some of the bigger ships actually had a schoolmaster on their complement. It was, however, a rough and ready environment, especially for an 11-year-old. Like many schools, especially those of the eighteenth century, bullying was rife. The midshipmen were traditionally housed, as their name suggests, amidships on the main gun deck under the paternal eye of the ship's gunner. The midshipmen lived here in a world halfway between the crew, who messed on the gun decks, and the officers in the wardroom. Being watched over by the ship's gunner did not necessarily prevent bullying as, with the best will in the world, a seaman who already had his hands full with other seagoing duties could not keep his eyes on them at all times. A certain degree of high spirits was considered an essential part of these young men's character development. The term 'skylarking' is derived from the eighteenth-century navy where the term was used to describe the young midshipmen's games of playing in the rigging of ships when off duty.

Thomas would have been thrown into this rough and ready man's world surrounded by members of a crew who represented a social class of men totally outside his previous experience. Typically, a crew were made up of a mixture of long-serving seamen, some with specialist skills such as gunners, carpenters and sail makers. At the other extreme were landsmen who were often 'pressed', that is inducted forcibly into the navy, and even criminals whom the courts had given a choice between jail or serving in one of His Majesty's warships. Another method used commonly to enlist men was known as 'crimping', whereby unwary young men were entrapped by free drink and/or the lure of female company only to wake up from a hard night's drinking or similar to find themselves enlisted on one of His Majesty's men-of-war. Thomas would have been thrown into this maelstrom and potentially violent world, and would soon have been expected to take charge of small numbers of the crew in command of a gun station or one of the ship's boats. It is difficult to think of a more complete change for a young boy, or a more complex and demanding education.

However, it would be equally wrong to suppose that life as a midshipman was totally brutal and unbearable. Most young boys, and Thomas going to sea at the age of 11 was by no means unique, managed to thoroughly enjoy themselves. Vice Admiral William Stanhope Lovell describes his own experiences as a midshipman thus:[9]

We lived in the gun room on the lower deck, and in fine weather had daylight, which was better in many respects than the old midshipmen's berths in the cockpit. Amongst the youngsters were some within a year or two as young as myself; nice boys, full of fun and mischief, who soon initiated me in the sea pranks of 'sawing your bed-posts,' – cutting you down head and foot; 'reefing your bed-clothes,' – making them up into hard balls which, if properly done, will take one unpractised in the art a good half hour or more to undo. It used to be a great annoyance to come off deck after a first or middle watch (from eight at night to twelve, or from twelve to four in the morning), perhaps quite wet through, thinking on being relieved, what a nice sleep you would have, to find, ongoing to your hammock, all your sheets and blankets made up into hard balls, and a good half-hour's work in the dark to undo them, particularly when tired and sleepy. During your labour to effect this, you had the pleasure of hearing the mischievous fellows that had a hand in doing it, laughing in their hammocks, and offering their condolences by saying what a shame it was to play such tricks when you had been sent on deck, keeping your watch, and recommending you to lick them all round, if you were able, or at all events to retaliate at the first opportunity.

Blowing the grampus (sluicing you with water), and many other tricks used to be resorted to occasionally. Taking it all in good part, from the persuasion that it was the customary initiation to a sea life, my torments were few, for when the art of tormenting ceases to irritate, it loses the effect intended, and it generally ends by your shipmates saying, 'well you are a good-natured fellow, and shall not be annoyed anymore.'

Thomas's first ship, the frigate HMS *Hussar*, was equipped with twenty-eight guns, twenty-four of which were 9lb guns situated on the main deck and four 3lb cannons on the quarterdeck. She was a standard Royal Navy frigate of the era, designed by Sir Thomas Slade who was the Royal Navy's chief surveyor and during the mid 1770s he was responsible for the standardised design of many of the navy's fighting ships. HMS *Hussar* was one of the 'Mermaid' class frigates designed more for their excellent sailing qualities rather than the ability to be involved in major naval battles. Frigates were not considered big enough to participate in the 'line of battle' but they were fast and manoeuvrable and their main task was to act as the eyes and ears of a fleet.

From the comparative luxury of his home in Buckinghamshire, Thomas's world shrank to that of a wooden ship just 124ft long by 33ft in breadth and he was to share this with nearly 200 other men. The Hussar had been built at Deptford and launched in 1763. In 1774 she returned to Woolwich Dockyard for a major refit and it was at the completion of this refit that young Fremantle joined her. She was commanded by Capt. Elliott Salter, who was also a Buckinghamshire man, coming from Stoke Poges. It may well have been the first example of the Buckingham influence working on behalf of Fremantle, as the Salters were well known to the Grenville family.

HMS *Hussar* was to join the fleet cruising off the coast of Portugal and for the next two years Thomas learnt the basics of life in His Majesty's Navy. He soon showed an aptitude for the job, which brought him to the attention of both his captain and other officers. During his time on board he had the excitement of being part of a diplomatic row between Britain and one of its oldest allies when HMS *Hussar* was in collision with a Portuguese ship, the *São Boaventura*, in the mouth of the Tagus. Her captain, Joaquin José de Lima, lodged a formal complaint with the Portuguese government and pending the account of the relevant authorities in Portugal, HMS *Hussar* was held at Lisbon.[10]

Unsurprisingly, the British crew were held to be responsible as the collision had occurred when HMS *Hussar* had forced the merchant vessel to 'hove to' pending their inspection of the cargo. Some years later this policy of stop and search would push neutral governments into more drastic action that, in turn, would play a key role in Fremantle's career. The matter was finally settled after some very high-level wrangling between the relevant Secretary of State, Lord Weymouth and his opposite number in Portugal. After a certain amount of posturing from both sides, Queen Maria I of Portugal relented and allowed Capt. Salter and his ship to sail. It was not to be the last time that Fremantle was in the midst of diplomatic rows and it would be interesting to know how much the strength of the British government's stance in refusing to pay damages influenced his thinking when, much later in his career, he was asked to negotiate with foreign governments.

There was a curious postscript to the story of Fremantle's first ship, HMS *Hussar*. A year after he left her she was under the command of Capt. Charles Pole, who unwisely tried to bring her through the treacherous straits between Manhattan Island and Long Island. In so doing, she was swept on to the Pot Rock and subsequently sank in more than 100ft of water. Salvage attempts were fuelled by rumours that she was carrying a fortune in British gold, although none was recovered. What was salvaged were some of her cannons and these were put on display in Central Park. Two hundred and thirty years later in January 2013, during routine maintenance, it was found that one of the cannons was still loaded with cannonball, wadding and black powder. It was disposed of by the New York Police Department with the comment that 'we silenced British cannon fire in 1776 and we don't want to hear it again in Central Park'.[11]

Thomas moved on and after two years, on 1 December 1779, he was posted to HMS *Phoenix* under Capt. Sir Hyde Parker, who was to play a significantly beneficial role in his early career. HMS *Phoenix* was part of the Jamaica squadron. The primary role of the British squadron was to safeguard British mercantile interests in this important market while at the same time trying to strangle that of the American states. America had commissioned a number of privateers, which were basically privately owned ships issued with a letter of authority by the provisional colonial American assemblies. The amount of British trade in the West Indies gave ample opportunity for the American privateers to make a nuisance of themselves and, incidentally, to make some money out of the war. It was during this phase of the war that Capt. John Paul Jones became the first American naval hero with his daring raids on British shipping and even an armed raid on British soil when he attacked the Cumbrian port of Whitehaven.

What really changed the situation, so far as the Royal Navy was concerned, was not the raiding of the Americans but Benjamin Franklin's successful spell as American ambassador to France. In 1778 he arranged a military alliance between France and America that saw French forces enter the conflict in July 1778 when a French fleet under the command of the Comte d'Estaing reached the eastern seaboard of America. In truth, Franklin had been pushing against an open door. With British forces facing military setbacks on land and the French desire to take over British colonies in the West Indies, the situation must have appeared ripe for intervention to French eyes.

The young Fremantle was, therefore, serving in an area of the globe that was of key strategic importance for British interests and one where there should be opportunities to expand his experience of naval combat. Despite this, it was the Caribbean climate that was to provide the next major challenge to the young midshipman.

While his early experience on HMS *Phoenix* was humdrum, the year was to end in the most dramatic way and provide him with possibly his closest brush with death prior to his battles under Nelson's command. During the first week of October 1780, HMS *Phoenix* was cruising off the coast of Jamaica midway in the channel between Jamaica and Cuba. She was struck by one of the most powerful hurricanes that the Caribbean region had seen for many years and blown helplessly towards the Cuban coast by winds that exceeded 100mph. An eyewitness account was provided by the ship's first lieutenant, George Archer:[12]

At eleven at night it began to snuffle, with a monstrous heavy appearance from the eastward. Close reefed the top-sails. Sir Hyde sent for me: 'What sort of weather have we, Archer!' 'It blows a little, and has a very ugly look: if in any other quarter but this, I should say we were going to have a gale of wind.' 'Ay, it looks so very often here when there is no winds at all; however, don't hoist the top-sails till it clears a little, there is no trusting any country.'

At twelve, the gale still increasing, wore ship,* to keep as near mid-channel between Jamaica and Cuba, as possible; at one the gale increasing still; at two, harder yet, it still blows harder! Reefed the courses, and furled them; brought to under a foul mizzen stay-sail, head to the northward. In the evening no sign of the weather taking off, but every appearance of

---

* 'Wearing' or veering is a method of turning a ship through 180 degrees whereby the stern passes through the wind rather than the bow, as happens when a ship tacks. It is a slightly simpler manoeuvre but requires more sea room and is usually a slower manoeuvre than tacking.

the storm increasing, prepared for a proper gale of wind; secured all the sails with spare gaskets; good rolling tackles upon the yards; squared the booms; saw the boats all made fast; new lashed the guns; double breeched the lower deckers; saw that the carpenters had the tarpaulings and battens all ready for hatchways; got the top-gallant-mast down upon the deck; jib-boom and sprit-sail-yard fore and aft; in fact everything we could think of to make a snug ship ... by sending about two hundred people into the fore-rigging, after a hard struggle, she wore; found she did not make so good weather on this tack as on the other; for as the sea began to run across, she had not time to rise from one sea before another lashed against her. Began to think we should lose our masts, as the ship lay very much along, by the pressure of the wind constantly upon the yards and masts alone: for the poor mizzen-stay-sail had gone in shreds long before, and the sails began to fly from the yards through the gaskets into coach whips. My God! To think that the wind could have such force!

Sir Hyde upon deck lashed to windward! I soon lashed myself alongside of him, and told him the situation of things below, saying the ship did not make more water than might be expected in such weather, and that I was only afraid of a gun breaking loose. 'I am not in the least afraid of that; I have commanded her six years, and have had many a gale of wind in her; so that her iron work, which always gives way first, is pretty well tried. Hold fast! that was an ugly sea; we must lower the yards, I believe, Archer; the ship is much pressed.' 'If we attempt it, Sir, we shall lose them, for a man aloft can do nothing; besides their being down would ease the ship very little; the mainmast is a sprung mast; I wish it was overboard without carrying anything else along with it; but that can soon be done, the gale cannot last for ever; 'twill soon be daylight now.'

Found by the master's watch that it was five o'clock, though but a little after four by ours; glad it was so near daylight, and looked for it with much anxiety. Cuba, thou art much in our way! Another ugly sea: sent a midshipman to bring news from the pumps: the ship was gaining on them very much, for they had broken one of their chains, but it was almost mended again. News from the pump again. 'She still gains! a heavy lee!' Back-water from leeward, half-way up the quarter-deck; filled one of the cutters upon the booms, and tore her all to pieces; the ship lying almost on her beam ends, and not attempting to right again. Word from below that the ship still gained on them, as they could not stand to the pumps, she lay so much along. I said to Sir Hyde: 'This is no time, Sir, to think of saving the masts,

shall we cut the mainmast away?' 'Ay! as fast as you can.' I accordingly
went into the weather chains with a pole-axe, to cut away the lanyards;
the boatswain went to leeward, and the carpenters stood by the mast. We
were all ready, when a very violent sea broke right on board of us, carried
everything upon deck away, filled the ship with water, the main and mizzen
masts went, the ship righted, but was in the last struggle of sinking under us.

As soon as we could shake our heads above water, Sir Hyde exclaimed:
'We are gone, at last, Archer! Foundered at sea!' 'Yes, Sir, farewell, and
the Lord have mercy upon us!' I then turned about to look forward at the
ship; and thought she was struggling to get rid of some of the water; but
all in vain, she was almost full below. 'Almighty God! I thank thee, that
now I am leaving this world, which I have always considered as only a
passage to a better, I die with a full hope of the mercies, through the merits
of Jesus Christ, thy son, our Saviour!'

I then felt sorry that I could swim, as by that means I might be a quarter
of an hour longer dying than a man who could not, and it is impossible to
divest ourselves of a wish to preserve life. At the end of these reflections
I thought I heard the ship thump and grinding under our feet; it was so.
'Sir, the ship is ashore!' 'What do you say?' 'The ship is ashore, and we
may save ourselves yet!' By this time the quarter-deck was full of men
who had come up from below; and 'the Lord have mercy upon us,' flying
about from all quarters. The ship now made every body sensible that she
was ashore, for every stroke threatened a total dissolution of her whole
frame; found she was stern ashore, and the bow broke the sea a good deal,
though it was washing clean over at every stroke.

Sir Hyde cried out: 'Keep to the quarter-deck, my lads, when she goes
to pieces, 'tis your best chance!' Providentially got the foremast cut away,
that she might not pay round broad-side. Lost five men cutting away the
foremast, by the breaking of a sea on board just as the mast went. That
was nothing; everyone expected it would be his own fate next; looked
for daybreak with the greatest impatience. At last it came; but what a
scene did it show us! The ship upon a bed of rocks, mountains of them
on one side, and Cordilleras of water on the other; our poor ship grinding
and crying out at every stroke between them; going away by piecemeal.
However, to show the unaccountable workings of Providence, that which
often appears to be the greatest evil, proved to be the greatest good! That
unmerciful sea lifted and beat us up so high among the rocks, that at last
the ship scarcely moved. She was very strong, and did not go to pieces at

the first thumping, though her decks tumbled in. We found afterwards that she had beat over a ledge of rocks, almost a quarter of a mile in extent beyond us, where, if she had struck, every soul of us must have perished.

I now began to think of getting on shore, so stripped off my coat and shoes for a swim, and looked for a line to carry the end with me. Luckily could not find one, which gave me time for recollection. 'This won't do for me, to be the first man out of the ship, and first lieutenant; we may get to England again, and people may think I paid a great deal of attention to myself and did not care for anybody else. No, that won't do; instead of being the first, I'll see every man, sick and well, out of her before me.'

I now thought there was no probability of the ship's soon going to pieces, therefore had not a thought of instant death: took a look round with a kind of philosophic eye, to see how the same situation affected my companions, and was surprised to find the most swaggering, swearing bullies in fine weather, now the most pitiful wretches on earth, when death appeared before them. However, two got safe; by which means, with a line, we got a hawser on shore, and made fast to the rocks, upon which many ventured and arrived safe. There were some sick and wounded on board, who could not avail themselves of this method; we, therefore, got a spare top-sail-yard from the chains and placed one end ashore and the other on the cabin-window, so that most of the sick got ashore this way.

As I had determined, so I was the last man out of the ship; this was about ten o'clock. The gale now began to break. Sir Hyde came to me, and taking me by the hand was so affected that he was scarcely able to speak 'Archer, I am happy beyond expression, to see you on shore, but look at our poor *Phœnix*!' I turned about, but could not say a single word, being too full: my mind had been too intensely occupied before; but everything now rushed upon me at once, so that I could not contain myself, and I indulged for a full quarter of an hour in tears.

The ship had been driven helpless on to the shore at Cabo de Cruz, a peninsula running southward from the south-eastern end of Cuba. There is a long reef running broadly south-westerly from the tip of the peninsula that, with the ship being driven helplessly northwards, inevitably caught her and completed the process of breaking up the hull, which had previously survived the 100mph winds. The crew were lucky in that the majority were able to struggle ashore, as described in Lt Archer's graphic letter.

They were ashore and, for the time being, safe from the hurricane. However, Capt. Hyde Parker and his officers were all too aware that Cuba was a Spanish colony and that, as Spain had declared for America, a rescue might well end with them imprisoned by the Spanish authorities in Havana. The next morning, when the hurricane had subsided as rapidly as it had previously arisen, they were able to assess their position more fully. One of the ship's boats had survived the foundering. With timber from some of the other wrecked ship's boats they were able to patch her up sufficiently for Lt Archer and a couple of volunteers to sail across the 100-mile channel back to British-held Jamaica. Within a matter of ten days of being shipwrecked, Fremantle, Capt. Hyde Parker and the majority of *Phoenix*'s crew were taken off the coast of Cuba by a British vessel called out from the Jamaica station by the redoubtable Lt Archer. They were taken back to Port Royal, the home port of the Jamaica squadron.

Midshipman Fremantle spent a few days in Jamaica, presumably gathering his wits after his recent experiences and buying himself a new set of seagoing kit. The Royal Navy was obviously a believer in the old adage of immediately remounting once thrown from a horse for, on 26 October 1780, Fremantle was metaphorically 'back in the saddle' on HMS *Ruby* and after four months he was transferred to HMS *Ramillies*, where, in an important step in his early naval career, he was re-rated to master's mate.[13]

HMS *Ramillies* was a seventy-four-gun third-rate ship of the line and Fremantle was to serve on her under Capt. John Cowling for just over a year. He obviously made quite an impression on the captain as when he moved to HMS *Sandwich* on 1 March 1782 he took Fremantle with him.

His rating as master's mate was not a formal rank. However, to be rated as a master's mate on the ship's complement demonstrated that Fremantle was now a competent mariner, ready for responsibility and, in all probability, to take his lieutenant's examination. This proved to be the case for, after just thirteen days serving as a master's mate on HMS *Sandwich*, Thomas came ashore to take this test.

Promotion to lieutenant was by formal examination. Officially, a prospective lieutenant had to be at least 19 years old with a minimum of six years' seagoing experience. He was expected to produce proof of his service, which would include certificates from his commanders and journals kept while a midshipman. Both of these qualifications were elastic. Boards often got around the age qualification by stating that the applicant appeared to be of a certain age and the concept of seagoing experience was abused routinely by a captain keeping a lad's name on the ships complement despite the fact he was somewhere completely different.[14]

The candidate was summoned before a board of three captains and questioned about seamanship, navigation and discipline. It was the last chance the navy had to formally assess the competence of their officer class. From this point onwards a navy officer's career was by appointment and the only recourse, should an officer prove to be professionally weak, was simply not to appoint him to ships.

The boards were usually rigorous although a degree of 'interest' still found its way into the proceedings on occasions, as in all other areas of eighteenth-century life. A midshipman by the name of Boteler reported that he was summoned before the usual board of three experienced post-captains to find that one of them was his previous captain. He persuaded the other two board members to pass him based on his experience with him on board and, indeed, answered some of the questions on his behalf.[15] The norm was probably more like that of Charles Middleton (later Lord Barham and destined to be First Lord of the Admiralty) who, when he sat as a board member of lieutenants' exams, had a list of thirty testing questions that he asked including things such as: 'You are sent to a ship ordered to be fitted out, the captain not having appeared; the lower masts and bowsprits are in, but not rigged; what parts of the rigging goes first over the mast heads?'

Despite the difficulty of the oral examination and the nerves he must have inevitably experienced, Fremantle was successful and passed at his first attempt, on 13 March 1782.[16] His first commission, as a Royal Navy lieutenant, was as commander of the *Port Antonio*, a twelve-gun sloop that the navy had chartered locally. She had a crew of thirty-five, all of whom were crammed into what was essentially a boat some 60ft in length by 20ft beam. Whatever her size, the 16-year-old Fremantle was in sole charge; he was in navy parlance, 'acting commander' at an astonishingly young age.[*]

---

[*] 'Master and Commander' was a temporary rank reserved for (usually) lieutenants who were placed in command of small vessels considered too small for post-captains.

The appointment lasted only three weeks before he transferred as a lieutenant to HMS *Vaughan*. He spent nine months serving on HMS *Vaughan* before joining HMS *Tickler*. Here the Fremantle luck in getting himself into scrapes reasserted itself when, cruising off the north coast of Cuba, the ship sailed into the path of the French sixty-four-gun ship of the line, the *Tonant*. The commander did the sensible thing and immediately 'struck his colours'.* There was no other possible course of action. The *Tonant* could have blown the *Tickler* out of the water with just half of her broadside. The end result was that all were taken prisoner and landed in Havana after travelling through the Straits of Bahama as guests of the French navy.

Fremantle's luck had not entirely deserted him. Within weeks, suitable French prisoners were identified as being held in British hands and an exchange was arranged, as was the custom of the time, and Thomas found himself back in the naval base in Jamaica. He was eventually shipped back to the UK in a merchant vessel but, after a short period on shore, he rejoined the twenty-gun HMS *Camilla*.[17]

As first lieutenant he would serve for a further three years on the West Indian station. The exact dates when Fremantle served on each of his earlier vessels are not clear as he left at least two documents in his legacy concerning his naval career that differ slightly. However, either shortly before or during his spell of duty on HMS *Camilla* there had been a mutiny when the crew refused to sail because smallpox had killed several men, worsening a shortage of seamen on a ship that was already under complement. The crew felt, not unreasonably, that they could not sail without more men because if they hit a squall or a hurricane, they would not be able to handle the ship. The mutiny was quelled with extreme violence and five men received 800 lashes. It must have had an effect on the thinking of the young Fremantle for it made a stark contrast to his own treatment of crew some twelve years later who also mutinied but were dealt with in a far more humane and efficient manner.

Meanwhile, back in the UK, political support for the war against the American States had plummeted after the military defeat at Yorktown. The Prime Minister, Lord North, had already resigned in early 1782 to be replaced by Lord Rockingham, who led a Whig administration that immediately called for and won a Commons vote to end the war.

* To 'strike one's colours' on board ship means to lower the national flag to indicate surrender.

The preliminaries were agreed and signed in Paris, and although separate treaties were required for the newly recognised United States and the other European powers, the whole thing was eventually drawn up and signed by September 1783.

Fremantle's service on HMS *Camilla* was the first, and one of the very few occasions in his career, that he had a prolonged spell serving on a Royal Navy vessel during peacetime conditions. The war had left Great Britain with another large debt but with the pace of Britain's industrial development and the power of her empire-powered economy it was well within the limits of what the economy could service. For France it was different as it incurred huge financial losses as a result of the war. This destabilised its economy to such an extent that it fed the revolutionary forces which, over the next decade, would tear French society apart and ultimately engulf most of Europe in warfare.

However, that was for the future. Now, Fremantle had the opportunity to learn his trade, polish his skills of seamanship and navigation and generally learn the principles of command. One of the distinguishing features of Fremantle's subsequent stellar naval career was his professionalism, his desire to improve professional standards, his hatred of sloppiness and what he regarded as undisciplined behaviour.

3

LONDON LIFE AND EARLY COMMANDS, 1787–1793

In December 1787 Fremantle returned to the UK from the West Indies, a fully qualified naval lieutenant, with a range of professional skills and knowledge. In short, he was a fully qualified naval officer, competent to stand his watch on board ship and to command men in battle or in storm. He was barely 22 years old and had spent the last eleven years of his life at sea. Now he wanted to study some of the other subjects that interest young men, principally wine, women and a good time, and, in his elder brother, John, he had the perfect tutor. Men of Thomas's age usually want to live a little and John was eager to help this willing pupil learn all he could of the seamier side of London living.

John Fremantle was an officer in the Coldstream Guards. When Thomas joined him, in his house in Titchfield Street, John was aged 27, some five years older than his brother and vastly more experienced in the ways of the world, or at least, in London society. It is also at this stage of his life that Thomas begins to correspond regularly with his younger brother, William, and it is from these carefully collected letters that so much of what we know of Thomas's early life is revealed.

Four years prior to Thomas arriving in London his father, John, had died. Despite the dowry he gained from his father-in-law, John died leaving debts and settling his affairs took some time for all of the sons. On 5 February 1788 Thomas wrote to William:[1]

> Your not answering my last letter makes me and John rather uneasy as you certainly should have let us know what was your opinion of the business suggested in my last. I have I now trust done my share of the task ... I have in all sunk £710 and have only to add on this affair that £100 more would pay off every incumbrance ...
>
> We have been at two Masquerades within this week past, one at the Opera, and the other at the Pantheon. I was much entertained with both of them. The Princes, Dukes, all the Young Men and Whores constituted the assembly ... My Sister comes to London to lye in some time in April.* Apropos I forgot to tell you I belong to the Club in St James's Coffee house which is improving every day. I mean to dine today at the Buckinghamshire Club at the New London Tavern. I have been in Town now near a Month, but do not find the Raking etc. agree with me so well as the Country.
>
> I believe I have now told you all the News of our Circle – and I do not think I can be made more happy but by a small addition to my income. Do pray let me hear from you as soon as you can ... and with my best Wishes for your health and Welfare believe me
> Your most Affectionate Brother
> Thos Fras Fremantle.

Despite his stated opinion that a rake's life in London did not suit him, which appears to be inserted in the letter more to impress his rather more sober brother than from real conviction, he remained firmly entrenched in the London demi-monde. Just under two months later he wrote to William again:[2]

> We spend our time much in the same way as when I wrote to you last. Jack and a party of us gave a Whores ball at the Barracks a few nights ago. I was as you may imagine much diverted and entertained, they danced better than any Modest Woman I ever saw, we were just 10 compleat

---

* This is his eldest sister Sarah, married to Captain Thomas Wells.

Couple and kept it up till very late. Jack goes on just as he used to do, that is to say *living fast* but I cannot say I am a bit better, neither do I think it is possible to live regular in this precious town. I confess I feel more for him than for myself as my constitution etc. is in so much better repair.

Further letters followed in similar style. By April he had set himself up with another man's mistress and wrote to William again:[3]

I am now in possession of the Girl I mentioned I was so much in Love with. She is kept in great Stile by a d---d fool, and I now contrive to have as much pleasant f----g as I can lay my sides to without it costing me a farthing ... I think Jack and I go on very regularly, drunk almost every day and seldom in bed before three o' clock – A strange difference this, from what I have been used to, however I think I stand it tolerably well.

Fremantle's energetic lifestyle continued for two years but, by 1789, it had obviously begun to pall. In addition, several factors came together to push him into a more productive lifestyle. There is little doubt that beneath all the youthful bluster and wild living he remained, at heart, a person who genuinely wanted to be a professional naval officer. His brother, John, was beginning to feel the financial pinch and needed to quieten down in order to get his own affairs into order, and war threatened. With war came opportunity and Fremantle had obviously been keeping his eye open as to naval opportunities for, in August 1789, he wrote again to William, only this time in a far more serious and sober vein:[4]

My reason for now writing to you, is that a Naval promotion will take place in a short time. You know my situation &c. and I must beg you to urge Lord Buckingham to get me if possible included in the Number to be prefer'd. There are to be twelve of each Rank – and when you represent to Lord B. that I have now been near eight years a Lieutenant, I trust I am entitled from time &c. to hope for his support.

A month after this letter was written the Marquess of Buckingham resigned his position as Lord Lieutenant of Ireland, having become extremely unpopular in Ireland for what was perceived as his expensive and autocratic tenure. From this point onwards he took no real active role in British politics, retiring to his country seat of Stowe. He retained political influence, however, and was still to prove extremely useful to the Fremantle family. Whether or not William's appeal to the Marquess of Buckingham on behalf of his brother was effective is hard to say but, by May 1790, Thomas had received his orders from the Admiralty to report to a newly launched ship, HMS *Brunswick*.

HMS *Brunswick* was a seventy-four-gun, third-rate ship of the line and her first captain was to be Sir Hyde Parker. It is therefore more than likely that it was Hyde Parker's preference that got Fremantle the third lieutenant's berth on the vessel rather than the Marquess of Buckingham's influence. HMS *Brunswick* was being made ready as a result of heightening tension between Britain and Spain, known as the Spanish Armament or the Nootka Crisis. The dispute was brought about by a series of events in the Nootka Sound in Vancouver during the summer of 1789. Traditionally Spain had always claimed sovereignty and trading rights to what is now the Western Seaboard of Canada and Alaska. However, in the late eighteenth century British fur traders were also beginning to trade in that area with valuable resources of beaver and bear skins proving to be an irresistible lure. British ships began increasingly to move into areas that Spain claimed as its own and soon British vessels were being seized by the Spanish authorities in its effort to assert its monopoly rights.

When eventually news of the plight of British traders reached London, the government immediately issued a strong protest to the Spanish government and asked for compensation and the release of the vessels, which Spain refused. Both governments prepared for war and, as a result, the navy began to step up its activities and to put itself on a war footing. HMS *Brunswick* was fresh off the slipway, having been built in Deptford and launched on 30 April 1790. Fremantle received his commission and joined her at Spithead on 11 May. As she began her shakedown cruises in the Channel, the government was working on the negotiations with the Spanish. By early 1791, the crisis was over and by October Fremantle was back on shore looking around for his next commission.

It was not until March the following year that he was successful in being appointed to a ship. HMS *Spitfire* was classified as a fire ship and Fremantle was again appointed 'commander', which demonstrated that although he was still waiting the vitally important rank of post-captain, he was now recognised as a senior and competent lieutenant.

Fire ships had originally been converted merchant vessels and out-dated naval vessels that had passed their 'sell by date'. Their purpose was to be filled will combustible material, set on fire and floated off in an attempt to burn enemy shipping. By the late eighteenth century they were re-rated as sloops and HMS *Spitfire* had been converted from her nominal eight 12lb cannons to be re-equipped with fourteen 18lb carronades, four light swivel guns and two 6lb cannons with a crew of fifty-five. She was used for harbour defence, where her shallow draft made her potentially lethal against small coastal vessels.

It was 26 March 1791 when Fremantle took up his appointment as commander of HMS *Spitfire*.[5] Immediately he seemed to be pleased with his lot. As was by now his habit, he wrote to William to express his feelings:[6]

I should have answered your last before this but that I have been ordered from Spithead here, where I am laying as a Guard Ship, to board all Vessels coming in through the Needles. I like my situation so well and the people here are so civil that I have wrote to Sir Hyde Parker humbly requesting he will be so good as to keep me here for some time longer. The first, and I might say only family that resides here is a Captain Ourry of the navy, who has a very good fortune and is the most hospitable man in the world.* His house is nearly surrounded by a white wall to which he has affixed sham guns and if you were not told they were so you would not be able to find it out. He has what I call a hickery face, and is about six foot high ... on the whole he is the greatest curiosity I ever saw, he has an only daughter who was at Queen Square with Marianne. She is brunette, rather pleasing in her way which is an uncommon one. She is about 18 years old and will have a very good fortune, I flirt with her, but She is I believe engaged to be married to an acquaintance of mine. The only thing I am at a loss for here is a Girl – no prostitution of any kind, but I think the less of it in consequence ... I begin to think I have the Gout whenever my toe or finger akes, we may all tremble knowing what sinners we have been ... You would be much amused were you here, the Weather has been so very fine and indeed the Island is so beautiful.

---

* Captain George Ourry fought with distinction in the Seven Years War. Later, during the American Revolution, he captained HMS *Somerset* off the North American coast. There she was driven on to the shallow Peaked Hill Bars on 2 November 1778, following which Capt. Ourry and his crew were taken prisoner, only to be exchanged days later.

His fondness for the retired captain's daughter grew more serious and she obviously reciprocated Thomas's feelings. If the ship had not been paid off in September 1791 he might well have finished up marrying, or perhaps being 'required' to marry, Miss Ourry. In the event, the next crisis, known as the Russian Armament, followed quickly after the Spanish Armament and was just as quickly resolved, resulting in HMS *Spitfire* being no longer required to guard the entrance of Portsmouth harbour. She returned to her home port and Fremantle was once again paid off and placed back on to half pay.

The Russian Armament crisis had been created when Pitt's administration had become alarmed over threats to the balance of power in Europe caused by Russia's aggressive stance towards the Ottoman Empire. It caused a great deal of hot air and took up a great deal of Parliamentary time but blew over just as quickly as it arose. Both the British public and a significant proportion of the British Parliament thought that war with Russia was both unnecessary and unwise. William Pitt, however, had used the traditional British diplomacy of negotiating while simultaneously putting the navy on to a wartime footing. With alliances in Europe proving remarkably short lived and fluid, there was never sufficient momentum for such a definitive move as moving a British fleet into the Baltic and the threat of war between Russia and Britain receded and finally faded completely by June 1791.

By September 1791 Fremantle was back in London, where he was to spend another two years on shore. His brother, John, was by this time off the social scene, doing all he could to behave as a respectable married man. He had taken the opportunity of his brother's absence to find an heiress and settle down. Fremantle, however, was obviously determined not to follow John's example this time around and continued to play the jolly bachelor with a trip to France, where he unfortunately contracted a sexually transmitted disease that he treated, as was common practice at the time, with a mercury compound.

On 21 January 1793 King Louis XVI was guillotined and the full horror of the French 'Terreur' was brought home to the British public. They were keen for Britain to declare war on revolutionary France but in the event matters were taken out of their hands when France declared war on Britain on 1 February. Prime Minister Pitt had tried initially to maintain a strictly neutral line to the French Revolution, but nine days later he was forced to reciprocate. He did not expect the war to be prolonged as Austria and Prussia both appeared to be militarily stronger than the rather haphazard French forces.

Pitt's war aims were to protect Great Britain from invasion, albeit not a realistic threat at this point; to finance a coalition that would defeat France, or at least hold it to its original borders; to bring the navy up to a state of war readiness; and, lastly, to encourage dissidents within France. British relations with Russia, which had deteriorated during the Russia Armament, now improved steadily as Catherine, the Empress of Russia, allied herself with anyone who would oppose the revolutionary, anti-monarchical movements that were sweeping through France. Together, Russia and Great Britain now agreed a pact of mutual defence whereby, should one party be attacked, the other would be required to co-operate in repelling the aggressor.

The Kingdom of the Two Sicilies also joined the coalition, as did Portugal. Pitt and his foreign secretary, Grenville, worked to enlarge the coalition in order to isolate and surround France with hostile monarchies. Britain sent a force under the command of the Duke of York to Holland to help in the struggle against the French forces. Ultimately, however, the combined allied army was split apart by internal strife and Pitt was forced eventually to order the evacuation of the British army from the Prussian port of Bremen. By December 1795 all British forces had been evacuated from the Continent to lick their wounds and to begin a long-needed overhaul of manpower, equipment and operating practices. It would be some time before British troops would reappear on mainland Europe. Until such time, Britain's contribution to the anti-revolutionary coalition would be limited to finance and sea power.

While Europe began to react to the events in France that were to shape the Continent for the next twenty or more years, Fremantle, having completed his commission on HMS *Spitfire*, was appointed as commander on HMS *Conflagration*, another fire ship, similar to HMS *Spitfire*. He was to serve as her commander for three months until 21 May 1793, when he was discharged having been told that the following day he was to take over as captain of HMS *Tartar* as a post-captain. The threat of a prolonged war was starting to affect the navy's build-up and Fremantle was to be an early beneficiary.

4

POST-CAPTAIN,
MAY 1793

On Wednesday, 22 May 1793, Capt. Fremantle RN stepped on board His Majesty's Ship *Tartar*. He climbed from a ship's boat as she was anchored out in Spithead anchorage. For the first time in his life he boarded a Royal Navy vessel as post-captain. The ship's officers, lined up on the deck to receive their new captain, would have looked on anxiously, for this man would be in total control of their immediate destinies. Capt. Fremantle was in charge and his word was law. The Articles of War promulgated on all Royal Navy vessels and the King's Commission, from which he derived his powers to command, gave him awesome powers over the men, both officers and crew.

The captain of a Royal Navy warship had considerable luxury compared to his crew and fellow officers. His own cabin gave him a degree of privacy unknown to any of the occupants of the ship but it also had its drawbacks. From the point when newly appointed Capt. Fremantle climbed on board he was a man apart, removed from the conviviality of the ward room and his fellow officers by the tradition that he could only dine in the ward room when specifically invited to do so. Of course, he could invite the officers to dine with him, and on many occasions he would do so, but these were meals governed by the strict

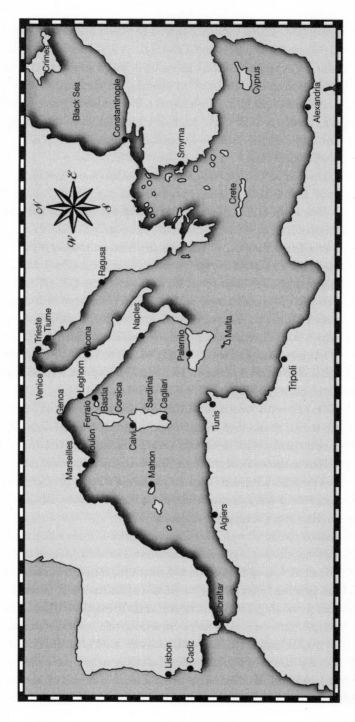

The Mediterranean, as Fremantle knew it.

formality of the times and by his rank. They would afford a captain no chance to unburden himself and to discuss his fears and anxieties. The same King's Regulations that gave him his powers also spelt out in detail that he was to be ultimately responsible for both the ship and everything that happened to it (Regulation 111). Should any significant disaster befall his ship or should he fail to attack the King's enemies with sufficient vigour the captain would be forced to account for his actions in a court martial.

It is no exaggeration to say that this lonely and responsible position drove some men to the point of paranoia. What was more common was the entirely natural desire, when seagoing duties allowed, for captains to invite each other to dine, no doubt to swap gripes and experiences. From this point of Fremantle's career his professional development was dependent on what he could learn from experience and what he could glean from fellow captains and flag officers, often over the dinner table. Convivial dining conversations were not just a way of staving off loneliness, they were also one of the finest learning opportunities. Indeed, he was soon to find out when he came within the orbit of Nelson that this was his favoured way of assessing his fellow captains and of both disseminating and dissecting tactics and strategies that would form the background to his battle plans.

Fremantle's command was one of the old-style frigates. HMS *Tartar*, a twenty-eight-gun frigate, had been launched in 1756 and was, by some considerable distance, older than her new captain. Despite her age she had a reputation as an excellent sailer. Although, in terms of new frigates, she was considered small and somewhat under-gunned, she was to prove an excellent ship and would serve Fremantle well during this early stage of his career as a post-captain.

From this point forward in his naval career, Fremantle's destiny would be governed by his date of seniority; nothing could hold him back from the senior flag ranks of the navy. Only premature death could halt his progress through the lengthy list of post-captains until eventually he would hoist his pennant as a rear admiral. His immediate task, however, was to weld the 193 men under his command into a cohesive team and ensure that, if and when required to fight, they would acquit themselves like a first-rate fighting crew, capable of upholding the reputation of the service. That involved practice at gunnery and, four days after taking over command, he called for live practice of the main guns.

What distinguished a good crew from a poor crew was a) the speed and dexterity with which they changed sails and b) the speed and accuracy of their gunnery. With these two elements working perfectly a captain would know he had a good ship, for both required teamwork of the highest order and an 'intelligent' crew who knew their jobs. The handling of sails required detailed knowledge and experienced sailors, and was considered a longer term objective for those captains unfortunate enough to have a high ratio of 'landsmen' among their crew.* Many sea captains have spoken admiringly of watching a vessel making ready to go to sea, hauling up their anchor and setting their sails with scarcely an audible order being made; each man knowing his job and co-ordinating their actions perfectly to achieve a smooth departure.

The art of turning a landsman into a competent able seaman was, therefore, a long-term project. It was commonly thought that to become a fully qualified sailor took five to six years. Gunnery, however, could be improved quickly as it only required one, or possibly two, members of each team to have any specialist knowledge. Providing a seaman was fit, with a certain degree of physical strength, he could be welded quickly into a member of an efficient gun crew. Practice really did make perfect. Anybody who has watched a Grand Prix team changing all four tyres within two to three seconds will have some idea of what a team can achieve when working in perfect harmony. This was certainly the case for the gun crew of a Royal Navy cannon. From the point when the cannon recoiled after firing, a complex series of actions needed to be carried out, all in perfect synchronisation, to ensure the gun was ready to fire again as quickly as possible.

For both battle and gunnery drill the opening sequence was the same. Marines drummers beat out the rhythm of all hands to quarters and the crew ran to their positions adjacent to each gun. Two of the lieutenants would also stand on the gun deck, one to the fore and one aft, with midshipmen taking up positions next to the group of guns for which they were responsible. The gun captains were issued with flintlocks and trigger lines, which enabled them to trigger the flintlock while standing clear of the recoil, and took with them powder horns of finely ground

---

* One of the first duties of the first lieutenant when taking on a new crew was to 'rate' each member of the crew aged over 15. Those with no knowledge of the sea were rated as landsmen, those with a basic knowledge were rated as ordinary seaman and those competent in all main shipboard duties were rated as able seaman.

black powder that would be used to prime the guns, plus a priming wire to pierce the canvas that enclosed the main charge.

The port lids covering the gunports were lifted and held in position against the hull like vertical trapdoors, and the tompions removed from the muzzle of the cannon.* On the order 'load', the 'powder monkeys' – usually the youngest members of the crew – would open the wooden case containing the canvas bag that contained the main charge. They would pass it to the assistant loader, who would stuff it into the muzzle, and the loader would then thrust it down to the breech of the weapon with the sponger. Wads were thrust down next, followed by the shot and another wad before the weapon was ready to fire for the first time. At that point, the crew would then run the gun out ready to fire.

As the gun fired it would recoil violently inboard, only halted by the breech ropes that were attached to rings fixed to the ship's sides, which were run through a brass ring behind the gun's breech and reattached to the ship's side on the opposite side of the gun. They were rigged so as to allow the weapon to recoil just enough for the muzzle to come inboard, thus allowing access to ram the next shot home. As the gun came to a halt, the loader at the side of the muzzle began the process known as 'worm and sponge'. The 'sponge' was a damp wad of rags attached to the end of a wooden pole, slightly longer than the barrel of the gun. This was thrust down the gun, twisted and then brought out before being tapped on the side of the muzzle to ensure there were no sparks or parts of the previous charge that could prematurely ignite the next cartridge. Any particles, blockages etc could be cleaned out with the 'worm', which was a corkscrew-shaped implement that could be used to pull out any foreign material caught in the barrel.

The cartridge was a flannel bag loaded with black powder that had been stitched up. Cartridges were kept next to the gun in a wooden box to prevent them being ignited accidently by a spark. They were placed in the muzzle of the gun and then pushed home with the reverse end of the sponger. The gun captain (the leader of the team) then pushed his priming wire down the touch hole at the base of the muzzle, 'feeling' for the cartridge. Once he was certain it had been thrust firmly down he shouted 'home'. A small amount of wadding was thrust down in the same way as the cartridge followed by the cannonball and then further

---

* A tompion was effectively a wooden bung that sealed the cannon muzzle when not in use.

wadding to hold the ball in place should the ship roll and depress the angle of the gun barrel.

The gun was then hauled out using the breech ropes and the gun captain was responsible for aiming, and altering if necessary, the elevation of the gun before pricking the canvas cartridge case to expose the powder down the vent. A touch more powder was then poured down the touch hole and the gunlock placed over the touch hole. The gunlock was essentially a flintlock, a spring-loaded mechanism released remotely by a lanyard, which struck a spark that, in turn, ignited the charge in the cannon. With everyone clear of the line of recoil the gun fired, recoiled and the whole process repeated. A 32lb cannon needed a seven-man team who, when well trained, could fire a shot every sixty seconds. For the first shot the orders were shouted out of 'load', 'run out', 'prime' and 'fire' but subsequent orders would become superfluous in the noise of the gun deck and the officers would rely on the men's training to carry them through the process.

A ship's surgeon serving on a Royal Navy sloop left this description having watched the crew run through their gun drill:

> On the beat of a drum, the men immediately fly to their quarters; and their being so constant in that point of duty, increases their agility, gives them confidence in their own powers, and prevents much of that confusion, which with those less disciplined must necessarily ensue – even the little powder boy would be ashamed of being reproached by his ship mates, for not knowing his duty. On these occasions a general silence prevails, all attentively listening for the word of command.

Royal Navy captains placed great importance on gunnery and the best ones made sure crews practised it incessantly. It was the major advantage they had over their enemies. Disciplined, accurate and fast gunnery were the keys to winning battles. Complex sailing manoeuvres counted for little when a captain was willing to get in close, 'lay close alongside' and pound the opposition to bits. Fremantle was about to start the most intensive part of his naval education and he was to be taught by some of the masters of the trade.

HMS *Tartar* was part of the fleet heading for the Mediterranean and in charge was Lord Hood. Also in the fleet was Vice Admiral Hotham and the then Captain Horatio Nelson in HMS *Agamemnon*. The captain of Lord Hood's ship, HMS *Victory*, was his old mentor, Sir Hyde Parker. There were two other admirals in the fleet, Rear Admiral Thomas Foley on HMS *Britannia* and Rear Admiral Goodall on HMS *Princess Royal*. In all, the Mediterranean Fleet comprised forty-three vessels, of which twenty were ships of the line, fifteen were frigates and the rest were made up of sloops, fire ships, etc.

Prior to departure Fremantle wrote to his brother William on 22 May 1793:

> I came on board last night, and am resolved on no account to touch the Shore again. I have been overlooking my Ship's books and find I have actually 193 Men on board, my complement 200. The Ship is lumbered dreadfully with 6 Months provisions but I am getting rid of some, and we shall eat our way through the remainder, I wish you could have seen my Ship before we sailed, you would have been well pleased with her. I want a good first Lieutenant very much (none appointed), the 2nd is a d----d stupid fellow, the 3rd very clever, all the other Officers I have every reason to be perfectly well satisfied with. The Victory has made the signal for unmooring and we shall if possible be off to St Helens this evening.* I have found out how I was so fortunate as to get this ship. Sir Hyde requested it of my Lord Hood who wrote to Lord Chatham. I fortunately happened to toady Lord Hood before I knew the circumstances, therefore all is well … My sheep, fowls and ducks are just come alongside, and I have got a capital Cook, my stock of wine 50 dozen. I cannot help saying I feel my consequences amazingly, and with the Assistance of my friend Sir Hyde I may perhaps take a prize or two.

His 'toadying' to Lord Hood was sadly to prove useless. The fact was, as he stated in his letter, that he had been given the commission as a result of Sir Hyde Parker's intervention. Gradually, he would realise that relations between Sir Hyde Parker and Lord Hood were frosty and were to get worse. As Fremantle was quite clearly Parker's man he was branded from the start, so far as the 69-year-old Lord Hood was concerned.

The voyage out to the Mediterranean started well for Fremantle, three days out, HMS *Tartar*, together with another frigate, HMS *Mermaid*,

---

* An anchorage used extensively by the Royal Navy situated just off the east coast of the Isle of Wight.

captured a French privateer. HMS *Tartar* was required to take forty-seven of the French crew on board as prisoners of war and in turn allocate some of their crew to the captured vessel to take possession of their prize.

They had been detached from the main fleet in order to escort a convoy of merchant vessels to Bilbao.* From Bilbao they sailed to Gibraltar and had two days on the rock before sailing with other frigates to Málaga. Here Fremantle watched a bullfight for the first time in his life. His letter to William indicates he did not find the experience totally enjoyable:

> We went to two bull feasts where there were near 6,000 people, it is the most savage and barbarous amusement I ever saw in my life, one bull killed three horses in five minutes, but the greater the blood spilt the greater the diversion.

Coincidently, Nelson also attended a bullfight that year, writing to Fanny, his wife, in June 1793 expressing his repugnance at the experience.

From Málaga it was back to Gibraltar where again they were sidetracked by another merchant convoy, which they escorted to Leghorn. Finally, having arrived at Leghorn, they found orders from Lord Hood to rejoin the main fleet at Toulon, where they rendezvoused in the second week of August.

While Fremantle was cruising around the western Mediterranean, Lord Hood's fleet sailed for Toulon direct from Gibraltar and arrived on 19 July to blockade the port. Toulon served as the home port for the main French Mediterranean Fleet and, to see what he was up against, Lord Hood sent in an emissary under a flag of truce overtly to arrange an exchange of prisoners but, in reality, to carry out a little reconnaissance. There were some twenty-one French ships of the line bottled up in the harbour but, despite Hood's fleet being dispersed for a few days due to gales, the French made no attempt to break out.

Inside Toulon, and unknown to the British fleet, there was a counter-revolution taking place. Forces sympathetic to the restoration of the Bourbon monarchy and milder republican forces sickened by the excesses of the 'terror', were positioning themselves within the city to take over control.

---

* At this stage of the war with France, Spain was a British ally.

To the citizens of Toulon threatened by forces both inland (the French revolutionary army) and from the sea (the British) and with food running short thanks to the British blockade, the situation must have appeared a nightmare. The majority were for a restoration of the monarchy and given the uncontrolled nature of the fearsome revolutionary army, the choice was probably made easier. On 25 August 1793 the Toulon citizens invited Lord Hood to enter their city and placed the safety of Toulon in the hands of the English admiral. HMS *Tartar* was the first ship to enter the port and Fremantle soon wrote to let his brother know what was happening:

I have much to say to you individually that I am at a loss what subject to begin on, but as I am certain this will be delivered safely I shall speak my sentiments as freely as if we were sitting together. For political News I shall refer you in some measure to Lord Buckingham's letter. How must you be surprised to find that we are actually in possession of Toulon without losing a man, such an event I believe is without parallel in history, and were you here ... you would admire Lord Hood's determination and spirit in having compass'd a thing beyond our most sanguine expectations. Thus much for him publickly – he has behaved to me in the most unprecedented and harsh manner I believe ever known in our service on account of a man I contrived to get rid of as he was totally incapable of performing his duty – it was the Surgeon of the *Tartar* who was appointed by him – he sent for the Ship from Leghorn to order a court of enquiry why he the Surgeon left the Ship, which was in fact censuring my conduct ... However I must do him the justice to say that since he has been remarkably kind and attentive to me ... I trust I know too much of the World to quarrel with a *great man*, particularly a man that has been so fortunate, and I flatter myself my attention and service has made the impression which has induced him to alter his sentiments and conduct towards me. Between ourselves the *Tartar* has been the most servisable frigate he has had, all the rest who were commanded by his particular friends he has sent to Naples Smyrna and in short on pleasant cruises. Sir Hyde and he seem to be on middling terms, and as I am considered a *friend* of the formers *party* will not allow me any favours. He Lord H – has frequently expressed himself much pleased with my conduct when chasing under the batteries or employ'd on any active service – and I take some merit to myself when I say that all the material information respecting Toulon came through the *Tartar* and

we were the only Ship any Shot went over. Luckily not one struck the Ship. We have taken two privateers one of 22 guns the *General Washington* in company with the *Mermaid* and another of only two guns under the Island of S. Marguerite. We have run two Vessels on Shore, and chased a French frigate of 28 guns exactly the same as the *Tartar*. You cannot imagine what a different life I lead – the most active possible and the more I have to do the better I am in health …
Adieu my Dear Will and with remembrances to all
Believe me most afftely. TFF

Having taken Toulon with barely a shot being fired, the situation began to unravel rapidly. The citizens who supported a restoration of the Bourbon monarchy were never numerous enough to create a significant counter-rebellion within France, neither were the British in a position to do much. Indeed, it was apparent from the start of the occupation that Lord Hood did not have enough troops to man the defences of Toulon. Nor was he a man likely to win support from any of the other agencies involved. His manner was autocratic in the extreme, alienating the army and, in an effort to get further troops, he fatefully sent Nelson with the *Agamemnon* to Naples to speak to the British Minister Plenipotentiary, Sir William Hamilton.

Lord Hood's manner was becoming increasingly difficult and Fremantle was not the only naval officer to suffer at his hands. He recorded his dissatisfaction later in the New Year as follows: 'He has had the ingenuity of making nine out of ten in this squadron his avowed enemy by his overbearing and tyrannical conduct.' Fremantle then went on to complain of Hood's treatment of Rear Admiral Sir Hyde Parker as being full of 'acrimony and vile humour'.

Meanwhile, Nelson was distanced from the acrimony going on in Toulon. He was detached from the main fleet by Hood, who used the fast-sailing HMS *Agamemnon* rather like a large, powerful frigate. On his voyage around the Mediterranean, carrying the dispatches from Admiral Hood, he came across Fremantle and HMS *Tartar*. It was almost certainly the first meeting between these two and took place on 31 August 1793. What either man thought of each other is not recorded. However, it is quite likely that Fremantle had already heard something of the reputation of Capt. Nelson for he was already beginning to make a name for himself.

On 1 September HMS *Tartar* was in Oneglia near Genoa. Fremantle was moved to write to William concerning the richness of the Genoese and the beauty of their women, a subject in which he claimed some expertise. Despite this, he was disgusted with them for having slave galleys with men chained to their oars and treated atrociously. Some of his father's whiggish sensibilities obviously still ran through the veins of his son. Of more immediate concern was a French frigate that was moored close to his ship. As Oneglia was a neutral port the rules of war forbade him from attacking. The French sailors compounded his misery every morning and evening by manning the rigging to shout taunts at their British foe.

He returned to Toulon to find the citadel was now coming under attack from the revolutionary army. While the British commanded the sea approach, they did not have sufficient armed personnel to man the citadel walls of Toulon. The French artillery, led by the young Capt. Napoleon Buonaparte, was beginning to make inroads in the Toulon defences. On 12 December 1793 Thomas again wrote to William:

I think I have now an opportunity of writing for a few days as the Gentleman who will convey this is going passenger with us from hence (Toulon) to Oneglia – since my last I have carried Sir Jas Erskine, his Brother and Major Koehler, formerly General in Brabant who is now deputy Quarter Master General at Toulon from Oneglia to this place. I confess I feel myself much gratified at the compliments and civilities I receive from these people to whom we are realy transports, but there is an expense attending this *trade* which my fortune is by no means adequate to, and my pride will not suffer that they should feel a want of any kind on board the Ship I command ... Lord Hood is by no means kind or attentive to me, and would I am sure if in his powers *crush* me, but I am on my guard, and seem pleased with all orders &c ... I still keep well in with my old friend Sir Hyde who is realy a staunch friend, tho sometimes very *Vinegar** but I cannot say he has ever been so to me, the fact is there is a kind of Jealousy between the two great men and it is difficult to avoid the one or the other and my having served so long with one makes me odious to the other, instead of finding Lord Hood as I had expected my

---

*   Sir Hyde Parker's father, also an admiral and also named Sir Hyde Parker, was known throughout the navy by the soubriquet of 'Old Vinegar'.

friend and patron, I have received every mortification, and nothing but my determination to persevere in *strictly* performing my Duty can keep my Spirits up under his command – this I mention merely *entre nous* ... To compensate for my disgust at the Commander in chief, I am exceedingly happy and comfortable with my Officers and Ships Company who are improving daily, the former are my friends and the only place where I can say I am really content is onboard my Ship ...

Nothing but having so bad an army and so bad a General as opponents could have kept us so long in possession of this place, no dependence whatever can be placed on the foreign troops, and I am much mistaken if we shall be in possession this day three months, our outposts are so numerous and unconfined, that with 20,000 Men we have not a relief – they extend 16 miles, and the besiegers encrease in numbers every day ... The policy of sending so large a force to the West Indies and leaving this place destitute of English troops is much condemned, and seriously if we are to keep the place I should think the troops much better employed here, but I am in hopes that it is the intention of Government to drive us to such extremities that we shall (for fear of the Enemys getting possession) be obliged to fire the French Ships and destroy the Town forts and Arsenal, such are my most sanguine wishes and tho I am perhaps singular in my wishes, I think it will ultimately be of more service to Great Britain than persevering in the plan we have adopted which must be attended with an enormous expence to Government ...

We are now just got out of Toulon Road, and there is the heaviest cannonade to the SW I ever yet saw – but that is not what we are in dread of, it is a *coup de main* where numbers may overpower us ...

The Misery of the poor French who have ran to this place for succour is not to be described, of 12 that belonged to Marseilles whom I brought from Genoa in the Tartar not one has been able to get a Shilling or scarcely procure sufficient to support Nature, I have from fear of their starving only been obliged to assist them materially for as distress is so only from comparison it is hard to see a woman at the age of forty having been bred to every luxury obliged to earn her sustenance by washing and ironing – such is the state of this place tho from Lord Mulgrave's account in the Gazette you would imagine it different both as to Security and Comfort. The town of itself is not very large, the houses generally about four stories high, the Streets very narrow, and a Drain running through the middle into which they discharge out of the Windows all kinds of

Devilment ...Nothing could surpass the good order and management of their Dock Yard so much more commodious and handy than ours, the Stores so much better and the Workman likewise, if I had not seen what I have done the partiality I have for my own Country would not have suffered me to believe it, but such is the case, and fortunate has it been that when they have built their Ships they do not know how to navigate them ...

13th Decr ... It is now eight o' clock and as the Wind is fair and I am standing in for the Land, am anxious – shall therefore wish you a good night – and as this long letter must excuse me to all the parenté desire you will remember me most kindly to them all ... so once more adieu.

A week later the British fleet was compelled to evacuate Toulon. The occupation had been a failure. The humiliation was completed by the fact the British exit was so abrupt that they were not able to complete the destruction of the French fleet. HMS *Tartar* was fully employed in the last few hours of the occupation in destroying both French ships and stores, and was one of the last British ships to leave the port. It sailed as the French army poured into the city. Of more immediate concern to Lord Hood and the British fleet was where they should be based to allow them to keep a military presence within the Mediterranean. Lord Hood decided that St Fiorenzo on the north-western coast of Corsica was the best choice. From a purely geographical point of view it was excellent. Close enough to France's Mediterranean coast to keep an eye on Toulon, far enough into the Mediterranean to keep both the Kingdom of the Two Sicilies and Austria in the coalition, also well placed to look after British mercantile trade while simultaneously harrying that of France.

The one fly in the ointment was that Corsica was currently under France's jurisdiction, having been ceded to it by Genoa in 1768. However, the French hold over Corsica was precarious for the island saw itself as independent and the leader of the nationalist forces, Pasquale Paoli, was pro-British having spent twenty years in exile in London. Lord Hood had little trouble in concluding an agreement with Paoli that would see the French thrown out with British assistance and Corsica then ceded to the British. Paoli was seen in a romantic way by the British public following his stay in their country. Indeed, he was seen as the very epitome of a proud and free island race, which was exactly how the British liked to picture themselves. Since returning to Corsica, Paoli had gathered together a force of freedom fighters possibly some 3,000–4,000 strong. The British, together with Paoli's forces, were opposed by some 3,000 French soldiers, the majority of whom were stationed in the northern Cape Corse peninsula at the fortresses of St Fiorenzo, Calvi and Bastia. The last named was a town of some 8,000 people and served as the capital of the island.

Nelson, together with Fremantle in HMS *Tartar*, and three other frigates, HMS *Juno*, *Romulus* and *L'Aigle*, were detached as a separate squadron to blockade Corsica and to assess the defences, Lord Hood took the main fleet to the Gulf of Hyères to await developments. With the French fleet free to move out of Toulon and harass British trade and the revolutionary army gaining success in Italy, the British urgently needed a base east of Gibraltar or there would be a danger of losing the Mediterranean completely. Hood needed success urgently.

Capt. Horatio Nelson, now commodore of a reasonably sized squadron, was able to harry the French in and around the coast of the island despite the wintery conditions. He kept his force in peak fighting condition by allowing one ship at a time to provision in Leghorn.[1] The weather was some of the worst that could be remembered, with constant gales and large seas making it a gruelling experience for the small British ships. Lord Hood eventually joined them towards the end of January and a flavour of what both the *Agamemnon* and the *Tartar* crews went through in that stormy month around the coast of Corsica is given in Nelson's letter to his wife:[2]

> I was blown off my station on the 28th, in the hardest gale almost ever remembered here. The Agamemnon did well, but lost every sail in her. Lord Hood has joined me off Corsica the day before; and would have landed the Troops but the gale has dispersed them over the face of the waters. The Victory was very near lost; however, we are safe. A number of Transports are missing. I am fearful the Enemy will get their Troops from France before I can return to my Station, which will be a vexing thing after my two months' hard fag.
>
> I hope to get my Ship to sea tomorrow. I direct this to Bath, where I desire you will not want for anything: my expenses are by no means great, therefore don't be afraid of money. A circumstance happened a few days past, which gave me great satisfaction. January 21st the

French having their storehouse of flour near a water-mill close to St Fiorenzo, I seized a happy moment, and landed sixty soldiers and sixty sailors threw all their flour into the sea, burned the mill – the only one they had, and returned on board without the loss of a man. The French sent one thousand men at least against them and Gun-boats, &c.; but the shot went over them, and they were just within reach of my guns. It has pleased Lord Hood, but this gale may have blown it out of his memory.

This coastal raiding or amphibious operations carried out, whenever possible, in co-operation with the army, became one of Nelson's trademarks and, in Fremantle, he had a keen pupil. A feature of Fremantle's career was his ability to soak up information and learn from whoever happened to be his commanding officer even when, in several instances, he did not personally like them. Sometimes, as in the case of Lord Hood's relationship with the army, these might be negative lessons in how not to do something, but always there was the impression from his writings and his letters that he was learning and improving his professional skills wherever and whenever possible. He worked his way through these lessons, not by mere imitation but by applying his mind in a concentrated fashion to the task of becoming an outstanding naval officer.

Fremantle's work around the northern coast of Corsica was, therefore, bound to bring him to Nelson's attention. On 6 February 1794 together with HMS *Fox*, he forced a French vessel ashore near to the town of Bastia but he had not been able to haul the vessel off and take possession of it thanks to a heavy fusillade of shots from the French ashore. Nevertheless, it was exactly the kind of aggressive action that Nelson appreciated.

The first recorded skirmish in which we know that Nelson and Fremantle fought together was on 8 February 1794 at the Corsican town of Rogliano, situated right at the northern tip of Cape Corse. Rogliano was a small town that was important to the French garrison on Corsica as it gave it the ability to monitor the ships passing around the northern tip of the island and it had installed a detachment in the castle specifically for this purpose.

The two vessels, HMS *Agamemnon* and *Tartar*, anchored just off the main town jetty and threatened the town with their broadsides. Under a flag of truce, Nelson offered the town liberty should it declare for the restoration of the monarchy. The French commander remained defiant despite the obvious threat from the two warships. Nelson himself led a shore party into the town from the ships' boats, at which the French garrison fled without a shot being fired. The British party proceeded to do as much damage as it could, destroying storehouses, some French merchant vessels and a store of wine. Three ships were also taken as prizes and although the French repossessed the town as soon as the British ships sailed off, the message was being brought home to the Corsican people. Undoubtedly, Pasquale Paoli's forces reaped the benefits of these British raids as more and more Corsicans joined the revolt against French occupation.

This communication and mutual benefit between Paoli's forces and the British fleet nearly paid off a few days later. The Corsican leader informed Nelson that a Ragusan ship was unloading goods contrary to the British blockade at L'Avisena, just north of Bastia.* Nelson and Fremantle sailed to see if they could seize the ship as it discharged its cargo, unfortunately arriving too late. Nevertheless, they again landed a shore party, who marched to a nearby French detachment at Maginaggio and drove them off before re-embarking. There was arguably little military value but it was demonstrating loud and clear to the Corsicans that British sea power was effective. The message was further reinforced when, a few days later, Nelson landed 400 muskets and ammunition[3] to be used by Paoli's forces against their French oppressors.

While Nelson and Fremantle continued their blockade on the eastern side of the Cape Course peninsula, Admiral Hood had not been idling and on 18 February 1794 he took and occupied the port of St Fiorenzo. French forces fell back from the British across the peninsula to Bastia, thus fortifying the port with the additional troops.

On 19 February 1794 Nelson wrote to Lord Hood summarising the defences of Bastia:[4]

---

* The Republic of Ragusa, otherwise known as the Republic of Dubrovnik, was a maritime republic centered on the city of Dubrovnik in modern-day Croatia. It was formed in the middle of the fourteenth century and finally came to an end in 1808 when it was conquered by Napoleon. It existed almost entirely on the proceeds from its merchant fleet and suffered badly from British navy 'stop and search' tactics. Even at the height of its powers it never had a population greater than some 30,000 citizens.

I had a good opportunity of looking at Bastia this morning; its means of defence are as follows: On the Town-wall next the sea, about twenty embrasures; to the Southward of the Town, two guns are mounted on a work newly thrown up, and an Officer's guard encamped there; they are also throwing up a small work commanding a large road to the Southward of the Town, which leads towards the mountains. I observed at the back of the town four stone works, all with guns; two of them appeared strong, the others are stone guard-houses. In the Mole is La Flêche, 20 guns, which came out from Tunis with the other Frigates; she is dismantled, and her guns are put on the outworks.

Yesterday a Flag of Truce, with a Note from General Paoli, came off from a place called Erbalonga, to say they were friends of General Paoli's, and wanted muskets and ammunition. I asked them how long they had been our friends? One of them, who called himself General Paoli's commander of Volunteers on Cape Corse replied, 'Ever since the day you took Maginaggio'. They may be good friends, if it is in their interest to be so; but I am rather inclined to believe that they will always cry, 'Long lives the Conqueror.' However, they are active fellows, and may be of great use, if we land near Bastia.

I have received information at Leghorn, that the cargo of the Ragusan vessel had been landed at L'Avasina. I therefore went on shore this morning but unluckily the cargo had been carried to Bastia thirteen days ago: had General Paoli's friends given him this information, we might have made a valuable capture. I have carefully examined the landing-places near Bastia, and can take upon me to say, that troops and cannon may be landed with great ease to the Southward of the Town at any distance you please, on a level country. If I may be permitted to judge, it would require 1000 troops, besides seamen, Corsicans, &c. to make any successful attempt against Bastia. The Enemy, from all accounts I could learn, have about four hundred Regulars; and altogether 2000 men carrying muskets.

If British forces were to take Bastia it would be as well to act quickly and, in Nelson and Fremantle, Admiral Hood had two officers who could do precisely that. On 23 February HMS *Agamemnon*, *Tartar* and *Romulus*, the last frigate captained by Capt. John Sutton, sailed just off the coast and proceeded to bombard the French defences being built to protect the city. Nelson, as ever, led the line and having bombarded the French batteries proceeded in line-ahead formation down and across the front of Bastia itself before starting an artillery duel with the town's batteries.

Both HMS *Tartar* and *Agamemnon* took some damage from the return fire but the chief casualty seemed to be HMS *Romulus*. Capt. Sutton insisted on returning to Leghorn for repairs, and although both Nelson and Fremantle were bemused by his attitude to such minor damage (in their eyes), Nelson agreed he could leave the squadron. He subsequently reasoned with Fremantle that it was better to have officers who wanted to be in the action rather than those who didn't. This would have undoubtedly made an impression on Fremantle for, not only did he see at first-hand how Nelson handled his fellow officers, he could not fail to take on the message that it was aggressive officers who Nelson wanted at his side and Fremantle was determined to be worthy of Nelson's regard.

Despite the obvious urgency in Nelson's dispatch to Lord Hood of 19 February, the admiral was busy doing what he undoubtedly had a talent for, making enemies for himself from amongst his own side. On the same day that Nelson had led Captains Fremantle and Sutton into Bastia to bombard the town, British forces had marched overland from St Fiorenzo and, reaching the pass overlooking Bastia, had a chance to observe for themselves the state of the town's defences. Leading the British troops was Lt-Gen. Sir David Dundas who, contrary to Nelson's tactical appreciation, felt that Bastia was impregnable without considerable reinforcements being brought in.

Considerable reinforcements were the one thing that Admiral Hood was unlikely to get. He had managed at Toulon and St Fiorenzo to alienate the British army and none of its officers were likely to put themselves out to help him out of the jam he was now in. In truth, it is unlikely that Lt-Gen. Dundas understood the importance to the Royal Navy of having a forward operating base. It was not just the army who felt that Lord Hood needed to improve his interpersonal skills as even some of his admirers amongst the navy felt that he had acted very badly towards the army.

By the middle of March, Lt-Gen. Dundas felt unable to continue and resigned his command to go back to England, but Admiral Hood's problems with the army were not over. His overbearing attitude towards the army generally had ensured that both sides took entrenched positions and Dundas's successor, Brig-Gen. Abraham D'Aubant, proved no more tractable over the use of army resources.

Both Fremantle and Nelson continued their blockade of Bastia while, on the other side of the Peninsula at St Fiorenzo, the army and navy continued to bicker. Finally, on 19 March, Admiral Hood called a council of war on HMS *Victory*. Sir Gilbert Elliot, who was the British viceroy to Corsica, Admiral Hood along with his flag officers, Hotham and Goodall, together with the army in the shape of Brig.-Gen. D'Aubant, who brought along nine of his senior officers, were all present.[5] Before the meeting was convened Hood had a pre-meeting with Capt. Nelson and invited him to brief the navy team on how Bastia could be taken. Predictably, the 'gung-ho' captain easily convinced them of the practicability of taking Bastia. Equally predictably, when the main meeting was held, the outcome was stalemate with the navy firmly of the opinion that Bastia could be taken and the army of exactly the opposite mind.

Hood had heard enough and was now determined to go it alone with a navy-led assault, but Brig.-Gen. D'Aubant had one more shot in his locker when he refused the admiral use of any army resources.[6] On 3 April, when the navy finally started to go ashore to commence the siege, army mortars and artillery lay redundant in St Fiorenzo but Nelson was confident the navy's cannons would carry the day. As the siege progressed Fremantle wrote to his brother William to provide his side of the story:[7]

It is now I believe near four months since I wrote a line – and I have heard only once from England since I have been in the Mediterranean.

I have been absolutely at Sea ever since I wrote to you last, and have scarcely a clean shirt left – and as for eatables I have long been used to have the pleasing variety of salt beef one day and pork the next, but thank God I am as well in health and Spirits as ever I was in my life. The unwearied persecution that is used towards the Tartar is I believe generally taken notice of in the Squadron, and is almost without precedent. We are kept at Sea without Sails ropes stores or even candles – but I bear up against everything, being fully convinced it cannot last for ever. I have had the employment of blockading this place for ten Weeks, and am now at anchor about three miles and a ½ from the town, our Troops to the number 1100 landed about a week ago, and our batteries and Mortars began playing the day before yesterday. The undertaking the siege is entirely Lord Hood's and the Troops landed are those only that appertain to the Squadron. Gen. Dundas you know has left the Army and the Command has devolved in consequence to Col. D'Aubant of the Engineers – who by the Advice of all the field officers except Vilettes has refused to give any assistance, of course this must be a subject much canvass'd both here and in England ...

I must say that the presumptuous and overbearing conduct of Lord Hood to Dundas and *all* the Army has been such as not to be borne with by any corps particularly from the Army who are so independent of us. When Fiorenzo was taken you must have heard that the Town was evacuated and that the Seamen in boats went first into the town. Without presuming to judge of the propriety of the thing, for the Town was pillaged before the Army entered, I must say the indelicacy of keeping the keys of the Magazine onboard the Victory four and twenty hours does not accord with my ideas of supporting that degree of harmony between the Corps so essential for the wellbeing of both. After this Lord H: came round here with the Victory and a few frigates without conveying his wishes or intentions to Dundas, the consequence was that like the King of France with 20,000 Men Lord Hood returned to Fiorenzo again. A council of War composed of flag officers and field officers of the Army was then called, to consider the propriety of attacking Bastia. All the Sea Officers voted for it, all the Army against it – that being the case Lord H: determined with the Troops embarked and the Squadron to attempt the place which I am sanguine enough to think that we shall succeed in eventually tho our force is scarcely adequate to such an enterprise ...

My good friend Sir Hyde is cruizing off Toulon, where he has been ever since he hoisted his flag onboard the Prince George, nothing can equal the acrimony and ill humour of Lord Hood towards him, so much so that he has not an officer of his *own* nor any one thing that is in general allowed an Admiral in hoisting his flag. The cry here against the Toulon business is very great, and I shall not be surprised if some parliamentary enquiry is made into it, as O'Hara and Dundas both wrote to him publickly requesting he would make some arrangements for the Destroying of the Ships as it was impossible for us to keep long the possession of the place ... judge then of the infatuation of this man who never would even think of it ... I have realy so much to say and so little time that I do not know which topic to open on – I shall therefore defer any further detail until Bastia is taken ... I am now amphibious, being half the day at the batteries on shore the other onboard.

As he stated in his letter, Fremantle spent much of his time ashore and it is undoubtedly during this period that the friendship between Nelson and Fremantle began to grow. Both had similar backgrounds, Nelson from a relatively poor parson's family and Fremantle from that of a country squire. They were both aggressive in their actions against His Majesty's enemies while, at the same time, 'thinking' officers, keen to see professional standards rise and both had ideas of their own. Both seemed to come alive in battle and put themselves in the front line when danger threatened. This was illustrated when they were walked around the batteries to inspect a newly dug position when a French cannonball smashed into the rocky ground adjacent to their path. Both were flung to the ground by the force of the explosion and Nelson was cut on his back by flying rocks. Fremantle was unhurt, apart from being covered in dirt thrown up from the impact, but showed sufficient coolness to remark to Nelson that he rather thought he would not take that particular shortcut again.[8] It was precisely the kind of coolness under fire that endeared him to Nelson. He was the exact opposite of the French Cdr Lacombe St Michel, who on 25 April fled from Bastia along with his military commander, leaving his troops to fight on. They did and for a further three weeks the siege dragged on, albeit with the British batteries creeping nearer to the walls of the city.

On 19 May 1794 the defenders of Bastia finally cracked and sent a party on to HMS *Victory* under a flag of truce. The preliminaries were signed and on 22 May 1794, after forty-five days of stiff resistance, Bastia formally surrendered. Freemantle was almost immediately detached from the main fleet to continue with one of the main duties of the frigate, acting as an escort to a merchant convoy bound for Smyrna (modern-day Izmir) on the Adriatic coast of the Ottoman Empire (modern-day Turkey). On the way to Smyrna the convoy put into Naples where, for the first time, Fremantle met both the King and Queen of the Two Sicilies and the British Plenipotentiary to the kingdom, Sir William Hamilton, and his exotic, and considerably younger, wife Emma.

Most men were immediately besotted on meeting Emma but surprisingly, given his reputation, Fremantle was unimpressed confessing 'she is not to my taste, much too large and masculine …' thus leaving the field free to the man whom he now counted as a friend, Horatio Nelson. By July the convoy had reached Smyrna where, not unnaturally in the eastern Mediterranean at that time of the year, he found it extremely hot. In his usual letter to William he informs him that, together with the other frigates, they have taken some enemy merchant vessels and that his share of the prize money amounts to £800. Given that a post-captain of a sixth-rate vessel received an annual salary of just over £200 per annum, this represented a considerable sum of money.[9]

In the first week of November 1794, Admiral Hood finally left the command of the Mediterranean Fleet and returned to England. His falling out with the army had certainly not been helpful to the British fleet but overall he had proved to be an able and thoughtful leader, albeit not one appreciated by Fremantle. He was old and tired and on his return to England he fell out spectacularly with the First Lord of the Admiralty, Lord Spencer. As a result, he was dismissed with the sop of promotion to viscount and a shore appointment as governor of Greenwich Hospital.

Vice Admiral William Hotham was left in temporary charge in the Mediterranean and, at about the same time, Nelson finally brought the battered *Agamemnon* into Leghorn for a much-needed refit. It was here that he met Adelaide Correglia, who became his mistress. While there is no doubt she would have been horrified to be described as a prostitute, her description by Fremantle as a 'dolly', a term he invariably used to describe prostitutes, was probably accurate enough. Nelson's records certainly show he was paying sums of money to her for her keep.[10] Later, in early December, Fremantle dined with Nelson and was horrified when Nelson invited his 'dolly' to eat with them. Fremantle was still a single man and was by no means shy of using the services of the many ladies who made themselves available to visiting naval officers. But to actually invite one of these 'ladies' to dine with a fellow officer obviously offended Fremantle's sense of appropriate behaviour.

On 23 January 1795 Fremantle returned again to St Fiorenzo in Sicily and two days later his first command as a post-captain ended and he was transferred from HMS *Tartar* to HMS *Inconstant*. This represented a step up, for while HMS *Inconstant* was still rated a sixth-rate vessel (frigate), she was more heavily armed and much newer than the near 40-year-old *Tartar*. HMS *Inconstant* had actually been launched in Deptford in 1783 but had immediately been sent into ordinary. Having then been commissioned into active service, she had recently gone in for an extensive refit in February 1793. She was, therefore, almost a new ship when Fremantle took command.

Before Fremantle assumed his new command he had the unpleasant duty of standing in judgement over one of his fellow officers. Capt. Smith of HMS *Berwick*, a seventy-four-gun third-rate ship of the line, was to be court-martialled following the dismasting of his ship. She had been refitting in St Firenzo Bay when a gale hit the area. HMS *Berwick*, with her masts unsupported by the usual stays and rigging, rolled violently and was dismasted. It was alleged that the officers had been negligent and as a result, within five days of the incident, Capt. Smith found himself in front of a jury of his peers.

The court martial was held in the great cabin of HMS *St George*, where Capt. Smith and two of his officers were found culpable and dismissed from the navy.[11] Unlike the officers, HMS *Berwick* was saved for further naval service. After fitting a jury rig,* she was placed under the command of Capt. Adam Littlejohn and sailed to join the British fleet at Leghorn.

This was not to be the only contact Fremantle had with the Royal Navy disciplinary system. Some six weeks after taking over command of HMS *Inconstant* he faced what was probably the greatest challenge of his naval career to date. In the first week of March 1795 Fremantle was summoned ashore to speak to Admiral Hotham. It transpired that the crew of HMS *Inconstant* had written to Admiral Hotham, accusing Fremantle of cruelty and ill usage and expressing their determination never to receive him on board as captain again.[12] Capt. Fremantle reacted well and asked the admiral if he could deal with the matter himself. He immediately took the letter and returned to his ship.

Fremantle called the men up on deck and addressed them from the quarterdeck. He asked any man who had been treated unfairly to step forward and state their grievance. Fremantle was going to say more when the crew shouted out and rushed below. He seized his opportunity and, before the men could discuss any concerted effort to usurp his authority, he was among them and in his own words 'immediately collared two of the ring leaders and handed them over to the Lieutenants.' Obviously shocked by Fremantle's prompt actions, and the sight of officers among them, the crew rushed back on deck and Fremantle was

---

* A jury rig is a temporary fix for a sailing ship that has, for example, lost a mast. Royal Navy vessels carried spare spars that could be used in lieu of broken masts to rig a structure that would at least be sufficient to give the vessel forward momentum in order for the rudder to have effect and allow the ship to be steered.

able to take out the five main ring leaders and send them in chains on to the flagship, HMS *St George*. He then took the precaution of getting some soldiers (marines) sent over from HMS *Terrible* to keep the crew under control and, within a quarter of an hour of getting back on board, Capt. Fremantle had suppressed the mutiny.

It is difficult to be clear what events really sparked off this outburst. Capt. Fremantle was known as a hard man who would stand no non-sense but he was not, by the standards of the eighteenth century, a cruel man. He was not an overenthusiastic or indiscriminate user of flogging as a means of controlling the crew. There was a mood of revolution in the air and Royal Navy crews were not immune to the propaganda that emanated from France. The Mediterranean Fleet was obviously the fleet that was most susceptible to such influences. There had been a mutiny on HMS *Tartar* after Fremantle had handed over control. In that case the men had been forgiven and it was perhaps the display of clemency that had sparked the attempted mutiny on HMS *Inconstant*.

It may be that the more famous mutinies at the naval anchorages of the Nore and Spithead, which took place during the spring of 1797, were symptoms of the same malaise. It is entirely possible that the spirit that spread through the home fleet in 1797 was already prevalent in the Mediterranean Fleet of 1795. Conditions in the navy were always hard and pay had remained static since being established in 1658. This had, with the recent burst of inflation caused by the war, become an issue with the men. All captains were essentially sitting on a potential powder keg of discontent and it would take only one of two influential malcontents to spark the kind of uprising seen on HMS *Inconstant*.

Fremantle, having dealt successfully with the trouble on his ship, was later to devote much of his professional expertise to thinking through the problems of discipline and control. Both he and Nelson had surpris-ingly enlightened views on what was required for the management of a man-of-war, being mindful that in the end, as a fighting force, it is discipline that counts and it is discipline that wins battles. His letter to his brother William after the mutiny is indicative of his thinking, even at this relatively early stage of his career:[13]

I am convinced that there is nothing like perseverance and fortitude to govern, if used properly ... I may perhaps have been the worse with respect to pecuniary advantages for having lived long in London, but I am convinced that a knowledge of the World and Mankind is of more service than any other quality you can mention when you are to govern 2 or 3 hundred people with perhaps as many different opinions.

These were not the words of a tyrant or a man deaf to the views of others. Rather, it is the considered view of someone who recognises the sheer diversity of a typical ship's crew and knows that it is necessary to show clarity and strength of mind in order to get them to pull together. Soon after the mutiny, events were to conspire to show another side to Fremantle that would demonstrate his knowledge of people, as referred to in his letter. The letter perhaps also shows an element of self-justification to his more sober and strait-laced brother in justifying his revels in London.

On 8 March news reached the British fleet that the French fleet under Rear Adm. Pierre Martin had put to sea and was heading for Corsica. Adm. Hotham immediately put out the signal to make ready to go to sea, and the next day the fleet sailed. Fremantle, along with his other frigate colleagues, would act as the 'eyes' of the fleet. With their greater sailing speed, they were able to range ahead of the main ships of the line.

On 10 March HMS *Moselle*, one of the scouting frigates pushed well ahead of the main battle fleet, saw the French had turned and were heading north-west, back to Toulon. Adm. Hotham signalled the British fleet to take up a general chase of the enemy, thereby allowing each captain to be free to make his best progress towards the French. By 12 March the British were divided into two main groups due to the vastly differing sailing speeds of their respective vessels. The faster sailing ships, including Nelson on HMS *Agamemnon* and Fremantle on HMS *Inconstant*, were becalmed some 10 miles east of the French fleet.

At this stage, the French were in the dominant position, being able to sail between the separated elements of Hotham's fleet and probably pick off the smaller element before Hotham himself, and the larger line-of-battle ships, could come to their rescue. The French, however, did not want to engage the British fleet. Perhaps they suspected a trap, for they ignored the potential prizes on offer and continued their flight back towards Toulon. By this stage a wind had freshened, making it easier for the French fleet to continue its flight. Early on the morning of 13 March, in a freshening and squally wind, one of the French ships *Ça Ira*, an eighty-gun ship of the line, managed to foul *La Victoire*, the vessel immediately ahead of her in the line, and in so doing lost the fore and main topmasts. By this stage the British fleet had again caught up with the French fleet, who were spotted four leagues to windward still trying to escape.* It was at 7.30 a.m. that the collision occurred and Capt. Louis-Marie Coudé of the unfortunate vessel soon found himself lagging behind the main fleet with his ship heeling over so that the lower deck gun ports could not be opened, thus rendering a portion of the broadside useless. Despite this impediment, the eighty-gun ship was still a dangerous opponent and as soon as the crew could untangle the rigging and cut themselves free of the broken masts, the ship, albeit somewhat slower, would be able to fight both sides again.

Being some way ahead of the fleet, Fremantle spotted his opportunity immediately. He quickly cleared HMS *Inconstant* for action and sailed her up under the stern of the *Ça Ira*. At approximately 9 a.m. HMS *Inconstant* opened the battle by firing a broadside into the stern of the stricken French ship, adding to the confusion that already existed on the ship's decks. He tacked and then re-passed on the starboard side, where the masts and rigging were fouling the guns, putting in another well-aimed broadside. The third time, however, Fremantle's luck ran out as the French cleared the debris and blasted the British frigate with one of its huge broadsides. Fremantle knew he could not fight the giant French ship, especially now it had been joined by the French frigate *Vestale*. He withdrew with seventeen of his crew either killed or wounded, and the ship's hull seriously holed, luckily above the water-line. As Fremantle withdrew he would have been cheered by the sight of Nelson, on the fast sailing *Agamemnon*, passing him to take up the fight. Fremantle had played his part in delaying the *Ça Ira* and thus allow at least part of the British fleet to catch up. Later on the following day, the *Ça Ira*, together with the *Censeur* who was trying to tow her to safety, were caught by the rest of the British fleet and both were captured.**

The chase never did develop into a full-scale battle but the British fleet prevented the French from retaking Corsica. The action fell short of the total defeat of the French that both Nelson and Fremantle felt was within their grasp. Hotham called off the chase and both fleets

---

* A league is 3 nautical miles (approx. 5½km), therefore four leagues would have been 12 nautical miles away (approx. 22km).

** The *Ça Ira* was subsequently assessed as too damaged to be taken on as a warship and served out her time as a hospital hulk.

returned to their respective bases. The truly decisive battle was to elude the British for a further ten years. Vice Adm. Hotham, however, was pleased with Fremantle's performance and his post-battle dispatch was suitably complimentary. It read as follows:[14]

> The signal was made for a general chase, in the course of which, the weather became squally, and blowing very fresh, we discovered one of their Line-of-Battle Ships to be without her topmasts, which afforded to Captain Fremantle, of the Inconstant frigate (who was then far advanced on the chase) an opportunity of shewing a good proof of British enterprise, by his attacking, raking and harassing her until the coming up of the Agamemnon, when he was most ably seconded by Captain Nelson, who did her so much damage as to disable her from putting herself again to rights; but they were at this time so far detached from our own Fleet, that they were obliged to quit her, as other Ships of the Enemy were coming up to her assistance, by one of which she was soon after taken in tow.

Captain Nelson describes his part in the affair more fully, although curiously pays little heed to the part played by the little-known frigate captain, Fremantle:[15]

> March 13th 1795 – At daylight the Enemy's fleet in the S.W. about three or four leagues with fresh breezes. Signal for a General Chase. At eight a.m., a French ship of the Line carried away her main and fore topmasts. At quarter-past nine, the *Inconstant* frigate fired at the disabled Ship, but receiving many shot, was obliged to leave her.

He continued at greater length on his own part in the action. Although he paid only lip service to Fremantle's part in the battle, it was obviously stored away in Nelson's memory for future reference as later battles were to bring these two men closer both as friends and as professional colleagues.

Fremantle, meanwhile, bathing in the glow of his admiral's approval, petitioned and received a pardon for the five mutineers. He wrote to the admiral immediately after the action with the *Ça Ira*:[16]

> The Ships Company of His Majesty's ship *Inconstant* under my command have behaved themselves in a very sober, quick and proper manner since the 5th of March, and having supported the same conduct this day by

their steadiness and good order in time of action, I have been induced to acquaint them that I would exert my influence with You to release their comrades the five seamen now in confinement on board the St George. Should this application Sir meet your approbation I shall consider myself personally obliged by your acquiescence and hope you will be enjoined that nothing but the disgrace attendant on their being punished on the innocent part of the Ship's Company, together with my conviction of their shame and remorse for having been guilty of such an offence, could have allowed me to become their advocate.

His reply arrived promptly from Adm. Hotham:[17]

I approve very much of what you propose with respect to the delinquents now in confinement belonging to the ship you command, and shall withdraw the order for their trial agreeable to your request.

I am glad to find the Inconstant has sustained so little damage in her action with the *Ça Ira*, your conduct upon which occasion has merited my warmest approbation, I shall not fail of taking due notice of it.

With a touch of the theatrical, of which surely Nelson would have approved, he announced the pardon after the funeral that he led for the five members of HMS *Inconstant*'s crew who had been killed in the fight with the *Ça Ira*. In his own words, the crew cheered him and declared they would never have any other captain. Fremantle, for his part, could see the humour in the situation and the fickleness of these men who a few days ago had wished to see him dismissed from the service.

5

SERVICE IN ITALY
AND MARRIAGE

By the summer of 1795 Fremantle had been marked out as an up-and-coming talent in the Royal Navy. At the age of 30 he was still a relatively young post-captain but he was fast becoming one of the select band of talented officers, in a period that was to become a golden age for the Royal Navy. The 'stars', all of whom were to serve under Adm. Jervis, included Nelson, Fremantle, Miller, Elphistone, Foley, Troubridge, Hallowell and Hood.* To varying degrees, these officers would revolve around Horatio Nelson as he gradually built his own reputation to a point when his fame would almost eclipse that of the navy itself. But these men did not only learn from the great man, but also from each other and from the endless blockades where they sought to refine the naval and seaman-like skills that would ultimately elevate the Royal Navy to a peak of wartime efficiency. By the end of the eighteenth and the beginning of the nineteenth century, it would be no exaggeration to say that the Royal Navy had become an educational centre of excellence, with Fremantle one of a number of star pupils.

The political situation at the Admiralty was also working to Fremantle's advantage. Earl Spencer, a Whig politician, was appointed

---

* Capt. Sam Hood, cousin to the rather more illustrious Lord Hood.

First Lord of the Admiralty in 1794 and was to remain in post until 1801. Being responsible for naval appointments and a close political ally of the Grenville family meant that Lord Spencer became a valuable 'friend' for Fremantle, and while there is no evidence of Fremantle receiving a direct career boost from the association it was never a bad thing to have friends in high places.

Fremantle's first task was to join the blockading fleet off Toulon. It was a thankless, boring job and one he, and indeed most captains, heartily disliked. With the British fleet under Hotham now based on St Fiorenzo, there was a strong naval presence along France's Mediterranean coast with a constant need for frigates to ferry messages between the ships of the line and to act as the in-shore eyes of the blockading force. Fremantle's seniority had been recognised by Hotham, who had appointed him acting commodore of a squadron of five frigates. Fremantle found that he could relate to Hotham in a way that had never been possible with Hood, as he told William in a letter dated 31 May 1795:[1]

> Nothing can equal the civility, attention and kindness I have received from Hotham ... is it not extraordinary that I should be so well with a man I never knew but upon service, and so much the reverse with another from whom I had reason to expect everything ... my good friend Sir Hyde continues staunch, and has realy been the means of my getting this ship.

However, despite liking the man, Fremantle was not entirely uncritical of the commander-in-chief. He recognised that he was probably too old and risk averse to make a great commander. His comments, recorded in a letter to his brother a month later, state:[2]

> My good friend Hotham who is certainly as worthy and as gallant a man as ever was born is grown too old and has not nerves sufficient for the situation in which he is placed, government can't do better than send somebody else here.

His wish was soon to be realised and with it he was to get exactly the type of firebrand for whom he so earnestly wished.

In the summer of 1795 Fremantle was detached from the Toulon blockade to join Nelson in the blockade off Genoa. From the word go it was obvious Nelson was prepared to take a more aggressive approach to blockading and within months Fremantle was telling his brother exultantly of shore raids and the taking of prizes. On 26 August 1795, as part of Nelson's squadron, Fremantle participated in the capture of two French gun brigs, two galleys and five store ships.

The situation was a typical Nelson-inspired piece of aggressive action. The Genoan ports of Alassio, Oneglia and Languelia were, legally, neutral ports and as such no acts of war should be committed within the boundaries of the port. However, they were by now in French hands, or at least behind the lines of the French advance, and were being treated openly as French ports, sheltering French supply ships. Nelson, together with five frigates, attacked Alassio and Languelia to attempt the capture of ships sheltering there, which they knew were carrying French military supplies. Nelson in HMS *Agamemnon*, together with the frigates, HMS *Meleager*, *Southampton* and *Ariadne*, attacked on the eastern side of the bay while Fremantle on HMS *Inconstant*, together with HMS *Tartar* commanded by Capt. Elphinstone, attacked Languelia on the western side.[3]

Nelson issued orders to Fremantle as follows:[4]

I beg leave to acquaint you that it is my intention to endeavour to take the above mentioned vessels if it can be done, without any material contest with His Majesty's Ships and Batteries.

You will therefore anchor with the *Tartar* close off the Town of Languilla which is about gunshot distance from Alassio, and if you can bring out all the vessels at that place, you are hereby directed to do so, but you are by no means to enter into such a contest as may greatly endanger the Masts and Yards of your Ships and the *Tartar*. You are not to fire on the Battery or Town unless fired upon, or by signal to engage from me.

I have the fullest confidence on You Sir as an officer that you will not endanger greatly His Majesty's Ships, and although the object of destroying those vessels is of great importance for the services of the Squadron will shortly be wanted on other Services equally important.

These orders were typical of Nelson for what he was proposing was an audacious action in what he knew to be, legally, a neutral port, albeit one that was not behaving in a neutral fashion. As Fremantle approached Languelia he saw there was a large French gunboat in the harbour that was guarding two merchant ships. He signalled to Nelson for permission to attack and, being answered in the affirmative, he took the three ships without incurring any casualties and, crucially, without involving the Genoese authorities.

The fact that Fremantle had signalled prior to capturing the French vessels demonstrated that he still required a little more self-confidence before taking decisive action. Nelson wanted captains to think for themselves, to take responsibility and to have the courage to take difficult decisions without constant recourse to a senior officer. Fremantle was still learning but his commodore's independent actions along the Genoese coast were gaining the plaudits of his admiral and British representatives in the Mediterranean, who could see how the French were abusing the neutrality of Genoa. The courage to take difficult and sometimes risky political decisions was just one of the lessons that Fremantle would learn from his time with Nelson.

Nelson was generous in his praise for Fremantle's actions and in his dispatch to Hotham paid tribute:[5]

> Having received information from General de Vins, that a Convoy of provisions and ammunition was arrived at Alassio, a place in the possession of the French Army, I yesterday proceeded with the Ships named in the margin to that place, where, within an hour we took the Vessels named in the enclosed list. There was but a very feeble opposition from some of the Enemy's cavalry, who fired on our boats after Boarding the Vessels near the shore, but I have the pleasure to say no man was killed or wounded. The Enemy had two thousand horse and foot Soldiers in the Town, which prevented my landing and destroying their magazines of provisions and ammunition. I sent Captain Fremantle of the *Inconstant*, with the *Tartar*, to Languelia, a Town on the west side of the Bay of Alassio, where he executed my orders in the most officer-like manner; and I am indebted to every Captain and Officer of the Squadron for their activity, but most particularly so to Lieutenant George Andrews, first Lieutenant of the *Agamemnon* who by his spirited and officer-like conduct saved the French Corvette from going on shore.

Despite the best efforts of the British navy, French coastal vessels were still able to resupply the French army by creeping along the coastline in waters too shallow for the British vessels. This led to one of the senior Austrian army commanders accusing the squadron of entering into an illegal agreement with the French coastal shipping to turn a blind eye to their activities.

Nelson was indignant in his defence of the captains under his command, acknowledging that it was perfectly true that the French were resupplying their army from the sea, but pointing out in no uncertain terms to the Austrians that it was because they possessed small coastal vessels, together with native crews who knew the coastal waters intimately and were therefore able to flit along the coast out of reach of the bigger British ships.

It was one of several incidents indicative of the fragile nature of the alliance fighting the French revolutionary forces. The problems of a disparate international coalition, against the cohesion and patriotism of the revolutionary French army, were surfacing yet again.

Despite the annoyance of their efforts being unappreciated by the Austrian army, it is hard not to believe that these months of operations off the coast of Italy were not the happiest and most fulfilling of Fremantle's career to date. He was surrounded by fellow officers with whom he got on socially and his immediate commander, Nelson, was someone he both admired and, on a personal level, liked. They frequently dined together and despite Fremantle's rather priggish disapproval of Nelson's mistress, it did not seem to stop him enjoying the delights of many other females of his own, especially when in the Italian port of Leghorn.

The situation changed dramatically in November when Adm. Hotham was sent home and the post of commander-in-chief of the Mediterranean Fleet was filled by Adm. Sir John Jervis.* Jervis quickly took stock of his new command and decided that things within the fleet had become lax. He sensibly started at the top and sent home those officers who he felt were responsible for the state of the fleet, in which both drunkenness and venereal diseases were rife. Captains who Jervis felt would not fit into his new regime were sent home and he spelt out exactly what he expected of those who remained. There were to be no illusions as to the standards he expected of them. This was exactly what both Nelson and Fremantle wished for and from now on they would be directed by an admiral who knew what he wanted and communicated clearly the standards he expected.

---

* After the Battle of St Vincent on 14 February 1797 Sir John Jervis was granted an earldom by the King and became known as 1st Earl of St Vincent.

He ensured ships stayed at sea for long spells and that training drills were carried out rigorously and frequently. Crews and officers were kept busy for, in Jervis's eyes, a busy man had no time to cause trouble or to think of revolution or mutiny. Repairs were carried out at sea and the replenishment system was overhauled and made more efficient.[6]

Orders spewed out of HMS *Victory*, sometimes two or three per day to the fleet, ordering every facet of life at sea to make them more businesslike, to get them ready for battle by ensuring that both crews and officers were fit and well trained for battle. Orders were given to ensure all ships completely filled their water butts when in port, that they replenished with food sufficient for a minimum of fourteen weeks. No sailors were to be sent back to Portsmouth sick without the explicit authority of the fleet surgeon and bedding was to be hung out every day in fair weather to ensure it was clean and dry whenever possible.* No facet of life at sea was too detailed that it did not come under Jervis's all-seeing eye and soon the message was rammed home to every officer under his command. It was either shape up or be shipped home; there was no other alternative in Jervis's fleet.

In the spring of the New Year (1796) Fremantle was ordered to cruise along the African coast. It may have been a low-key warning by Jervis to keep the ever-ready Fremantle out of the fleshpots of Italy but there was an operational imperative as the Mediterranean coast of Africa had long been a threat to British commerce with pirates from Tunisia, Algiers and Morocco always alert for stray merchantmen. In the course of his passage along the coast, Fremantle was passed information that the French frigate *L'Unité* had been seen cruising off the same coast adjacent to Cape Mabera near Tunis. His dispatch to Sir John Jervis tells the story:[7]

I have the honour to inform you, that on the 19th cruising near Tunis, I received an Account that a French Frigate had been seen off Cape Mabera near Bon; I therefore made sail for that Place, and, on the Evening of the 20th, perceived a Ship under French Colours at Anchor on the Coast, which I came to, by, and directed to Strike; this was prudently complied

---

* Many years later, when serving as an admiral in the Adriatic, Fremantle received a missive from the Admiralty cautioning commanding officers of the unacceptably high replacement bills for bedding and canvas sleeping bags that had been put out to dry but had blown away in windy weather!

with: She is called *L'Unité*, a Corvette of 34 guns and 218 Men. The crew had made an Attempt to set her on Fire, but by the Exertions of Lieutenant Hutchinson it was soon extinguished. Had the Ship been of equal Force with the *Inconstant*, I have every Reason to believe it would have afforded me a further Proof of the Spirit and Steadiness of every Officer and Person on Board the Ship I command.

From the last sentiment expressed in his dispatch it is obvious that, in the year and two months since he had been captain of HMS *Inconstant*, crew morale had improved dramatically and that the dark days of the attempted mutiny were far behind him. Fremantle had achieved to what he had always aspired, a crew that understood him, respected his authority and acted promptly when required. He could count himself among the elite, both Jervis and Nelson recognised his ability and accordingly his confidence grew. As an added bonus, *L'Unité* was taken on by the Royal Navy and renamed HMS *Surprise*. It was, therefore, both a lucrative and effective operation.

If things appeared to be going well for Fremantle, the same could not be said for the land forces opposed to France. While Austria was more than holding its own against the two French armies with Archduke Charles von Habsburg, younger brother of the emperor, commanding the Austrian army, the Piedmont and Austrian forces facing the French Army of Italy were doing less well. The Directory, France's government under the leadership of Barras, had appointed a new general, a comparatively unknown 26-year-old named Napoleon Buonoparte. He soon changed his name to the better-known Bonaparte to give it a more Gallic sound. At this stage in his career he was still far removed from the political power he was eventually to assume but he was to prove an astonishingly effective military commander, despite being so young, and he was to turn around rapidly the fortunes of the chronically underfunded and despondent Army of Italy.

By mid June 1796, Napoleon had strengthened and reinvigorated his army. He had been able to push eastwards from the Genoese Republic into Piedmont and the lands of the Duke of Palma, and was threatening Milan and the Austrian forts that protected the Alpine passes. More worryingly for the British, he was threatening to move southwards and as a result had nullified the possible threat from Naples by signing a treaty with the King, freeing his forces to threaten the Cisalpine and

Vatican states. In June, Pope Pius VI was forced to sign an armistice with Napoleon, who occupied both Modena and Bologna. In order to boost his standing in the ever-changing political climate in Paris he was 'liberating' art treasures and tributes from the conquered states to send back to France to fill the ever demanding government coffers.

Trying to keep ahead of Napoleon's all-conquering forces were a flood of refugees and emigrées, amongst them an English family consisting of Richard Wynne, his wife and four daughters. Wynne was the son of a well-to-do family originally from Wales. By the middle of the eighteenth century the family had large estates in Falkingham, Lincolnshire. His mother, a Venetian named Anna Gazzini, christened her fourth child Riccardo Gulielmo Casparo Melchior Balthazaro Wynne, otherwise to be known as Richard Wynne. The first three children were all girls so on the death of his father it was Richard who inherited the estate. Richard lived in Falkingham until the last of his five daughters had been born in 1786. He then sold the estate and, with the proceeds, moved to the Continent to start a peripatetic life with his wife, the four youngest daughters and a considerable retinue of servants and hangers-on.

Two of his daughters, Elizabeth, known to all as Betsey, and Eugenia, became avid diarists from the start of their travels, providing amusing commentary on the doings of this strange travelling circus. Their mother was a Roman Catholic, a pious and self-effacing woman, but it was their eccentric father, Richard, who pranced through the pages providing much of the material for the girls' diaries. Richard was a hypochondriac, afflicted by piles, gout and rheumatism. He frequently drank too much and was seemingly addicted to practical jokes.[8]

As Napoleon's army moved further south, the British Minister to Florence, the Hon. William Wyndham, wrote to Jervis to appraise him of the rapidly changing scenario:[9]

That there are many reasons to suppose, that on this point either His Royal Highness's Ministers, thinks it politic, to deceive one, or are themselves deceived, by the French, or perhaps both, and once fairly in Tuscany, I much doubt, if the French will resist the temptation of going to Leghorn.

As this blow (if struck) will probably be sudden and violent, I should hope that your Excellency will continue till such time, as the Alarm subsides to let such Frigates as you can spare from your Fleet remain at

Leghorn to carry off such persons and merchandise, as it may be necessary to be conveyed from hence in case of Invasion.

Jervis responded to the threat posed to British interests in Leghorn by dispatching Fremantle with two frigates, *Romulus* and *Dido*, with orders to ensure that British naval stores and English traders' merchandise did not fall into French hands. Shortly after HMS *Inconstant* sailed into Leghorn the Wynne family, together with some of their entourage, arrived with other English émigrés from Florence to escape the rapidly advancing French forces.

Fremantle reacted to the potentially fraught situation of frightened English tourists, merchants, civil servants and the hundred and one hangers-on with exactly the kind of phlegmatic confidence that was becoming his trademark. He successfully evacuated everything of value out of Leghorn, together with all the English citizens, finally sailing out of the port at 1 p.m. on 27 June as the French forces were already pouring into the town right behind the fleeing British. Among his passengers was the Wynne entourage. As he left the mole, the French were already occupying the town and he was fired on by French artillery. His report to Jervis explains:[10]

I had the honour of acquainting you in my letter of the evening of the 23rd inst. accompanied with despatches by the Blanche of the supposed forcible entry of the French Troops into Tuscany and their intended invasion of Leghorn.

On the 24th I attended a meeting of the Consul and factory, where the information that had been received was communicated, and having assured them that I would remain at anchor in the Road for their protection, until the Enemy obliged me to weigh, the Merchants prepared to embark their Goods on board the Ships and Transports, which were ordered immediately out of the Mole and I requested Captain Craven would use every Despatch in getting the large Ships lower Masts, Spars &c. launched and secured on Board the Transports

On the 25th many of the Merchant Vessels and the Elizabeth Transport, which was sheathing in the inner Mole, were got out and the Masts lashed alongside the latter.

On the 26th the Gorgon arrived about Noon, and the remaining large Spars were launched and sent to the Ship when having got certain

Information of the Intention of the Enemy, who slept at Pantedera only Eighteen Miles from Leghorn, I ordered the whole of the Convoy amounting to Twenty three Sail of Square rigged vessels and 14 Tartans to be got underway at day light on the 27th.* A little after Noon on that Day the French Troops entered the Town of Leghorn, and began firing on the Inconstant about One, when I got under Weigh with the only Vessel remaining, which was the Prize to L'Aigle a Brig laden with Ship Timber. Two small Privateers endeavoured to cut her off, which obliged us to tack to support her, and occasioned some few Shot being exchanged, which however did no Damage.

Commodore Nelson with the *Captain* and *Meleager*, who had received Notice of the Enemy's Design, anchored here on the 27th at Ten o' Clock, and the Commodore added the *Meleager* to the Convoy which was of much Importance as the Enemy's Small Privateers were numerous and enterprising.

All the Shipping, nearly the Whole of the English property, and all His Majesty's Naval Stores and Provisions, have been saved, and every English Person and Emigré desirous of leaving Tuscany, have been received on Board some of the Ships.

Commodore Nelson, in the *Captain*, remained at anchor at Malora, and will doubtless stop any English Ships who may not be informed of the French being in Possession of Leghorn.

I feel myself particularly obliged to Lieutenant Grey, employed in the Transport Service, for his great Exertions in getting the Stores, &c. off, and great Credit is due to Mr Heatly, Agent Victualler, who was indefatigable in saving the Provisions, Wine, &c.

I have Cause to be satisfied with the Unanimity and united Efforts of every English Subject on this Occasion, where so little Notice could be given, and considered that no certain Accounts were ever received that the French were absolutely in Tuscany until the 25th, I hope, Sir, you will believe that nothing has been wanting to accelerate the Embarkation, or to accommodate and protect both the Persons and Property of His Majesty's Subjects and the unfortunate Emigrés, all of which I left safe off Cape Corse Yesterday at Noon; Lord Garlies having promised to see them in Safety into San Fiorenzo, with the *Lively*, *Meleager*, *Gorgon*, *Comet* and *Vanneau*.

---

* A tartan is a lateen-rigged, usually single-masted, vessel with a shallow draft that was used extensively in the Mediterranean for coastal trading.

Admiral Jervis was more than satisfied with Fremantle's efforts. He recognised that the young post-captain had succeeded in carrying out a tremendous feat of logistics in the most difficult of circumstances. He forwarded Fremantle's dispatch on to the Admiralty, adding his own fulsome praise:[11]

> The *Inconstant* joined this morning from Leghorn; and I enclose for the Information of the Lords Commissioners of the Admiralty, Captain Fremantle's Reports of the Proceedings of the Enemy in Tuscany, their taking Possession of Leghorn, and the Retreat of the British Factory with most of their Property, which they owe to the unparalleled Exertions of Captain Fremantle, the Officers and Crew of the *Inconstant*; Commodore Nelson, owing to Calms and light Winds, not having reached Leghorn Road until the Enemy was in possession.

Equally important to Fremantle's professional future was Nelson's opinion, which he expressed in a letter to Sir Gilbert Elliot on 1 July 1796:[12]

> I know you must be anxious to hear what has been passing at Leghorn, therefore I send you information just as I received it, without form or order. You may depend Buonaparte is gone, and I hope on account supposed, that General Beaulieu is reinforced. The English are under infinite obligations to Spannochi, who is suffering for it. And to Captain Fremantle they are much obliged, for his great exertions in getting all their shipping out of the Mole ...

The speed at which the French had moved to take Leghorn is illustrated in Betsey Wynne's diaries, where her entry for 24 June reads:[13]

> Papa's fears began to be greater than ever Thursday and nothing could prevent him from resolving to set off for Leghorn in the evening. Everybody laughs at his being so great a coward and says it is very foolish to go away when there is not the least apprehension to be had in this place ...
>   We arrived at Leghorn at eleven in the morning we went to Mr Udney's* and found there a most terrible bustle and noise – All packing up and

---

*   John Udney was the British consul, post-master, victualler and even, on occasions, the 'procurer' of women for the officers in Leghorn.

getting on board the ships. We hardly had time to get a little breakfast, they hurried us so terribly to quit the place and Captain Fremantle took us on board his Frigate the *Inconstant* a most beautiful ship.

So began the short, romantic interlude that would eventually end with Betsey Wynne marrying Fremantle. It would be nice to think the whole affair was one beautiful example of serendipity but, given Fremantle's notorious ability to spot a beautiful girl at 100 paces, it was more than likely that he took the decision to take the Wynnes on board his own ship having already spotted the attractive and vivacious Betsey. What is certain, however, is that it did not take Betsey long to form a very favourable opinion of her saviour, for her diary entry for the same day read:[14]

How kind and amiable Captain Fremantle is. He pleases me more than any man I have yet seen. Not handsome, but there is something pleasing in his countenance and his fiery black eyes are quite captivating. He is good natured, kind, and amiable, gay and lively, in short he seems to possess all the good and amiable qualities that are required to win everybodies hearts the first moment one sees him.

Betsey was quite obviously smitten from the moment she saw Fremantle, but what of his feelings? Having rejoined the fleet and passed the Wynne family on to Capt. Garlies, Fremantle, as on all important occasions in his life, wrote to his brother William seeking his views:[15]

I have now to mention to you a circumstance which from your regard for me I am sure you will feel much interested in, and as I mean to let you into the whole history I shall begin with its origin and continue, not that I can benefit from your advice, as that will be too late, but that nothing gives more consolation than communicating to a friend one can perfectly rely on – from this preface you will expect it is of great importance, I think it is of all others that on which a man ought most seriously to consider, namely marriage.

On the evacuation of Leghorn a family with 4 Daughters came from Florence with letters from our Minister Mr. Wyndham requesting they might be received on board some of the Ships to escape from the French.

Civility rather than anything else in the first instance induced me to receive them on board, where I found them so pleasant that except three days they have remained ever since. The family are English and I believe of good property, and the Eldest daughter a girl of eighteen. You will now suppose [me] to be going to break out in all the transports of a man violently smitten, no such thing, I will tell you the real truth and not exaggerate, and I trust I have not yet gone so far but I shall with some little difficulty, be able to get the better of my attachment. There is but one impediment which is *fortune*. Without getting a sufficiency to keep her in the way I think necessary you may depend upon it I never will engage myself, however I may be distressed in the event. For the Girl she is short, speaks and writes German Italian French & English, plays incomparably well on the harpsichord, draws well, sings a little and is otherwise a very good humoured sensible dolly, not particularly handsome, but a little healthy thing more the appearance of my sister Cathcart than any person I can immediately recollect.

The family altogether very pleasant, and much attached to each other. I should imagine a few days must determine one way or other. You may conceive I am made very unhappy in having so accidently tumbled into a snare not to be guarded against. God knows how it will end, I have my fears. Now don't you think that everything is concluded, I give you my word of honour everything is as I have related, and I think it will be prudent in you to conceal it, as I shall from you the name for the present, that I may not afford you the grounds to laugh at me. When I consider my friends are married, and I certainly shall not live in the same way I have formerly in London I confess I feel great pleasure in thinking a man may live perfectly happy with a sober sort of Dolly in the Country, I am sure all this will make you laugh – do so – and pity me for five minutes after, for the horrid confinement of a Sailor's life is insupportable. I shall seal this up for I am ashamed of my weakness.

At first glance, this is not the letter of a totally besotted lover and certainly does not contain the emotional sincerity of Betsey's diary entries. However, in its own way Fremantle's letter inadvertently gave an indication of his true feelings while simultaneously trying to hide what he perceived as weakness and thereby prevent him becoming the butt of his brother's humour. After starting the letter protesting that he has promised nothing, he is by the last paragraph beginning to imagine the domestic happiness that a wife could bring him. It would be rare for Fremantle to bare his soul, even to someone as close as his brother, but this letter was probably as close as he felt able to go.

Fate was yet again to play a part when Adm. Jervis played the unlikely role of Cupid in the affairs of one of his favourite protégés. He dispatched Fremantle on a mission to negotiate with the Dey of Algiers. In doing so, he was not unmindful of the possibility of Fremantle perhaps picking up a few prizes and thus adding to his attractiveness as a potential suitor. As things stood, Richard Wynne favoured the older Capt. Thomas Foley as his daughter's suitor rather than the impoverished Fremantle.

The Wynnes stayed with the fleet while Fremantle was carrying out his duties along the African coast and, as can be imagined, Betsey proved to be exceedingly popular with a number of the single officers. She was, however, protected by the kindly and paternal attentions of the grizzled, 61-year-old admiral. Betsey relates one of the invitations the family received during Fremantle's absence on duty:[16]

Sir John Jervis wrote us a note at four o'clock in the morning to ask us to dine with him. We accepted with infinite pleasure of his kind invitation, and having had several visits Ct. Ogle, Captain Hood, Captain Troubridge, the Commissioner from Ajacia (who brought us a letter from Captain Fremantle) we dressed to go to the Victory. The Admiral was on the Deck to receive us with the greatest civility and kindness nothing stiff or formal about him and we were not at all embarrassed as I feared we should be. He desired we should pay the tribute that was due to him at our entering his Cabin, this was to kiss him which the Ladies did very willingly. Lord Garlies came soon after us. The Admiral abused him for not having yet saluted us, the consequence was that we were kissed a second time ...

He [Admiral Jervis] made the greatest commendation of him [Fremantle] and applause to Papa and Mama and said he would wish *him* to marry me. Papa answered he had not what was necessary for the marriage state, Sir John Jervis replied he was in a very good way to get one, and he was besides such an excellent honest man that he could wish nothing better for my happiness. The good Admiral has a very high opinion of me. He told me I should make the best wife in England.

While this was going on Fremantle remained oblivious to the fact he had one of Britain's most senior admirals fighting his corner. From Jervis's point of view, it was possibly not quite the altruistic move it first appears. It is inconceivable that he was unaware of Fremantle's womanising reputation and, in order to assist his naval career, he probably thought that a strong, independently minded wife was exactly what Fremantle needed. It was fortunate that Betsey remained unaware that just days before she arrived in Leghorn, Fremantle had been entertaining Adelaide Correglia, Nelson's mistress, on board HMS *Inconstant*. Obviously, to Fremantle, all was fair in love and war.[17]

Prior to Fremantle's negotiations with the Dey of Algiers the military situation in the Mediterranean had been turning rapidly against Britain. In July 1796 Spain allied herself with France and, in October 1796, declared war on Britain. Spain, despite possessing a significant empire, was a far smaller economic power than Great Britain but she did possess a powerful navy and, together with the French navy, posed a real threat to Britain. It would not be long before Britain was forced to pull back from the eastern Mediterranean.

All of this was unknown to Fremantle, who was about to conduct his own inimitable brand of international diplomacy with the Dey of Algiers.[18] His orders from Jervis stated:[19]

You are to use any means consistent with the Dignity of His Majesty to appraise the Dey of the most sincere desire of the King to preserve the Friendship and Amnity, which for the benefit of both Countries have strongly and happily existed between the Sovereigns and subjects of the two powers.

Should you find it necessary you are to enter into a full explanation and justification of the Capture of the French Republican ship *L'Unite* by His Majesty's ship under your Command, upon the ground of the report you made to me thereon, with the addition of any other circumstances which may lend to remove the wrong impression the Dey has received from Intriguing and Mischievous spirit of the French and Neutral Residents at Algiers.

In a letter to William, Fremantle explained his unorthodox negotiating technique:[20]

I was directed to present His Majesty with a Vessel from the Viceroy of Corsica* which conveyed the Dog would not accept of her and refused to grant me an audience. You may easily conceive I was not the *sort of Man* to submit *quietly* to such an insult, and as I knew His Highness required being talked to pretty stoutly, I got all the Ships moved nearer the Town to his great annoyance, when he began to cry out that it was a mistake, and that he begged to see me, as I found how things were going, and I felt my ground sufficiently solid, I sent on shore to His Highness a note or whatever you may chuse to call it ... I said that I should not wait on him until he sent an Officer off to the Ship I commanded to make an attonement for the Insult offered, which he did, and on Shore I went among these fellows with the plague raging as I have told you, and had about an hours' talking with him on *matters of state*, particularly of my taking L'Unite in his jurisdiction &c. &c. ... What do you think of my Embassy – it kept me on thorns for 24 hours, his works and batteries were manned and I was in momentary expectation of his firing on us. I do sincerely believe that nothing but our determination which surprised him made us carry it with so high a hand.

From Algiers, Fremantle moved on with dispatches for Britain's chargé d'affaires at Constantinople before picking up a convoy at Smyrna to escort it back to the main British fleet in Corsica. Prior to sailing, he received orders from Jervis that clearly showed the international scene had turned decisively against the British presence in the Mediterranean. Jervis was forced to point out to Fremantle that it now should be regarded as a hostile sea. In his letter of 25 September he orders Fremantle to:[21]

Proceed with the upmost caution, and to avoid the European side of the Mediterranean, and keep mid-channel between Sardinia and the coast of Africa, avoiding Sardinia, where the enemy is paramount. In truth, there will be no security or protection from the powers on either side.

Despite the dire warning from his commander-in-chief, Fremantle had succeeded and had returned to the fleet safely. Adm. Jervis was pleased with his efforts. His subsequent dispatch to the Admiralty stated:[22]

* Sir Gilbert Elliott.

'The manner in which Captain Fremantle has acquitted himself of his mission in the Levant adds greatly to his former merit.'

The problems that beset the British fleet were not so much on the high seas but where they could position themselves with a base to support the fleet. Corsica was obviously threatened; even Gibraltar could not be considered wholly safe now that Spain had joined France. Troops were embarked from Corsica, which the British now evacuated, and Fremantle was ordered to Elba while the rest of the fleet sailed for Gibraltar to replenish. The Wynne family rejoined Fremantle on HMS *Inconstant*, but if Betsey was expecting a rapturous reunion with the man she was by now sure that she wished to marry, she was to be cruelly disappointed. Fremantle was cold and stand-offish in his manner to her. Unfortunately, we have to take her sister Eugenia's description of the next few months as, some time later, Betsey's own diary for the period late September 1796 until January 1797 was lost.

However, the extent of her mounting feelings for Fremantle is contained in her diary entry for Thursday, 1 September:[23]

> Since I am on board I have never been so gay and good humoured as I feel now. From the moment I heard the admiral expects the *Inconstant* soon returned from her cruise my lonely thoughts changed into the most pleasing ones. All hopes of seeing Fr. before sailing for England have forsaken me, now I flatter myself soon to see the *Inconstant* join the ship. I am an odd girl! For all I only think of Fr. I can hardly live without him I scarcely believe I am in love. I should like to know whether he thinks so often of his Betsey as I do of him? And whether he wishes as much as I do to meet again? Surely if all he said before he went away is true (as I cannot doubt of) it must be so.

Betsey was only 18 years old when she wrote this but, because of her unorthodox upbringing and mixing constantly with people older than herself, she was mature and sensible. Fremantle, on the other hand, was a 30-year-old man used to making life or death decisions. He was the one paralysed by his own emotions and by the thoughts that he would not be able to keep a wife in the manner he would wish. For the next few months he seems to have oscillated between his already admitted desire to marry Betsey and his lack of belief that he could keep a wife in, what he considered to be, the appropriate style. Perhaps there was also the thought of giving up the rather strenuous love life that he so enjoyed. Whatever the reasons, he kept Betsey on a string alternately dangling between happiness and despair.

The Wynnes sailed on HMS *Inconstant* to Elba, where Fremantle's duty next took him. In Elba, Richard Wynne rented a house just outside the town of Porto Ferraio. It was from here that Fremantle wrote to William sounding as if he had given up the whole idea of marriage:[24]

> On the subject you last wrote to me I feel every minute more and more distressed, but after very serious reflection I think I have determined finally about it in the negative, not from any alteration in my opinions of the person alluded to in my letter from Ajaccio, but for want of a sufficiency to make the remainder of one's life comfortable. I think you know me sufficiently to be convinced that I shall not commit myself or do an act I shall have cause to repent the remainder of my life, and having thus stated the whole circumstance I shall quit the subject all together.

The letter sounds more like that of a man afraid of committing himself and subsequently trying to rationalise his fears rather than one who has actually made a decision. This was supported by the fact that on Thursday, 28 December, when Fremantle was ordered to Naples, the Wynnes were once again back on board HMS *Inconstant* and sailed with him to Naples. Again the loss of Betsey's diaries dictates that Eugenia's is the only record of Betsey's emotions. However, the two sisters were extremely close and, when they arrived in Naples, it was Eugenia who took over the main assault on Fremantle's indecisiveness regarding matrimony. Her diary entry for Wednesday, 4 January 1797 reads:[25]

> I had again a great deal of talk with Fremantle, he gives his word that his intentions, his sentiments are the same as they were when he went to Smyrna, and then he adds what would [you] do if you were in my position? As far as delicacy will permit it, I try to hint to him what I would do, if I were in his place. He understands me perfectly and says that he does not want inclination but power to do it. I own that I am quite out, yet the idea of seeing him a member of our family, is too dear to me, is grown too favourite, that I should give it up at once. So many unexpected things happen! And since sometimes I have been taught to look only towards improbabilities, therefore why should I give up hope? I am afraid that if

time does not justify this hope B will have forfeited her happiness, because she is too far gone, her affections are very deeply engaged.

Thus the battle lines were drawn. On one side, against marriage, was an ambivalent Fremantle with a, possibly hostile, Richard Wynne. On the other side was Mrs Wynne, the Wynne sisters, the commander-in-chief of the Mediterranean Fleet and probably, William Fremantle, who wished to see his brother married and settled down. Events moved rapidly and on 10 January, Fremantle bowed to the inevitable and wrote to his future father-in-law to set out his proposals and to ask for Betsey's hand in marriage. Richard Wynne recognised that the forces mounted against him were too powerful and on 11 January the matter was brought to a satisfactory conclusion with him agreeing to the marriage and settling £5,000 on the happy couple,* with an undertaking of a further £10,000 on his death.

The settlement having been agreed, the couple wasted no time in getting married. The ceremony took place on Thursday, 13 January 1797 with King George III's sixth son, Prince Augustus, giving the bride away.** It was followed the next day by a Catholic blessing. After the ceremonies Fremantle was almost immediately called back to duty and he and his wife left on HMS *Inconstant* to take Sir Gilbert Elliott back to Porto Ferraio in Elba.

A few days after they arrived in Elba both the captain and the crew were invited over to their respective messes on HMS *Minerva*. The next morning, Capt. Fremantle was required to discipline some of the crew who had got drunk and behaved badly. It was Betsey's first experience of naval discipline and she records them crying out as they were flogged and how sick it made her husband to have to both order and witness the punishment. It certainly did not accord with the image of an indiscriminate user of corporal punishment.

The Fremantles then moved ashore and lived in a small house close to the water's edge. The two-month period, from late January 1797 to late March, must have been a wonderful opportunity for the couple to settle down and really get to know each other. Their courtship had been so brief

---

*   Worth some £330,000 in today's currency.

** Prince Augustus was 'exiled' in Naples considering the alternative of renouncing his morganatic marriage to Lady Augusta Murray or giving up his place in the royal family, including his pension.

that this quiet period of togetherness served to reassure Fremantle that he had made the right choice. He was comforted by the fact that Betsey was such an excellent sailor and was able to amuse herself with music and suchlike when he was detained on board with his official duties. His words to William expressed his happiness:[26] 'We go very little out and if I am to judge of the future by the present time I think I shall never have cause to repent of being married. *My Wife* is perfectly what I could have wished.'

Fremantle's command was now Britain's sole naval presence in the Mediterranean and in Toulon the combined French and Spanish fleets numbered some thity-eight ships of the line. It was inevitable that strategic realities would break up this idyll and on 16 April HMS *Inconstant*, together with numerous merchant ships, sailed in convoy out of Elba westwards towards Gibraltar. On the way they were met by Nelson, who records in his dispatch to Jervis:[27]

> To Admiral Sir John Jervis, K.B. from Admiral Nelson on HMS Captain off Cape Pallas 1st May 1797 – I have not interfered with Captain Fremantle's charge and arrangement of the Convoy, it could not be in better hands, therefore I could only overshadow them with my wings.

At Gibraltar on 1 June 1797, Fremantle left HMS *Inconstant* to be posted to another frigate, HMS *Seahorse*. She was slightly bigger than HMS *Inconstant* but was significantly more heavily armed, with the addition of heavy carronades to add to her more traditional cannons.* The vessel was barely 3 years old but, that apart, Betsey would not have noticed a significant improvement in her living quarters as the captain's cabin was barely a foot broader than that on HMS *Inconstant*. Unknown to Fremantle, HMS *Seahorse* was to be his last frigate command, for after leaving her in September all his future commands would be ships of the line.

While the Fremantles had been enjoying their extended honeymoon in Elba, Britain, in the form of Adm. Jervis, had been to war. The Spanish, under Adm. Don José de Córdoba, had left Cartagena on 1 February with a fleet of twenty-seven ships of the line in order to protect a merchant convoy coming into Cádiz. The fleet were blown further out into

---

* Carronades were becoming a popular addition to Royal Navy ships' armament. They were short-barreled cannons that were only useful at very close range but threw an extremely heavy load of shot. This made them the perfect weapon for the navy, who strongly believed in getting closely alongside the enemy vessel before firing.

the Atlantic than they wished, thanks to an easterly gale. The British, having received intelligence of the Spanish intentions, had also put to sea and Jervis's fleet of ten ships of the line were bolstered by five ships joining him from the Channel Fleet. On 14 February 1797 the two fleets came into contact and, in the resulting battle of the Cape of St Vincent, Nelson achieved fame by sailing out of the line of battle, in apparent disregard of Jervis's orders, to engage and prevent the escape of the Spanish fleet. HMS *Captain*, Nelson's ship, was involved closely in the capture of two of the four ships that were taken by the British.

Fremantle was not involved, but the battle was to affect his future. Nelson, who was promoted to rear admiral just days after the battle, saw for the first time the effects of rigid tactics and the futility of trying to command centrally a major fleet engagement of the size and complexity of the Battle of St Vincent. From now on, as Nelson refined his thinking, he would demand more and more initiative from the captains who served under him. The tactics that would culminate in the melee of the Battle of Trafalgar were born in the escape of the major element of the Spanish fleet off Cape St Vincent.

When Fremantle joined the fleet off Cádiz he did so with a newly promoted admiral (Nelson) who, given the paucity of personal publicity in the post-battle dispatch, was determined to make a name for himself. More significantly, Nelson was determined to free up the rigid tactics of the past and grant freedom of action to captains operating under his command. He would set the overall objectives and strategy and then expected the men under his command to have the initiative and respond to unfolding events without constant referral back to a senior officer. Fremantle was about to begin the tertiary stage of his naval education. The first part, as a midshipman and junior lieutenant, had been about learning the basics of seamanship and command. The second part, as a junior post-captain, was learning how to command a man-of-war. Now would come the third and most important period that would end with Fremantle becoming one of the navy's great fighting captains.

By April, Jervis, now Earl St Vincent, was blockading the Spanish fleet in Cádiz. He handed over command of the inshore blockade to Nelson and in early June 1797 Fremantle joined him, having successfully evacuated the British from Elba, It was by now increasingly clear that the last thing on earth the Spanish wished to do was to come out of the harbour to face Lord St Vincent's fleet.

Nelson was temperamentally unsuited to accept stalemate and on 3 July he mounted an assault on the city of Cádiz with HMS *Thunderer*, a bomb vessel equipped with a 12½in mortar and a 10in howitzer[28] that he hoped would goad the Spanish into coming out of harbour to fight. Bomb vessels were the only Royal Navy vessels designed to throw explosive shells rather than solid cannonballs. The vessels themselves, weighed down with heavy artillery, were frequently difficult to manoeuvre and the range of the artillery was comparatively short. Owing to the dangers of the explosive canisters with fuses exploding prematurely, the bomb ships were often accompanied by small craft to hold the ammunition.

What was proposed was essentially a 'terror attack' on the city, targeting civilian and military buildings in an indiscriminate fashion, in the hope of provoking the Spanish fleet into action. HMS *Thunderer* was towed into position by small boats at about 9 p.m. Despite problems in getting her into the planned position, she began to fire salvoes into the city by 11 p.m. Within an hour, the Spanish had mustered up a small boat flotilla, commanded by Don Miguel Irigoyen, to row out to HMS *Thunderer* with a view to putting her out of action.

Capt. Miller had charge of the British flotilla of small boats, dispersed around HMS *Thunderer* for just such an eventuality, and as the Spanish approached, the British readied themselves to fight them off. Nelson, however, watching from HMS *Theseus*, was not happy with the British efforts. He called on Capt. Fremantle and eleven members of his crew and ordered the ship's barge to pull him over to HMS *Thunderer* to allow him to lead the defence.

As the admiral's boat pulled into the mass of Spanish craft, Nelson and Fremantle found themselves assaulted by the Spanish commander's barge, the *San Pablo*. The Spaniards outnumbered the British sailors by approximately three to one and, for a moment, it looked all up for both Nelson and Fremantle. They fought toe to toe with the Spaniards and, on two occasions, Nelson's life was saved only by the brave and selfless actions of his coxswain, John Sykes, who interposed his own body between the admiral and a Spanish sabre. Fremantle was cut around the face on several occasions. Eventually they were saved by the intervention of Capt. Miller, who pulled alongside the far side of the Spanish boat, boarded her and took the Spanish commander prisoner. In 1806 the painter Richard Westall exhibited a painting of this small boat engagement, featuring both Nelson and Fremantle. On being shown the picture for the first time Betsey was delighted that her young children recognised their father in the picture immediately.[29]

The fight had been desperate with all the participants, both Spanish and British, in danger of their lives. From the British side, Nelson singled out Fremantle along with Capt. Miller and Coxswain Sykes for their gallantry during the action:[30]

In obedience to your orders, the Thunderer Bomb was placed, by the good management of Lieutenant Gourly, her present Commander, assisted by Mr Jackson, Master of the Ville de Paris who volunteered his able services within 2500 yards of the walls of Cadiz; and the shells were thrown from her with much precision, under the direction of Lieutenant Baynes, of the Royal Artillery; but, unfortunately, it was soon found that the large Mortar was materially injured, from its former services; I therefore judged it proper to order her to return under the protection of the Goliath, Terpsichore, and Fox, which were kept under sail for that purpose, and for whose active services I feel much obliged.

The Spaniards having sent out a great number of Mortar Gun-boats and armed Launches, I directed a vigorous attack to be made on them, which was done with such gallantry, that they were drove and pursued close to the walls of Cadiz, and must have suffered considerable loss; and I have the pleasure to inform you, that two Mortar-boats and an armed launch remained in our possession.

I feel myself particularly indebted, for the successful termination of this contest, to the gallantry of Captains Fremantle and Miller, the former of whom accompanied me in my Barge; and to my Coxswain, John Sykes who, in defending my person, is most severely wounded; as was Captain Fremantle, slightly, in the attack. And my praises are generally due to every Officer and man, some of whom I saw behave in the most noble manner; and I regret it is not in my power to particularize them. I must also beg to be permitted to express my admiration of Don Miguel Tyrason the Commander of the Gun-boats. In his Barge, he laid my Boat alongside, and his resistance was such as did honour to a brave Officer; eighteen of the twenty six men being killed, and himself and all the rest wounded. Not having a correct list of killed and wounded, I can only state, that I believe about six are killed and twenty wounded.*

---

* Admiral Lord St Vincent's final dispatch to the Admiralty records one killed and twenty wounded.

Betsey Fremantle was still with her husband on board HMS *Seahorse* at this stage and her calmness under pressure must have been tested to the utmost as her husband went out on these night raids. After all, they had only been married six months. She records in her diary for Monday, 3 July:[31]

> Fremantle was out all night he went with Admiral Nelson to bombard the town, much firing all night. I was anxious for Fremantle and did not go to bed until he returned. Spanish gun boats and a barge were taken, many people killed and wounded. Fremantle received a blow.

By 14 July 1797 it had become apparent that the close inshore blockade of Cádiz and Nelson's attempts to draw out the Spanish fleet were doomed to failure. The harbour was now effectively defended by the Spanish with a large flotilla of small craft to guard themselves from further attacks. It was obvious, even to the ever-pugnacious Nelson, that his inshore blockade was becoming less and less effective. The squadron was withdrawn and sailed back to rejoin Adm. the Earl St Vincent, and the main fleet.

Nelson, however, was far from finished with his attempts to weaken Spanish desire to remain allied to France. Earlier in the year he had sailed with a small squadron to intercept what they believed was a Spanish treasure ship with the Viceroy of Mexico on board. The mission had been abortive but Nelson now believed the ship was moored in the Canary Islands in the port of Santa Cruz du Tenerife. The lure of such a prize was almost irresistible to any eighteenth-century naval officer. Not only would such a prize weaken Spain's economic strength to wage war but could mean untold wealth and financial security for life to the successful captor.

He had spoken to both his old friend Capt. Thomas Troubridge and to Adm. Lord St Vincent, and subsequently had drawn up a plan that he had passed to the admiral, detailing how a joint army-naval assault on Santa Cruz could be carried out. He drew heavily on his successful assault on Capraia, a small island just north of Corsica. There he had acted on his own initiative in assaulting and taking the small island successfully. Using two companies of infantry and his own ship's crew, Nelson had landed and manhandled into position a battery of cannons that, in concert with a pincer movement from the army troops, succeeded in convincing the Genoese forces to surrender and hand over the island without bloodshed. It was a brilliant *coup de main* and later Nelson himself described it as follows:[32] 'I do not believe the two services ever more cordially united than on the present occasion.'

In the assault on Capraia, Nelson had been so confident of the admiral's approval of his actions that he had acted without consulting his superior officer. He rightly judged that speed was of the essence and his judgement had been vindicated by the immediate surrender of the Genoese forces. When he subsequently reported on his mission to Lord St Vincent, he had been backed to the hilt. Nelson was therefore confident that, in these similar circumstances, he would support him again and he was not to be disappointed. The ulterior motive of financial gain applied equally to Lord St Vincent for, as the Admiral of the Fleet, he also stood to gain from the capture of Spanish gold.

His plan envisaged a detached squadron, together with some 4,000 troops who would be landed to the north of Santa Cruz, seize the high ground behind the port and, together with the threat of bombardment from the navy ships, they would force the Spanish governor into capitulation and the handing over of the ships in harbour. Lord St Vincent issued orders:[33]

> For taking possession of the Town of Santa Cruz by a sudden and vigorous assault. In case of success, you are authorised to lay a heavy contribution on the inhabitants of the town and adjacent district if they do not put you in possession of the whole cargo of *El Principe de Asturias*.

He also allocated to Nelson's detached squadron a generous force of three seventy-four gun ships of the line, three frigates, including HMS *Seahorse* commanded by Fremantle, and two other small vessels.

However, one crucial element was missing and with it possibly the squadron's best chance of success. There were to be no troops seconded to the venture as there had been in the original successful venture at Capriai on which Nelson had based his planning. With no troops the chances of a successful outcome diminished significantly.

One other factor that Nelson also failed to take into account, which he may have been not fully aware of, was that Capt. Thomas Troubridge had been seriously ill. Despite his apparent recovery, he was far from his peak – a factor that was to have a significant effect on the whole operation. Troubridge had fought with distinction at the Battle of St Vincent and was one of Nelson's closest friends. Both had served as midshipmen on HMS *Seahorse,** had known each other since childhood and trusted each other implicitly. The events that were about to unfold would be affected enormously by Troubridge's uncharacteristic indecisiveness, which was almost certainly due, either wholly or partially, to his illness.[34]

When the squadron departed Cádiz it was blessed with a favourable northerly breeze and made excellent progress over the 850 nautical miles to the Canary Islands. Leaving the fleet on 15 July 1797, it reached Santa Cruz by the morning of 21 July, at an average speed of just over 6 knots, which was excellent progress for a fleet including three relatively heavy battleships. Fremantle and his fellow captains were, for the first time, subject to the newly promoted Adm. Nelson's philosophy and methods of command. He was now in a detached squadron away from the Mediterranean and was able to command a squadron in a way he thought fit and which was to make his name famous.

A key element in Nelson's philosophy of command was the involvement of all his captains, however junior, in an informal and free discussion of ideas usually, if the weather allowed, over a convivial meal. He used these occasions not just to refine his own planning but also to get to know his commanders in a social setting. What he achieved can best be described in modern parlance as a 'buy-in'. All the subordinate commanders would know and have agreed to the final plan by the time it was activated.

Prior to sailing, the fleet had received intelligence from two frigates that had sailed to Santa Cruz in late May 1797. Under the pretext of bringing in a letter about the exchange of prisoners, they had surveyed the fortifications and subsequently, under cover of darkness, had sent in a raiding party to seize a French corvette. This added to Nelson's confidence for, although well fortified, it did appear as if Santa Cruz might be susceptible to a surprise attack. Certainly Nelson paid little heed to Adm. Lord St Vincent's parting words,[35] 'God bless and prosper you. I am sure you will deserve success. To mortals is not given the power of commanding it.' Nelson was of the opinion that a bold and audacious leader made his own good fortune.

---

*   This was an earlier vessel with the same name as that commanded by Fremantle.

Santa Cruz de Tenerife is situated right up in the north-east of the island. Although sheltered from the main force of the Atlantic by being east facing, the bay in which the town is situated does not afford great protection from the trade winds that blow through the narrow valleys of the mountainous hinterland; just one more factor that was to affect the fleet's plans adversely. On arrival the British were greeted by pleasant weather and, with the squadron safely anchored some miles from the town and out of sight of any lookouts, the captains were invited over to the flagship, HMS *Theseus*, for a final planning conference. Here, Fremantle and his colleagues had their last opportunity to contribute any final ideas for the forthcoming assault.

It was typical of Nelson's strategies and thinking that while he placed enormous confidence in all of the officers who served him and expected personal initiative from them as events unfolded, he still planned for every eventuality that he could possibly foresee prior to the forthcoming battle. The attack would be launched from as close inshore as possible with the ships' boats loaded with 740 men, who were to attack in three companies, each equipped to be self-sufficient. They were provided with scaling ladders to take the fort and 18-pounder guns on specially constructed sleds so as to ease the task of dragging them into position. Those carrying muskets were issued with specially constructed metal ramrods because it was thought that standard issue wooden ramrods often break in the heat of battle.*

The assault party gathered from all of the ships were then transferred to the three frigates, HMS *Seahorse*, *Emerald* and *Terpsichore*. These three ships would then take the main assault force, together with their assault boats, into the bay during the hours of darkness to get them as close inshore as was practicable, shortening the distance to be rowed. The objective was the outlying fortress, the Castillo de Paso Alto. The intention was to seize the fort by speed and surprise and then threaten the town with bombardment from both the north and from the sea. While this was going on Nelson would bring HMS *Theseus*, *Culloden* and *Zealous* within range of the town and threaten it with bombardment from two sides. Nelson hoped that Commandant-General Don Antonio Gutiérrez would then agree to an ultimatum demanding the Spanish

---

* It had usually been considered that wooden ramrods were better in the maritime environment, as metal ramrods were deemed susceptible to corrosion in salt air.

galleon and her cargo in exchange for sparing the town from bombardment, or as Nelson's draft document put it 'the horrors of war'.

Unusually for Nelson, he chose not to lead the assault himself but awarded the honour to Troubridge. Fremantle and his colleagues on the other two frigates took the boats towards the shore. The boats cast off some 2 miles from shore, roped together to ensure they were not separated in the darkness and began the long pull to the shore. The trade winds were strong that night and coming down from the high mountains in sudden gusts that whipped up the surface of the sea, making progress extremely slow.

At first light when Nelson's ships arrived off the town, they discovered the assault party were still almost a mile from their objective. Soon they were spotted and the alarm was raised. The Spanish commander, however, still had problems. He had nearly 800 professional soldiers and to make up the rest of his defence force, he was reliant on a local militia who, being part-time soldiers, would take some time to muster. Even when finally mustered at their battle stations, it would have been reasonable to suppose that they would be of a relatively wide range of military competence. All of these factors had contributed to the attackers' supposition that the island would be vulnerable to a sudden, determined assault and this was a something that Nelson regarded as his own speciality.

At the critical moment, with the assault in jeopardy, Nelson was onboard his flagship, HMS *Theseus*, totally unable to influence events. He had trusted the mission to an extremely competent officer, one who had proved his ability to act with initiative. In the event Troubridge, for whatever reason, acted completely out of character. At the first sign of the assault boats being discovered, instead of pushing on with all speed, he turned the boats around and ordered them back to the frigates while he made his way to HMS *Theseus* to consult Nelson. It is arguable that at this point the attack on Santa Cruz had failed, all surprise had gone and Gutiérrez now had time to muster the militia.

Now anything attempted by the British squadron would entail a frontal assault without army assistance or the element of surprise that had been vital components of Nelson's original plan. By withdrawing the boats quickly Troubridge had removed those vital elements of speed and surprise. Whether he was still ill and therefore acted out of character or whether it was simply a bad call is difficult to say but his actions were atypical for an experienced captain of ability and drive.

The hurried consultations that took place on HMS *Theseus* now reconsidered an option they had previously discussed at the conferences around Nelson's dining table. The revised plan would see an assault force land further north of Castillo de Paso Alto, move round on to the high ground, which lay behind the fort, and occupy it. They would drag ships' cannons on sleds and place them in a position of such dominance that the fort would be forced to surrender or face annihilation.

The boats and the assault party were relaunched at about 10 a.m. and this time made it ashore. The sailors then began the laborious job of hauling their guns up the steep, rocky slopes of the Jurada heights. They were doing so at midday in midsummer with very little water to slake their thirst. By the time they reached the summit they were exhausted or, as one contemporary account put it, 'excessively fatigued'.[36] Worse was to follow. Having reached their allotted summit they found they were in no position to threaten the fort. What had seemed the peak overlooking the fortress from the seaward side was, in fact, one deep valley away from the position they wished to occupy. The opposite ridge where they had hoped to place their artillery was already occupied by Spanish militia, who were equipped with four field artillery pieces.

The ridge where the British were halted was bereft of any shelter and left them totally exposed to the midday, tropical sun and, to add to the discomfort, there was no breeze. Some of the British tried to make their way down to a stream at the bottom of the valley but were either killed by artillery fire or succumbed to the heat.

Yet again, Troubridge was forced to call off the attack but it was to be 10 p.m. before the exhausted party arrived back on the frigates and again, the assault had ended in complete failure. On Sunday, 23 July the wind picked up to gale force and all the ships were forced to sail out of the bay to allow sea room, and avoid being blown on to the lee shore. One factor, however, which arose from the retreat on the 22nd, now began to influence events and Fremantle, together with his newly married wife, were to play a key role.

During the retreat from Jurada heights, Capt. Thomas Oldfield had taken a deserter into his custody and now, back on board ship, Fremantle and Miller took upon themselves the task of interrogating him. It turned out that he was German (Prussian) and, because she was the best linguist in the fleet, Betsey Fremantle was called upon to translate. Betsey records it in her diary entry for Sunday, 23 July:[37]

A German that was brought off yesterday says the Spaniards have no force, are in the greatest alarm all crying and trembling and that nothing could be easier than to take the place, only 300 men of regular troops, the rest are peasants who are frightened to death.

Having received this intelligence, Miller, Fremantle and the other captains discussed how to put this to Nelson. They were in total agreement that, given this latest intelligence, another frontal assault on the town should be attempted and that Fremantle, having the most influence with Nelson, should be the one to pass on their views to the admiral. Fremantle duly went onboard HMS *Theseus* to acquaint Nelson with the latest intelligence and the views of his subordinate commanders.

The circumstances now conspired to commit Nelson to make one of his, admittedly few, bad decisions. Nelson's strengths as a commander, his aggression, his democratic and open decision-making style, his concern for both his own public image and that of his country, plus the care he took in surrounding himself with equally aggressive commanders, conspired against him. The sensible decision would have been to withdraw. There were good reasons to do so. The strategic gains, if a further attack were to be successful, were not huge and would do little to hamper or lessen Spain's ability to wage war, whereas the downside of a defeat was obvious. Any military leader worth his salt would counsel against house-to-house battles in an unknown built-up area unless possessing overwhelming force and heavy artillery. However, this was what Fremantle and his fellow captains were proposing to Nelson based on an unsubstantiated source from an individual of unknown reliability.

To add to the pressure, HMS *Leander* joined the squadron on the morning of the 24th and Thompson, her commander, was familiar with both Tenerife and the layout of Santa Cruz. The one person who was now against a frontal attack was the German deserter who, having been recruited by Nelson to act as a pilot for the attack, was rapidly revising his ideas as to the weakness of the garrison.

It was true that Nelson did have misgivings about a frontal assault now there was no element of surprise left to the attackers. However, his pride would not allow him to back down in front of Fremantle and his colleagues. He admitted as much[38] in a subsequent letter stating, 'My pride suffered.' The British were now committed to a full frontal assault upon the town. They hoped to seize the mole that was central to the town's main square and the fort immediately to the south of the mole. If they could they would once again be in a position to dictate terms to Don Antonio Gutiérrez and the Spanish authorities. In an effort to introduce some element of subterfuge the plan was to head initially to the north-east, as though the intended point of attack was again Castillo de Paso Alto, before swinging south and attacking the mole in the centre of town. To add to the element of diversion, Miller was to direct the frigates offshore to bombard installations to the north of the intended assault point.

This time, as if to prove that this really was the last throw of the dice, Nelson would lead the boats in. It was by no means normal naval practice for a rear admiral to personally lead a shore attack from the ships' boats but Rear Admiral Sir Horatio Nelson was no ordinary admiral.

At an early hour on the evening of 24 July Fremantle and his wife, Betsey, entertained Nelson and the other squadron captains to a dinner on board HMS *Seahorse*. Betsey records in her diary:[39]

> The Admiral supped with us, he then went with Fremantle on their expedition. They are all to land in the Town, as the taking of this place seemed an easy and almost sure thing, I went to bed after they were gone apprehending no danger for Fremantle.

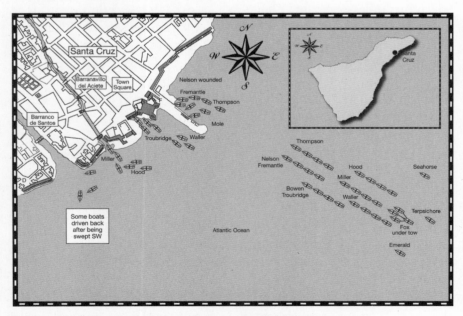

Santa Cruz in Tenerife showing the last unsuccessful attack.

At approximately 11 p.m., six divisions of men (nearly 1,000) under Troubridge, Miller, Waller, Hood and Thompson, with Nelson leading the sixth boat, pushed off from the mother ships. Fremantle and Bowen were with Nelson and were expected to act as beach-masters, to regulate the attack. Despite their amazing sangfroid at the supper table, which had so totally convinced Betsey of the ease of their mission, it appears from later correspondence they were by no means as confident of victory as they appeared. While it is true that a massed attack of 1,000 well-armed and disciplined seamen could possibly overwhelm the town's defences, to do so they would need to arrive simultaneously and in small boats hampered by a heavy swell that was unlikely to happen.

Nelson subsequently wrote to Hammond, 'I felt the second attack a forlorn hope.'[40] It has been suggested that the presence of Betsey at the dinner table prevented a full discussion of the possible pitfalls in the planning. But, even with a full and frank discussion it seems probable, with the captains being in favour of one further attempt, that Nelson would have been unable to resist a third attack.

The barge from HMS *Seahorse*, with both Nelson and Fremantle on board, began the 2-mile row to shore. The darkness allowed the party to get quite close to shore before the alarm was raised. The alarm bells ringing signalled the batteries to start firing out to sea almost immediately. The boats cast off the ropes that held them together during the row and made their own way towards the mole. Bowen was first ashore with some fifty men. They did well to fight their way towards the first gun battery and spike (i.e. disable) some of the guns. They probably had the best of what surprise remained, for as the second wave arrived, led by Fremantle, they found themselves in an inferno of artillery grapeshot from both the town square, aimed straight down the length of the mole, and from the flanks.* In addition, musket fire from buildings adjacent turned the mole into a killing zone. How far Fremantle made it down the mole before being hit by a musket ball is uncertain. Nelson was hit before he had even exited the boat and Capt. Richard Bowen and his first lieutenant, George Thorpe, were cut to bits by grapeshot sweeping the length of the mole.

---

* Grapeshot was the term used to describe a canister filled with musket balls that exploded when fired from a cannon, spreading into a deadly hail of anti-personnel missiles.

Nelson was fighting for his life as one of the main arteries in his right arm had been severed. Fremantle was slightly more fortunate in that a musket ball, which coincidentally had also hit him in the right arm, seemed to have missed anything vital. Nevertheless, in exiting his arm it had caused tremendous damage through loss of muscle tissue and nerve damage.

Nelson's life was saved through the prompt action of Lt Josiah Nisbet, Nelson's stepson. He had insisted on accompanying his stepfather on the raid despite Nelson's misgivings. As Nelson collapsed into the boat, Nisbet grasped the wound to apply direct pressure and, tying neckerchiefs over the wound, staunched the worst of the blood flow. The rudimentary first aid was sufficient to save the admiral from bleeding to death, which, in Nelson's own words, would have probably happened within ten minutes had his stepson not shown such a cool head.

Nelson was rowed back to HMS *Seahorse*, where he refused to go on board to be treated as he did not wish to distress Betsey, especially as at that time he had no news of her husband. He insisted that the boat crew row him to his flagship, HMS *Theseus*, where he would be operated on by the ship's surgeon, Thomas Eshelby. Fremantle was taken to HMS *Zealous* to be treated before returning to his own ship, HMS *Seahorse*, at 4 a.m. It is a measure of the physical resilience of Nelson that a day after traumatic surgery he was fit enough to attempt his first left-handed writing when he wrote to Betsey.

Meanwhile, in the town, things had gone from bad to worse. Apart from Nelson's division, most of the other boats had missed the mole in the swell and confusion and had been swept to the south, some landing on the small shingle beach immediately south of the mole and some south of the fort of Castillo de San Cristóbal. The parties were split up, some had no dry powder and were forced to rely on bayonet and swords. They were forced to accept the inevitable and by morning the British commanders ashore commenced the formal surrender procedures.

Their opponent, Gutiérrez, proved to be as generous in defeat as he had been skilful in mounting his defence. He ensured all the British wounded were cared for adequately and that food and water was provided to the survivors. He then provided boats to ship them back to their vessels. Nelson, ever appreciative of an opponent who proved so magnanimous in victory, sent him a present of beer and cheese in his message confirming the conditions agreed by Troubridge. Gutiérrez responded with a gift of Malmsey wine and, with the niceties over, it only remained for the British to bury their dead, treat the wounded and depart with their tails firmly between their legs. One hundred and fifty-three men had been killed and more than 100 wounded. Even Nelson's renowned powers of self-publicity would have a problem putting a positive spin on this.

As the squadron sailed northwards to rejoin the main fleet, Nelson and Fremantle had ample time to consider their positions. For Nelson, with his highly developed sense of the dramatic, his injury was the end of his naval career. He wrote to Lord St Vincent on 16 August:[41]

> I rejoice at being once more in sight of your Flag and with your permission will come on board the Ville de Paris, and pay you my respects. If the Emerald has joined you know my wishes. A left handed Admiral will never again be considered as useful, therefore the sooner I get to a very humble cottage the better, and make room for a better man to serve the State; but whatever be my lot, believe me, with the most sincere affection.

Fremantle, in stark contrast, was making a far slower recovery. Paradoxically, Nelson's injury, at first the most life threatening was, by dint of a quick and relatively clean amputation, a far less troublesome wound than that sustained by Fremantle.[42]

The problem was not just the rudimentary care that went with receiving a gunshot wound in the eighteenth century; it was the nature of the damage done to the human body. One had to be extremely unlucky to be hit by an individual musket marksman as the weapon itself was inaccurate over anything more than point blank range. Obviously, a platoon of soldiers massed together and producing a volley of musket fire raised the chances of being hit considerably.

Lead balls fired from unrifled barrels using black powder had low muzzle velocity but, because of the weight of the lead shot, could do considerable damage to the human frame. The comparative low velocity produced its own problems. They had sufficient velocity not just to rip flesh apart but also to shatter the bones they struck completely but then, frequently, failed to exit the body, thus complicating the subsequent surgery. On entry they usually took with them debris and dirt, producing a very dirty wound and heightening the risks of infection.

Nelson was hit just above the elbow by a cannon loaded with grapeshot. Fremantle's wound was slightly higher, through the right biceps, and was probably the result of a musket ball. The ball had luckily missed bone and any major blood vessels and had passed right through the arm. It had, however, caused a massive wound and damaged the nerves internally such that the surgeon on HMS *Zealous* who first treated him and subsequently on HMS *Seahorse* described his condition:[43] 'In great pain in the hand and extremities of the fingers which are much swell'd. Great irritability of the nervous system, had been kept very low. Ordered a more generous diet and more port wine.'

He later added: 'The wound continued to get better; pain in the hand as severe as ever. The nerves affected by touching the other hand or even mentioning the wound produces most violent pain.'

The squadron finally arrived back at Cádiz to rejoin the fleet on 16 August. With both Nelson and Fremantle obviously unfit for active service the decision to send both back to the UK to recuperate more fully was a foregone conclusion. Adm. Jervis ordered both officers home and, together with Mrs Fremantle, they sailed on HMS *Seahorse*. The voyage home was a nightmare, with even the normally optimistic Betsey finding it difficult.

In addition to Nelson and Fremantle, the ship carried many of the other wounded sailors from the attack so it was filled constantly with the moans and cries of the patients. To add to Betsey's problems, she was pregnant and beginning to experience morning sickness. From contemporary records of the surgeon on board, and from Betsey's own diary entries, it was obvious that Fremantle was not an easy patient. He did not get up from his cot during the voyage home and, in common with Nelson, he began to experience depression thinking that he might well have to resign his commission. To add to the misery, the winds on the voyage to Portsmouth were contrary and it was 1 September before they arrived. Prior to departing the main fleet for Portsmouth, Betsey recorded in her diary:[44]

20th August 1797 – Fremantle was very unwell this morning, he heard that Lord St Vincent was determined to come on board which made him quite nervous and miserable. However he did not come at last, but Captain Wells, Foley and Martin were with me all the morning and all the others came to take leave of us as the ship got under way. Admiral Nelson came on board at twelve o' clock, he is quite stout but I find it looks shocking to be without one arm. He is in great spirits. Fremantle was pretty well in the afternoon. Mr Eshelby the surgeon seems a sensible young man, he gave me some pills to take, for I am not well at all, but I don't mind it as it is easy to guess what is the matter with me.

August 24th 1797 – A foul wind which makes the Admiral fret, he is a very bad patient, poor Fremantle is still the same, no sign of the wounds healing up yet.

By the time HMS *Seahorse* finally reached Portsmouth, some two weeks later, Betsey must have been quite exhausted. New trials now faced her as she prepared to meet her new family, get used to an England she last saw when she was 9 years old and, of course, nurse her husband while simultaneously preparing for the birth of her first child. The legendary feminine ability to multi-task must have been stretched to the limit! Although Fremantle had retained his right arm he had little use or control over it for some considerable time and it was left to the indefatigable Betsey to draft all the correspondence and bring the Fremantle clan together.

However, it was his mentor and faithful friend, the Marquess of Buckingham, who took charge of getting him financial compensation for his injuries. In a letter addressed to William Fremantle, Buckingham writes:[45]

In the first place he must make his wife or someone write, so he must sign a letter to the Lords of the Admiralty stating the sense he entertains of their goodness in giving him a month's leave; but having been confined to his bed ever since he was wounded at Tenerife and having been reduced by his former wounds and by his accident which has proved much more serious than was at first imagined, to a very dehabilitated state of body, he understands from his Surgeon that he will not be able to use his arm to any extent for eight or nine months.

Buckingham then continued to describe how it was vital that Fremantle laid it on thick as to the nature and severity of his disability, mentioning that a Capt. Grimsdale had been awarded £250 per annum for a similar wound just one year ago. He even went to the trouble of stating exactly what wording Fremantle should use in the pleading letter before finally ending the letter with one final injunction to William: 'That all this should be done without a word to him (i.e. Thomas).'

He further suggests that Fremantle should go to Aston Abbotts to recuperate. All in all it is a letter that shows eloquently the care that Buckingham had for Fremantle with perhaps a hint that they consider him too much of an innocent to play the system adequately. There are further letters suggesting that William should push his brother to get more money from the merchants of Leghorn whom he had rescued, following the French invasion, pressing William to get more publicity from the *Gazette* believing that his brother was 'due more than a ceremonial sword worth £100'.[46]

The Fremantles stayed initially in Portsmouth in rented lodgings. Thomas, at this stage, was still in considerable pain and had no real control over his right hand. He remained under the care of the surgeon from the naval hospital in Portsmouth but while the wound itself healed cleanly they could do little for the pain other than to prescribe opiates. Two days later William arrived to see his brother and his new sister-in-law. He was himself about to be married to a rich widow, Mrs Selina Felton Hervey.* The arrival of his brother seemed to do little for Thomas's well-being for, in Betsey's words,[47] 'William's arrival in the afternoon affected his nerves considerably'.

The following Wednesday Thomas's eldest brother, John, arrived and Betsey immediately took to him rather more than the staid, serious-minded William:[48] 'I like his brother Jack better than William he is not half so formal, and I got much sooner acquainted with him.'

Luckily for Betsey, her introduction to the Fremantle family was further enhanced when Thomas's mother arrived a few days later and the two immediately get on well together. She was further comforted and made to feel at home by the friendship and kindness of Admiral and Lady Parker. Adm. Parker had been Thomas's commander-in-chief when he had been a young midshipman in the West Indies and Lady Parker had acted as a surrogate 'mother' to many of the young midshipmen. Nelson and Fremantle had both benefitted from her maternal kindness.

Some four weeks after arriving in Portsmouth the Fremantles rented a cottage in Purbrook, a few miles out of Portsmouth on the London Road. Betsey was pleased when they also rented a piano so she could play and relieve some of her boredom. Together the couple, cheered by the occasional visitor, stayed in Purbrook until the end of October, when

---

* See footnote on page 19.

Thomas felt sufficiently recovered to move up to London. They moved into No. 1 Bolton Row.

Here, instead of going on to half pay as would usually be the case, Fremantle was given a year's full pay and an additional pension of £200 per annum. He had to go through a thorough examination by the naval surgeons that, with their pulling his arm about, put him into a bad mood such that he had to go home rather than watch the play they had planned to attend. By late November, however, Betsey was able to note in her diary that Thomas was recovered sufficiently and able to stop his daily dose of laudanum.

During their stay in London the Fremantles carried out a series of social functions and met many influential people, particularly prominent members of the Whig party. With his wife proving so adept and at ease in social circles Fremantle was gradually beginning to build up the circle of contacts and political friends that would prove so useful to him in later years. At Christmas of 1797 they were invited down to Stowe to spend the festive season with the Marquess of Buckingham, a visit that, at least for Betsey, was to become an annual ritual.

After the New Year celebrations the Fremantles returned to London and on 11 March 1798 Betsey gave birth to the couple's first child, a boy, who was subsequently christened Thomas Francis. Betsey was further delighted by the news that her family were intending to come back to England and on 24 May they arrived back safely from Naples.

The domestic happiness of the new Fremantle family was finally sealed when in late July 1798 Thomas identified a house in Swanbourne, only some 6 miles from the old family house in Aston Abbotts and conveniently close to Stowe House. He was able to purchase the house for £900 and, shortly after, the family moved in to start the 200-year relationship between the Fremantles and Swanbourne that continues to this day.

Betsey recorded in her diary for 30 July 1798:[49]

We all went to see the house Fremantle wished to buy, it is two miles from Winslow, about two miles from the turnpike road in the village of Swanburn, very agreeably situated on a hill, it is a very nice place which would suit us on all accounts. It is to be sold for 1,000 guineas but we are endeavouring to get it for less – it is very cheap even at that price.

Betsey's joy at everything that had happened was marred on the last day of October when her beloved father died. Eventually, when his financial affairs were sorted out, it left the Fremantles in an enviable financial state. Having moved into Swanbourne in the late summer of 1798, the family was added to when Betsey gave birth to a daughter on 13 June 1799. She was born three weeks premature but, other than being a small baby, was perfectly healthy. She was christened Emma. Shortly after her birth, Betsey had to endure the frightening prospect of a smallpox epidemic sweeping through Swanbourne but luckily Emma remained untouched by the disease. Unusually for this period, with Jenner's ideas still in their infancy, Betsey had already been vaccinated albeit she had obviously not had Emma inoculated at this point.

Thomas was unexpectedly enjoying the life of a country squire and on 11 September Betsey wrote in her diary:[50] 'Fremantle for the first time in his life shot a bird, but could not show his prize as he lost it in the corn.'

Despite losing his 'prize', the fact that Fremantle was now able to handle a musket and shoot sufficiently accurately to bag a bird showed he had recovered much of the use of his right arm.

As was the custom, they spent Christmas at Stowe despite heavy snowfalls making the journey difficult. Betsey, in particular, enjoyed herself and had the additional pleasure of showing off her son, Tommy, as she referred to him. It was to be the last Christmas for a while that Fremantle spent with the Buckinghams as, now fully recovered from his wound, he wanted to go back to active service. The timing was excellent from his point of view as Earl Spencer was still First Lord of the Admiralty and by now, having served some six years in post, he was in a position to grant Thomas his wish. Thomas had started by writing to the Marquess of Buckingham asking him to speak to Earl Spencer on his behalf. As usual his brother, William, followed up with a further letter to the marquess:[51]

My brother Tom is extremely anxious for a ship and tells me he has written to your Lordship to intercede on his behalf with Lord Spencer. I am delighted that he has now determined on the subject, as I think him quite re-established in his health and with his professional character it is a matter of surprise to all who know him, that he should continue to neglect his profession. He is now contented to accept a good frigate and I should imagine Lord Spencer would not refuse him one of the best; but whatever he procures, he must always owe it to the continuation of that support and goodness which you have ever shewn to him and all of us.

On 31 May 1800 Betsey gave birth to their third child, a boy, who was christened Charles Howe. Betsey's joy at yet another healthy child was soon marred, however, when a letter arrived from the Admiralty signalling that her husband would shortly be leaving again to take command of HMS *Ganges*.

6

SERVICE IN THE BALTIC AND THE BATTLE OF COPENHAGEN

The start of the nineteenth century saw significant changes for Britain with the Act of Union bringing Ireland into the kingdom. It had been created at some personal cost to the Prime Minister, William Pitt, as he had promised Catholic emancipation as part of the package and this was a step too far for King George III, who regarded it as breaking his coronation vows. William Pitt was forced to resign and after two months of confusion, mostly caused by one of the King's bouts of mental instability, Henry Addington was asked to form an administration, which he did on 17 March 1801.* He invited Pitt to join his Tory administration, who sensibly refused.

On the international front, Napoleon had left his army in Egypt and returned to France. He arrived back in Paris on 16 October 1799 and having sorted out his matrimonial problems with Josephine he set about the task of taking over the reins of political power from the French government (the Directory). The government was in a parlous state as it had been weakened by internal divisions, incompetence and corruption.

---

* Henry Addington was perhaps better known as Viscount Sidmouth, a title he took in 1805.

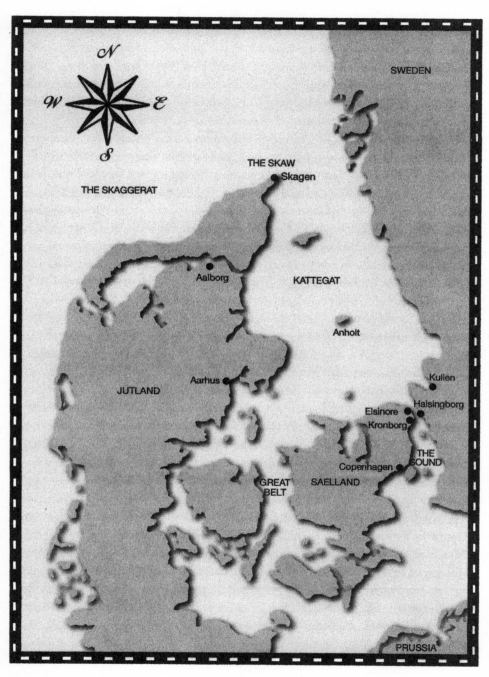

The Baltic approaches where Admiral Hyde Parker's indecisiveness almost led to disaster.

With the aid of his fellow conspirators Abbé Sieyès, Ducos, Fouché and Talleyrand, Napoleon plotted to overthrow it by force if necessary and seize power in an act that became known as the coup of Brumaire. The 'civilian' conspirators saw Bonaparte as their military 'enforcer' who would give the force of arms to their coup. They anticipated that on the successful conclusion he would be conveniently sidelined. They had sadly misjudged their man!

On 9 November 1799 the coup was initiated and by the 11th the government of France rested in the hands of three provisional consuls, Sieyès, Ducos and Bonaparte. The resulting months saw Bonaparte sideline, bribe and force his co-conspirators into the background such that from 1800 onwards he would gradually expand and strengthen his power base, culminating in his coronation as Emperor in 1804.

The second coalition against France, formed after Nelson's victory at the Nile,* was beginning to creak. Napoleon led the French army against the Austrians and, after his stunning victory at Marengo in June 1800, he had achieved exactly what he wanted, ensuring that any pretence of unity among the allies disappeared swiftly. The Russians were unhappy, both with Britain for holding on to Malta, rather than returning it to the Knights of St John, and with Austria for its part in the Italian campaign. While Russia saw the campaign as designed to restore the old order it suspected Austria was participating for territorial gain.

Britain's hopes of holding together a coalition to defeat revolutionary France were in tatters. The coalition had been formed with the specific aim of defeating French forces on land. But Britain, Austria, the Kingdom of Naples, the Ottoman Empire, the Papal States, Portugal, Russia and Sweden faced a France that was beginning, under its new first consul, to pull together. Thanks to British naval blockades, France was short of funds. What it did have was Napoleon and he was at the very height of his military powers during the early part of the new century. It was crystal clear who the enemy was but not so easy to come up with ideas as to how he could be stopped. Napoleon was no longer just a brilliant military officer of the Republic. He was effectively the personification of France and the only meaningful power.

---

* Napoleon's fleet was destroyed in the Battle of the Nile (sometimes known as the Battle of Aboukir Bay) on 1–2 August 1798.

The coalition was different. The factors that held such a disparate collection of European states together were British funding, fear of revolutionary France's potential occupying forces and the reactionary kings', emperors', princes' and Popes' understandable desire to hang on to their thrones. These self-serving links were insufficient to hold the coalition together when it came under the strain of military defeat. Individual states were more than happy to make separate peace treaties if they felt that was the lesser of two evils. Napoleon based his strategy on taking on individual members of the coalition in a series of lightning strikes that saw armies defeated and rulers suing for peace before their coalition partners could reinforce them.

Britain was forced to fight back with what she had, which was the navy. Whatever Napoleon did, whatever his brilliance on the battlefields of Europe, the British navy remained unchallenged at sea. The British answer was to reinforce the blockade and, hopefully, force Napoleon to negotiate by strangling his trade and his outlet to the rest of the world. From the Baltic, through the North Sea, the English Channel, the eastern seaboard of the Atlantic, the length of the Mediterranean and the Adriatic, Britain stretched a thin wall of ships. Neutral shipping, potential trading partners and French shipping were all alike to British naval captains. All could be ordered to heave to in a peremptory fashion, backed up by fearsome firepower, holds searched and papers inspected; any cargoes that fell outside that which the British defined as allowable were liable to seizure. No better example exists of this than orders Nelson supplied to Fremantle during their time cruising off the coasts of the south of France:[1]

Nelson to Fremantle Agamemnon August 2nd 1795
The following is the substance of a letter which I received from Mr Drake at Genoa of yesterday's date, that the French ships are riding at single anchor in the middle of the port, waiting for a wind from the eastward. They are intending to escort some vessels laden with corn for France. I need not urge your keeping a good look out for them.

The Lowestoft has joined me this morning, I shall order her to keep about 24 miles off Point Vardo to prevent the French ships passing in shore unseen, and the Agamemnon is in readiness to come out at a moment's notice.

And the next day he followed up with fresh injunctions to keep up his guard to ensure no freight slipped through to France:

> Nelson to Fremantle Agamemnon Aug 3rd 1795
> In addition to your former orders from information which I have received from the General, that Vessels loaded with corn clear out for Barcelona although actually bound to Marseilles. In case you meet with any such vessels, I am to desire you will send them here, that I may send a convoy with them if they are really bound to Spain.

Nelson was perhaps renowned for the freedom in which he interpreted the rules on international blockade. Nevertheless, he was not alone in interpreting the rules of blockade as giving him the powers not just to search ships, but to unilaterally form merchant ships into convoys and escort them to the place that they claimed as their destination. These orders to Fremantle left little doubt that Britain regarded the high seas as its national fiefdom.

The effects of this policy were obvious. Those countries whose allegiance had been bought with British funds and those who counted themselves as being completely outside the conflict were united by what they saw as British arrogance. The policy was hitting friend and foe alike and was costing them money. Trade, where it did continue, consisted of small, fast vessels scuttling along a coastline in sight of land, always fearfully looking over their shoulders for possible sight of a British frigate.

The situation was complex and fraught with potential legal problems. There was no real body of international law and precedent on which to base a judgement as to what was allowable and what was blatantly illegal. Britain, based mainly on the 'might is right' principle, insisted that denying their enemies sustenance from the sea was a legitimate weapon of war. However, neutral trading states were equally adamant that free trade on vessels sailing under a neutral flag was lawful. Both sides would probably accept that trading in weapons of war was likely to lay a vessel open to seizure, but what items of cargo constituted contraband was debatable. To enforce its own broad definition of goods likely to be of assistance to an enemy power, Britain insisted, even in international waters, of the right to stop and search.

In January 1798 a British frigate intercepted a Swedish convoy escorted by a Swedish naval vessel. The Swedish ship offered token resistance only, more to satisfy honour than serious military action, and when the British insisted on searching the Swedish merchant ships they found cargoes of tar, pitch and hemp (all used extensively for the maintenance of warships) and, accordingly, seized the cargoes. However, these cargoes were equally essential for peaceful purposes, being used in the maintenance of their merchant fleet. The Swedish government lodged a formal protest with the British government but the policy was regarded as sacrosanct by the British and they were determined to continue with it, making further incidents inevitable.

In December 1799 and July 1800 Danish merchant vessels were seized in similar circumstances. While the British government felt compelled to continue its insistence that they were acting in accordance with international precedent, they also wished to keep the Baltic/Scandinavian governments from outright hostility. Timber, pitch and other vital naval supplies came from these countries and their continued goodwill and trade was essential to Britain if she was to keep her massive fleet at sea and in good repair. One product in particular made the Baltic trade vital to Britain's interests and that was hemp, which was made into rope and provided the very sinews of the British warships. The sole supplier was Russia[2] and this, if no other reason, meant that the Baltic must be open to British commerce.

Despite efforts to keep neutral countries on good terms, Russia, Denmark (which at this stage included Norway), Prussia and Sweden were determined to stop the high-handed British approach to the embargo and, under the influence of Tsar Paul I, they formed a League of Armed Neutrality. Tsar Paul of Russia was the leading figure in the formation of the League and he had an ulterior motive for being anti-British. Not only did he wish to see Britain allow unimpeded trade but also, as Grand Master of the Knights of St John, he wished to gain control over Malta so that he could hand it back to the knights. Napoleon, in an inspired piece of diplomacy, having lost control of the island to the British, promptly formally handed it over to the Tsar in his role as Grand Master. The British were singularly unimpressed with this symbolic hand over for they certainly had no wish to see the Russian navy dominating the eastern Mediterranean. This was not a scenario that the Admiralty could view with any equanimity and the island remained firmly in British hands.

Tsar Paul's response was to seize all British vessels in Russian ports, send the crews off to prison camps and take British merchants hostage, thereby freezing trade in the Baltic. With Napoleon controlling many of the Mediterranean ports, British trade was hampered severely. As explained previously, the trade embargo was particularly significant for the navy, and the navy was equally the sole credible British weapon against Napoleon. The major problem for the British, of which Malta was a symptom rather than a cause, was that Tsar Paul was moving closer and closer to a rapprochement with Napoleon. He had started off regarding revolutionary France as the font of all evil but, with Napoleon becoming first consul and taking on all of the trappings and power of an old-fashioned autocratic ruler, it became obvious to the Tsar that the revolutionary Jacobinism of early France was dead and buried.

The League of Armed Neutrality and the Tsar's apparent willingness to ally himself with Napoleon presented a clear hostile threat to Britain's safety and ability to protect itself from Napoleonic France. The League's five objectives or principles were:

1. All neutral states were to be allowed freedom to navigate from port to port and on the coasts of nations at war
2. Goods belonging to subjects of belligerent powers, with the exception of closely defined 'contraband' to be traded freely on neutral vessels
3. The blockade to be recognised but exercised by close watch
4. Neutral vessels should only be arrested 'for just cause and in view of the evident facts'; and
5. The declaration of officers in command of armed escort vessels accompanying a merchant convoy that no cargoes contained contraband should suffice and prevent any visit or inspection.

While the League was purported not to be aimed specifically against Britain but against any potential belligerent power, Britain's almost total reliance on naval power effectively made it the chief target, whatever the League's governments might say. Pitt's government had demanded from Denmark a 'plain, open and satisfactory answer'[3] as to whether or not Denmark would allow current practices of embargo to continue, but poor Denmark was now hemmed in on two sides. On the one side was Britain demanding the right to embargo trade to France and on the other it had the powerful northern state of Russia, who threatened military intervention if it failed to comply with the terms of the League. The Danish minister, Count Bernstorff, tried to fob the British ambassador off with vague statements and referrals back to the similar situation that had occurred in 1780 during the wars with America. Obviously Denmark felt that the geographical proximity of Russia made it the principal threat and it remained within the League.

Neither Pitt's, nor subsequently Addington's, governments were prepared to sit by and let the Alliance carry out their objectives. In the last days of Pitt's administration he had ordered the Admiralty to prepare a fleet for the Baltic that would add force to whatever diplomatic efforts would take place next. When Pitt resigned and Addington formed a new government, he attempted one final diplomatic move. He appointed Lord Hawkesbury as his Secretary of State for Foreign Affairs and, in a move that he subsequently regretted, the redoubtable Lord St Vincent as First Lord of the Admiralty. Lord Hawkesbury appointed an emissary, Nicholas Vansittart, to go to Denmark to see if there was any final possibility of a peaceful solution.

Vansittart had been educated at Christ Church, Oxford, from where he had been called to the bar at Lincolns Inn. His interest in politics and public finances led him to become a keen supporter of Pitt. He had been brought to public notice when he published a series of pamphlets in defence of Pitt's financial measures during the first anti-revolutionary coalition. In May 1796, Vansittart became an MP for Hastings but his first important post was as junior secretary to the Treasury in Addington's administration. The new Prime Minister then showed great faith in his junior Treasury secretary by selecting him for his special ambassador to the court of King Christian VII in Demark.* He had no previous experience of diplomacy but it was probable that, whoever had gone, the result would have been the same. Without the clear and obvious threat of a British fleet anchored off Copenhagen, Denmark would have to stick to its position of being an active member of the League.

While diplomatic efforts continued, Fremantle was in the happy position of taking over command of his first line-of-battle ship. His brother's

---

* Denmark was effectively ruled by Crown Prince Frederick, due to the mental incapacity of the King.

letter to the marquess had asked if he would use his influence to gain Fremantle a 'good frigate' but the Admiralty had gone one better and had awarded him him the command of HMS *Ganges*, a seventy-four-gun third-rate ship of the line. At just under 170ft in length and with a beam of approximately 50ft, she was considerably larger than anything he had commanded before. He took over on 24 August 1800 and would have noticed immediately the comparative luxury of his own quarters that, stretching across the full beam of the ship, dwarfed the comparatively cramped captain's quarters on a typical frigate. His brother, William, who had no doubts as to who was responsible for Fremantle's appointment to a ship of the line, wrote to Lord Buckingham:[4]

> I see by the paper that my brother has got the 'Ganges'. I am delighted at it, as I was fearful that he had remained idle so long, that he would not be inclined to go to sea again. I am told by the navy officers here that she is as fine a seventy four as sails. I think him very fortunate to have had the appointment to so good a ship. I understand Lord St Vincent is exerting himself to get all his old Mediterranean friends about him in the Channel Fleet, from which I take it for granted the 'Ganges' will belong to his squadron.

This letter and other evidence would suggest it was not just Buckingham's influence with Earl Spencer that gained Fremantle his appointment for it was true that John Jervis, now the Earl St Vincent, was indeed gathering around him those captains he was familiar with and, more importantly, of whom he approved. It seemed, therefore, Fremantle's first appointment to a line-of-battle ship owed as much to his technical competence as his political mentors exercising the power of influence.

Six days after joining his ship on 30 August 1800 Fremantle wrote to the Marquess of Buckingham:[5]

> My ship is to be quite perfect I am told. I have every reason to be perfectly satisfied with her and my appointment, as both Lord Northesk and Lumsden were making applications for her, I hear. My Officers are all appointed and I have not a single person of any description that I ever sailed with before. We are getting on very fast and preference is given to ships of the line. I keep very steady to business and if it was necessary, could be ready in a very short time. Nothing can be more gratifying to

me than the accounts I hear of the state and discipline of the fleet,* I feel as much confidence, and there seems as much respect and obedience in every ship here as at any period of my service. It is said there are three or perhaps four ships in the Channel Fleet that are not so well regulated as they ought to be but I think a short time will see an end of them. I have had the good fortune to get four tolerable midshipmen and a coxswain from Wallace, out of the Brunswick. My lower masts are rigged and we stow our ground tier** on Monday. Ville de Paris goes to Spithead on Monday. She is in high repute as to discipline, fitting etc. I don't think they have lost three men since she had been in harbour. The *Triumph* is in dock but will be out next week. I dined with Captain and Lady Louisa Hervey yesterday. The ship is so well manned and so established that a few days after will equip him for Spithead. Our Commander-in-Chief here is a perfect imbecile; he never gives an order and seldom admits anyone into his house.

Before I left Swanbourne I endeavoured to get some boys from thence, Winslow and Mursley, to go with me to Portsmouth, and though I talked to the overseers of the parishes, and the boys themselves, particularly two from Winslow, who came to me for relief, the sons of a man of the name (I believe) of Higgins, whom you discharged, at my request from the militia; still I could not persuade any of them to go, nor did any of the overseers dare to urge them on the subject. I can only say that I should most willingly receive any lads from Buckinghamshire who are, in my opinion, preferable to the wicked vagabonds that are to be picked up at Portsmouth. By the way of inducement to the boys to go, I consented to take the son of a farmer at Swanbourne, whose name is Hutchings.

Fremantle was probably being a touch optimistic in expecting Buckinghamshire boys to become enthusiastic converts to a seagoing life. With the nearest coastline some 70–80 miles in any direction from Buckingham there has never been much of a tradition of a seafaring life in the county. Swanbourne had seen its common land enclosed under the Enclosure Acts in 1762,[6] therefore the trauma that accompanied such acts had been absorbed into village life and there was no large rump of

---

* This statement reflects the almost paranoid obsession of all ships commanders at this time. Following the Nore and Spithead mutinies of 1797, they all feared possible mutiny and the continued threat of revolution spreading from across the Channel.

** Anchors, cables, etc.

displaced agricultural labourers who might be susceptible to the lures of a life at sea.

Two years before Fremantle sought to recruit, a survey of men between the ages of 15 and 60 who might be useful to defend the country should Napoleon invade, revealed ninety-one such men in Swanbourne, none of whom were unemployed. It is therefore difficult to see what Fremantle expected and what had given him hope that young men would move from the land and be prepared to go to sea. Certainly if that was his expectation he was to be disappointed. Despite the fact that the navy offered generous food and drink to impoverished younger members of large families, north Buckinghamshire was never a hotbed of naval recruiting.

Sadly, Fremantle's cheery optimism on joining his ship at Portsmouth as reflected in his letter to the Marquess of Buckingham, was to be undermined by one of his officers, Lt Rice. Events were to be triggered as the ship was being made ready for sea and stores being brought on board, while the crew were being paid off from the previous voyage.

It was the norm in those days for Royal Navy crews to be paid in cash and often some time in arrears. Therefore, although comparatively poorly paid, each of them had a healthy bundle of cash in their pockets and was anxious to find ways of getting rid of some, or all of it. In such circumstances, the ship would be surrounded frequently by a flotilla of small craft bringing cheap goods for sale, drink and, of course, the inevitable prostitutes all eager to relieve the crew of some of their hard-earned wages. It is a well-established fact of seagoing life that when sailors, money and strong drink are brought into close proximity an explosive mixture results and Fremantle was all too aware of the potential problems, even though by this stage having received his orders to join the Channel squadron, he was anchored out in the roads at Spithead.

He was, therefore, surprised and disappointed to note that his first lieutenant, Rice, had brought guests on board. On questioning the lieutenant as to names he was informed they were relatives and that if the captain was unhappy with guests being on board he wished to request shore leave so he could spend the night with them ashore.[7] Reluctantly, Fremantle agreed to his lieutenant's request, despite the fact that he had previously issued written orders to all his officers not to allow ship's boats to go ashore and to be constantly alert to the possible problems of desertion.

None of these orders were unreasonable or draconian. Indeed, Fremantle himself had asked Betsey not to come to Portsmouth as he did not wish to be seen as having double standards with officers being given special privileges that he had prevented the crew from enjoying. He was, therefore, understandably annoyed at Lt Rice's attitude and had ample reason for being so.

HMS *Ganges* sailed in the first week of October to join Admiral the Earl St Vincent in the blockade off Brest. It was while they were off Brest that the troubled relationship between Fremantle and his lieutenant began to grow and fester. Late in October, Fremantle had reason to question the technical and professional abilities of Rice to stand watch on a man-of-war, especially in rough weather. Rice was also guilty of arguing publicly with Fremantle, who felt the necessity of having another officer with him when issuing orders to Rice to act as a witness. It was obvious that the situation was untenable within the claustrophobic atmosphere of a man-of-war and on 16 December the affair reached its climax.

Fremantle's professional relationship with Rice was finally fractured when he noted that the lieutenant had called up the men from their dinner in order to change the sails. It would have been customary as soon as the men had carried out their duties to send them below again to complete their meal, allowing them the full hour to do so. Rice, however, in direct contravention to his captain's order, kept the men on deck hanging around in poor weather despite the fact there was nothing for them to do. He was observed to be chatting to other officers while the presumably hungry men were kept waiting. The break between the captain and the lieutenant was total and after consultations with the commander-in-chief, Earl St Vincent, Lt Rice was sent back to England on another ship. That, so far as Fremantle was concerned, was the end of the matter. He had rid himself of an officer who he honestly felt was not up to the job of taking responsibility for standing a watch on a ship of the line and the problem as to what to do with Lt Rice was for the Admiralty. However, subsequent events were to prove that Lt Rice had a long memory. Meanwhile, HMS *Ganges* and her new captain were ordered to leave the Channel Fleet to join the newly formed Baltic Fleet. It was the Marquess of Buckingham who kindly wrote to Betsey Fremantle on 12 February 1801 to tell her of her husband's new posting:[8]

Dear Mrs Fremantle,

Orders were sent by Ld. St Vincent the day before yesterday for recalling from sea, some of the Channel ships who are ordered for Spithead (as supposed) for the Baltick Service. Amongst them is the *Ganges*: Their arrival and their stay are uncertain, but I should think the latter must be very short: And as it seems difficult at this season of the year to trust large ships in Yarmouth Roads you will have but little chance of seeing your husband unless you can catch him at Portsmouth. But at all events you will lay aside every idea of moving to Torbay or to Plymouth* as it is clear that the *Ganges* will continue on the Baltick duty.

I am, Dear Mrs Fremantle, Your faithful and obedient servant
Nugent Buckingham

The Baltic Fleet had been assembled by Pitt's administration and was commanded by Adm. Sir Hyde Parker. The admiral's second in command was to be Nelson who, although not fully trusted by the Lords of the Admiralty, was thought to counterbalance the older, more politically astute, Parker. It should have been, in the Admiralty's eyes, a 'dream team'. In the event, it proved anything but. The newly promoted Vice Admiral Nelson had just been through the throes of casting off Fanny, his legal wife, in favour of his mistress, Emma Hamilton. For someone as deeply religious as Nelson this was an extremely painful episode in his life but one that he felt he had to do if he was ever to enjoy conjugal happiness. His mood of depression was exacerbated by the fact that he knew it was wrong and that his open liaison with Emma was making him a laughing stock with many of his Royal Navy colleagues.

Parker was also going through matrimonial change for, having been widowed, he had recently married Frances, the daughter of his old friend Adm. Sir Richard Onslow. She was just 24 and Hyde Parker was 61 so he, too, was coming in for a certain amount of ribald merriment from his naval colleagues. The newly-weds had made their home at the manor house in Benhall on the Suffolk coast. Parker wanted the Channel Fleet as he felt he deserved it and, being stationed so close to Great Britain, had many attractions given his marital status. He was not pleased to

---

* Ports much frequented by naval wives whose husbands were serving in the Channel Fleet, as there were often opportunities for their husbands to come ashore.

be put in command of the Baltic Fleet, especially with Nelson as his second in command, and was showing some natural reluctance to move from the matrimonial bed to the rather colder, bleaker atmosphere of the Baltic. Indeed, Nelson was becoming seriously worried at Parker's reluctance to quit England and had already started to intrigue by writing letters to both Troubridge and to Lord St Vincent complaining about Parker's reluctance to move quickly.* In a letter of 12 March addressed to Admiral the Earl of St Vincent he came perilously close to accusing him of cowardice:[9]

> Time, my dear Lord, is our best Ally, and I hope we shall not give her up, as all our Allies have given us up. Our friend here is a little nervous about dark nights and fields of ice, but we must brace up; these are not times for nervous systems. I want Peace, which is only to be had through, I trust, our still invincible Navy.

As the recently appointed First Lord of the Admiralty, Earl of St Vincent was finally moved to write privately to Parker, pointing out to him that further delay would do irreparable damage to his reputation, so eventually Parker did sail on 12 March. In St Vincent's reply to Nelson he wrote:[10] 'With many thanks for the spur you have given to the movement of the Ships at Spithead.'

For Fremantle the mission was potentially awkward for he was dining with both Nelson and Parker at several lunches prior to the departure. He must have found the whole thing highly embarrassing, being extremely friendly with both while, at the same time, being well aware that Nelson did not have a favourable view of his commander-in-chief. Parker had been his commanding officer on at least two of his earlier ships while Nelson had been his squadron commander for many of his earlier Mediterranean battles. Ultimately, the following months would resolve his split loyalties in the most dramatic and final manner.

Fremantle had other worries to add to his perception of the rift between Parker and Nelson. His eldest brother, John, was seriously ill. He wrote to Betsey on 20 February 1801 to tell her of his anguish:[11]

---

* Addington's incoming administration had moved Earl St Vincent from commander-in-chief of the Channel Fleet to First Lord of the Admiralty.

You may imagine how uncomfortable I have been all yesterday and today, having received a letter from my brother William, dated from Oxford the 6th inst. Giving me little hopes that my brother Jack would be alive at this time, I have canvassed his letter over and over and have endeavoured to twist it to my wishes, yet I dread my next account, tho' I am anxious to receive it and am miserable in this state of anxiety and dread for an event that will so much add to or diminish my happiness in this world.

Fremantle had hopes that, as one of the senior post-captains and with his friendship with Parker still close, he might be appointed to lead the fleet but this honour was to go to Capt. George Murray due to his intimate knowledge of the Baltic. Nobody within the fleet was better qualified than Murray who, in April 1791, had been employed by the hydrographers department in the navy to survey and chart the Great Belt and the approaches to Copenhagen.[12] The Baltic had always been notorious for its shallows and the relative narrowness of several passages, all of which, for ships at the mercy of the wind, posed considerable problems. When the fleet sailed it had only three captains, including Murray, who had previous knowledge of operating in the treacherous northern waters.

The fleet made slow progress towards the Baltic. As a result, the diplomatic talks that should have taken place in Copenhagen under Nicholas Vansittart, with British warships anchored just off Copenhagen to add muscle to Vansittart's words, were already completed with a Danish refusal by the time Parker and the fleet arrived. Parker's orders made clear that if Vansittart's diplomacy failed he was then to destroy the Danish arsenal and all the Danish warships that were in harbour. There is little doubt the Danes may have considered the British fleet an elaborate bluff as the fall of Pitt's government and the mental incapacity of King George gave the Danes cause to think the British would seek to make peace with Napoleon, which in turn would remove much of the *raison d'etre* for the League of Armed Neutrality.

Parker further weakened the negotiating position when on 19 March he anchored the fleet in the Kattegat, north of the narrows guarded by Kronborg Castle at Elsinore, and on the eastern side in Sweden by Halsingbord Castle. Having not forced their way through the narrows to a point off Copenhagen gave the Danes a further dose of optimism that Britain was not seeking conflict.

By this stage of the mission Nelson was beside himself with anxiety that Parker was simply not moving fast enough. The admiral's mind and determination to act seemed to change daily and the longer he took to make a clear decision the more time he granted the Danes to strengthen their defences.

Nelson was clearly in favour of attacking the Russians as they possessed the largest fleet and because they were the driving force behind the League. However, the fleet was overwintering in Revel, protected by the ice sheets, and from a geographical perspective, Denmark was the key to the Baltic. Perhaps if there had been a greater degree of trust between the commander-in-chief and his second in command it would not have exasperated Nelson to quite the degree it did. Fremantle explained the relationship in a letter he wrote to William just before they sailed from Yarmouth:[13] 'My friend Sir Hyde is not a man to be reasoned into anything, and I think seems mortified at being tricked out of the Command of the Western squadron.'*

Keeping Nelson at arms length, however, was not going to answer Parker's conundrum. Eventually he would have to act and the longer he delayed the more prepared were the defences that would have to be overcome. On 19 March the fleet anchored just off the northerly tip of the Danish peninsula (the Skaw). From this point onwards for the next few days Parker, Capts Domett and Murray, and Nelson became key players in a farce of indecision and changing orders that allowed the Danes the time to prepare defences that ultimately would extract such a heavy toll on the British ships.

The next day (20 March) the fleet sailed south into the Kattegat. At this stage the British had two options: to force the Sound, a narrow strait to the east of Copenhagen that was only some 5 miles in width between two fearsome fortresses, or to sail to the west of Saelland, the island on which Copenhagen is built, through the Great Belt and approach the city from the south.

Initially, Parker favoured forcing his way through the Sound. It was certainly the most direct approach and would allow the fleet the option of attacking from either the south or the north of the city. However, having virtually reached the mouth of the Sound, Parker appeared to lose his nerve and anchored just off the Kullen peninsula in Sweden,

---

* Another term used for the Channel Fleet.

where during that night an onshore wind forced the ships out to sea in order to avoid being driven on to the lee shore.

For the next few days the fleet fought against storms but on 22 March the fleet reformed and sailed once again to the mouth of the Sound. On the evening of the 22nd the frigate *Blanche* returned with the envoy, Nicholas Vansittart, and the ambassador, William Drummond, on board with news of the failed diplomatic initiative. They also brought with them all the military intelligence they had garnered and their summary of the preparations being made at Kronborg, the fortress at Elsinore on the western side of the Sound. Parker wavered again and on 23 March he called a conference on the flagship HMS *St George*.

Nelson believed he left this conference with an agreement that they would now sail around the western side of Saelland via the Great Belt in order to attack Copenhagen from the south. However, things were never that straightforward. The increasingly indecisive Parker summoned Nelson again on 24 March to explain that, in discussions with Capt. Domett, he had now decided that the problems of navigating the Great Belt were such that they should think again. Nelson, with commendable patience, convinced his commander-in-chief that it would be alright and, once again, left the flagship with what he thought to be a plan of action. On returning to his ship he confirmed his conversation with Parker by letter:[14]

> My dear Sir Hyde
> The conversation we had yesterday has naturally, from its importance, been the subject of my thoughts; and the more I have reflected, the more I am confirmed in opinion, that not a moment should be lost in attacking the Enemy: they will every day and hour be stronger; we shall never be so good a match for them as at this moment. The only consideration in my mind is how to get at them with the least risk to our Ships.

On 25 March the fleet weighed anchor at sunrise and sailed west-north-west for the entrance to the Great Belt. Fremantle and the rest of the captains were amazed as they knew very little of the complex negotiations and the dithering that had gone on and had naturally assumed having anchored that they would force the Sound. At approximately 10 a.m. the fleet had reached the small island of Hesselo, some 12 miles due north of Saelland, where HMS *St George* hove to and a boat came over from the flagship to tell Nelson that Parker had changed his mind yet again. He was now minded to force the Sound so, at 11.15 a.m., the fleet was ordered to retrace its course back to the mouth of the Sound.

What the rest of the fleet thought of these manoeuvres is difficult to say, apart from the signals Parker had not communicated with it. Nevertheless, it would have been obvious to all that a certain amount of indecision existed at the highest levels of command. As it tried to retrace its course, back to the mouth of the Sound, contrary winds ensured it was not until 29 March that the fleet had regathered at the mouth of the Sound. It was back where it had been some nine days ago and these were nine precious days for the Danes to strengthen their already impressive, defences. By now the constant to'ing and fro'ing was beginning to suggest even to the most unobservant of crew members that everything was not right with the leadership of the fleet. Fremantle wrote to Betsey on 29 March:[15]

> You find us almost in the same situation as we were when last I wrote to you, [the 22nd March] except that we are a few miles nearer the Castle, which the Danes are making as formidable as they can, Sir Hyde in his present disposition means to pass the Castle, and Lord Nelson with the Van Division of the fleet is to attack the floating batteries. I confess myself I think if we had had the good fortune, to have undertaken this business a week ago we should have more probability of succeeding; however, to it we shall go whenever the Wind shifts to the Northward; if I were to give an opinion on this business, I should say the Danes are exceedingly alarmed, but Delay gives them courage, and they will by degrees make Copenhagen so strong, that it may resist the attack of our fleet.

He also wrote to the Marquess of Buckingham on 29 March in the same vein:

> Since I wrote you, we have had two or three different plans for attacking Copenhagen, and I think whenever we pass Cronsberg Castle, we may probably have to alter it again. I told you in my last, that my private opinion was, that we ought to pass Cronsberg, take up a position off the island of Möen, and from thence form our mode of operations. I confess I feel the difficulty of explaining exactly all that *has passed* on this business, which I hope may yet succeed. At first, it was intended to get through the

Belt, and make our attack on the Danish floating batteries from the other side. We were under way for one day, and then it was determined we were to pass the Castle, and anchor off Möen. This would have taken place if the wind had permitted us, but it has hung so to the southward that we could not lay through the channel. This plan, I am assured by Lord Nelson, still is to take place.

It is difficult to tell whether Fremantle was being loyal to his commander-in-chief or whether he truly believed that the delays were solely due to unsuitable winds but there is surely a clue in his opening words when he refers to the changes of plans and the fact that delays were counting against the chances of success. He added later in the letter to Buckingham: 'I am aware that every hour we lose is of serious importance to the country and ourselves; and this I have said on every occasion.'

Despite the differences between Nelson and Parker, Fremantle remained on close personal terms with both, referring later in his letter to Buckingham that he would be dining with Parker on the day he wrote and with Nelson the day after.

Prior to their arrival at the northern end of the Sound Parker had, at last, issued formal orders to Nelson that he would take command of the squadron that would attack Copenhagen with ten of the smaller ships of the line and eight frigates. While the attack took place, Parker would anchor off the northern end of the city with the ten larger ships of the line to create a diversion and to guard against any possible attack from Russian or Swedish sources.

On 30 March 1801, with a favourable northerly breeze, the fleet left its anchorage and sailed through the straits between Helsingborg in Sweden and the great Danish fortress of Kroneborg. Having already approached the fortress at Kroneborg to enquire as to their intentions, and having been told that the fortress would fire on them should they try to navigate the narrow channel, the British fleet prudently kept well over to the eastern (Swedish) side of the Sound well out of the range of the Danish guns.

The ships that were chosen to take forward the attack on Copenhagen needed to be able to sail into the narrow channel between the Middle Ground Shoal and the mudflats that guarded the city side of the channel. The ideal vessels were the seventy-four-gun ships of the line that had a sufficiently shallow draft to navigate the channel but still packed a fair punch. Nelson had seven such vessels in his squadron, HMS *Edgar*, *Elephant*, *Monarch*, *Defiance*, *Russell*, *Bellona* and finally HMS *Ganges* with Fremantle in command. Nelson transferred his flag to HMS *Elephant*, which was captained by Thomas Foley.

Having safely negotiated the Sound, the British fleet anchored 5 miles below Copenhagen, allowing the senior officers to reconnoitre the city's defences in a small lugger. During this reconnaissance buoys and navigational aids, removed by the Danes, were replaced by the pilots who had been recruited from the Baltic merchant fleet to aid the Royal Navy to navigate these tricky waters.

Attacking the Danish fleet in harbour was going to be no easy task. The delays had, as Fremantle had feared, allowed the Danes to prepare their defences in some depth. The majority of the Danish ships were not fit to sail, indeed many were de-masted hulks, but they were protected on the landward side by a sandbank and still more than capable of defending the city. At the northern end of the line the position was strengthened by a fort built on stone pilings. The Trekroner fortress was armed with sixty-eight guns (equal to twice the broadside of a ship of the line). Just to the north of the fort and in the entrance to the inner harbour were two ships of the line, a large frigate and two brigs, all rigged for sea, plus two more hulks.

Nelson's plan was that his ships would sail up this channel in line astern with the current with them and, hopefully, a southerly breeze, firing broadsides as they travelled up the line and anchor opposite their allocated enemy vessel before engaging them in what would be a stationary artillery duel. Typically, Nelson wished to anchor as close as possible to the enemy line and rely on the discipline and the constant practice of British gunnery crews to simply overpower the Danish crews. The problem was that they possessed no reliable charts. Capt. Thomas Hardy tried to rectify this by spending the night of 1 April taking soundings in the channel up to the Danish line.

By approaching from the south the British would be coming into the weaker end of the Danish defence. Nelson's plan was for the lead ship to draw alongside the most southerly Danish ship, anchor and engage that vessel. The remainder of the line would in turn pass outside the ships already engaged until they arrived at their allocated station, thus effectively reversing the British battle line in an elaborate nautical version of leapfrog. The frigates, commanded by Capt. Edward Riou, would attack the northern end of the line opposite the Trekroner fortress, which it was hoped would be assaulted by the troops carried onboard HMS *Ganges* once the fleet had battered the Danish fleet into submission. Bomb vessels would sit outside the British line and bombard the Danes by firing over the top of the British ships. It was hoped that, even if the fleet could not destroy all the Danish defences, it would achieve superiority at the southern end of the defences thereby allowing the bomb vessels to approach within range of the city and force the Danes to capitulate in order to prevent the bombardment of the city.

Owing to the complex preliminaries necessary to get the British ships into position for the intended battle, and because it would be against a stationary foe, Nelson promulgated detailed written orders, which Fremantle subsequently sent back to Swanbourne to be kept among his papers. The operational order is interesting for what Nelson was planning was not a sea battle in the traditional sense with all the intricacies of movement, tides and enemy manoeuvres, but an artillery duel with fixed guns on both the Danish and British sides. The seamanship involved was all about getting into position and, once successfully accomplished with the British ships anchored, the slugging match would begin. Parker was to remain to the north of the shoals with the heavier ships whose draft precluded them from entering the inner channel. The ships that would accompany Nelson into battle were set out in the operational order.[16]

Nelson's orders to his captains at Copenhagen were as follows:

The arrangements of the attack is as follows, but as the Vice Admiral Lord Nelson cannot with precision mark the situation of the different descriptions of the Enemy's floating batteries and smaller vessels lying between their two decked ships and hulks, the ships which are to be opposed to the floating batteries &c. &c. will find their stations by observing the stations of the ships to be opposed to the two decked ships and hulks.

Above: Admiral Sir Thomas Fremantle wearing his red sash denoting his appointment to the Order of the Bath. (Edward Duncan Smith)

Right: Marquess of Buckingham, the faithful mentor to the Fremantle family. (© National Portrait Gallery, London)

Mrs Maria Teresa Fremantle and Mr John Fremantle, grandparents of Sir Thomas Fremantle. (Edward Duncan Smith)

William Fremantle, Thomas's younger brother and recipient of many of Thomas's letters. (Edward Duncan Smith)

The young Post-Captain Thomas Fremantle. (Edward Duncan Smith)

Portrait of Elizabeth (Betsey) Wynne painted when she was aged 17, prior to her marriage to Thomas. (Edward Duncan Smith)

Richard Wynne, Betsey's eccentric father. (Edward Duncan Smith)

The city of Algiers where Captain Thomas Fremantle dealt robustly with the Dey of Algiers. (Reproduced with the kind permission of Mr A. Tibbits)

General view of Algiers. (Reproduced with the kind permission of Mr A. Tibbits)

British naval vessels anchored in Leghorn harbour where Thomas first met Betsey Wynne. (Reproduced with the kind permission of Mr A. Tibbits)

Rochfort at anchor in Gibraltar bay.

HMS *Ganges* in port. (Reproduced with the kind permission of Godfrey Dykes RN); Lieutenant (later, Admiral) Andrew Pelham Green, one of Thomas Fremantle's favourite naval colleagues and his flag lieutenant at the Battle of Trafalgar. (Reproduced with the kind permission of Mr A. Tibbits)

Tom Grenville, MP, who was First Lord of the Admiralty during Thomas Fremantle's brief flirtation with politics. (© National Portrait Gallery, London)

Admiral Lord Horatio Nelson. (© National Maritime Museum, Greenwich)

Opposite page. Top to bottom: the Rock of Gibraltar – western base for the British Mediterranean Fleet; the lighthouse at Leghorn; British warship leaving Gibraltar; the port of Valletta in Malta. (All reproduced with the kind permission of Mr A. Tibbits)

Admiral Sir Alexander Inglis Cochrane RN. Thomas Fremantle argued violently with him and was eventually forced into an apology in order to save his career. (© National Galleries, Scotland)

Royal Naval vessels anchored in Naples Bay. It was here that HMS *Rochfort* was anchored when Admiral Sir Thomas Fremantle died. (Reproduced with the kind permission of Mr A. Tibbits)

HMS *Rochfort*, Admiral Thomas Fremantle's flagship at Spithead. (Reproduced with the kind permission of Mr A. Tibbits)

HMS *Rochfort* off Palermo. (Reproduced with the kind permission of Mr A. Tibbits)

HMS *Rochfort* in a gale in the Mediterranean. (Reproduced with the kind permission of Mr A. Tibbits)

HMS *Rochfort* dressed overall in honour of the Emperor of Austria. (Reproduced with the kind permission of Mr A. Tibbits)

HMS *Rochfort* with her yards crossed in mourning following the death of the admiral. (Reproduced with the kind permission of Mr A. Tibbits)

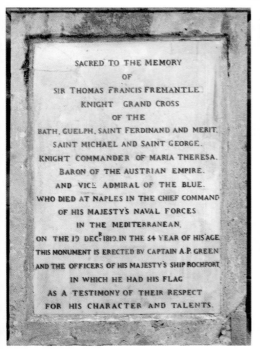

SACRED TO THE MEMORY
OF
SIR THOMAS FRANCIS FREMANTLE
KNIGHT GRAND CROSS
OF THE
BATH, GUELPH, SAINT FERDINAND AND MERIT,
SAINT MICHAEL AND SAINT GEORGE,
KNIGHT COMMANDER OF MARIA THERESA,
BARON OF THE AUSTRIAN EMPIRE,
AND VICE ADMIRAL OF THE BLUE,
WHO DIED AT NAPLES IN THE CHIEF COMMAND
OF HIS MAJESTY'S NAVAL FORCES
IN THE MEDITERRANEAN,
ON THE 19 DEC.R 1819, IN THE 54 YEAR OF HIS AGE.
THIS MONUMENT IS ERECTED BY CAPTAIN A.P. GREEN
AND THE OFFICERS OF HIS MAJESTY'S SHIP ROCHFORT
IN WHICH HE HAD HIS FLAG
AS A TESTIMONY OF THEIR RESPECT
FOR HIS CHARACTER AND TALENTS.

The plaque in Valletta harbour, Malta, in memory of Thomas Fremantle.

IN REMEMBRANCE OF
VICE-ADMIRAL SIR THOMAS FRANCIS FREMANTLE
(THIRD SON OF JOHN FREMANTLE OF
ASTON ABBOTTS, IN THIS COUNTY, ESQUIRE)
KNIGHT GRAND CROSS OF
THE BATH, GUELPH, ST. FERDINAND AND OF MERIT,
AND ST. MICHAEL & ST. GEORGE,
KNIGHT COMMANDER OF MARIA THERESA,
BARON OF THE AUSTRIAN EMPIRE,
SOMETIME A RESIDENT LANDOWNER IN THIS PARISH,
WHO FOUGHT UNDER NELSON AT COPENHAGEN AND
TRAFALGAR, AND IN CO-OPERATION WITH THE AUSTRIAN
LAND FORCES RE-TOOK FROM THE FRENCH TRIESTE
AND THE TOWNS OF THE DALMATIAN COAST 1813.
BORN 20TH NOVEMBER 1765, DIED AT NAPLES WHILE
COMMANDING HIS MAJESTY'S NAVAL FORCES IN THE
MEDITERRANEAN, 19TH DECEMBER 1819
AND OF
ELIZABETH MARY, HIS WIFE, DAUGHTER OF RICHARD WYNNE
OF FOLKINGHAM IN THE COUNTY OF LINCOLN, ESQUIRE,
BORN 19TH APRIL 1778,
DIED AT CIMIER NEAR NICE, 2ND NOVEMBER 1857.
THE GLORY OF CHILDREN ARE THEIR FATHERS.

Thomas Fremantle's memorial plaque placed on the wall of Swanbourne Church in Buckinghamshire. (Tim Parker)

Above: Admiral Sir Charles Fremantle. (Edward Duncan Smith)

Left: Admiral Sir Thomas Fremantle. (Edward Duncan Smith)

Clockwise from left: Commander Charles Fremantle RN, the latest, but perhaps not the last, Fremantle to captain a Royal Naval vessel. (Commander Charles Fremantle RN); Admiral Sir Edmund Fremantle. (Edward Duncan Smith); Admiral Sir Sydney Fremantle. (Edward Duncan Smith)

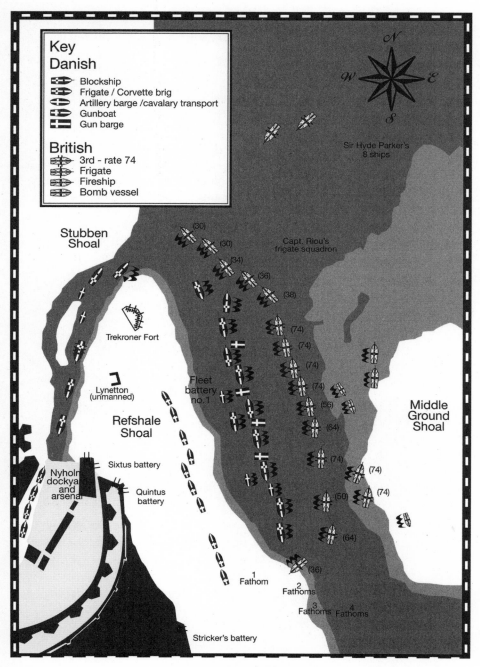

Nelson's squadron lined up against the Danish at the commencement of the Battle of Copenhagen.

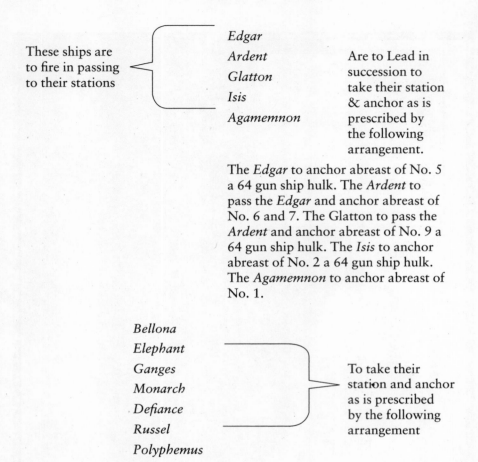

These ships are to fire in passing to their stations

Edgar
Ardent
Glatton
Isis
Agamemnon

Are to Lead in succession to take their station & anchor as is prescribed by the following arrangement.

The *Edgar* to anchor abreast of No. 5 a 64 gun ship hulk. The *Ardent* to pass the *Edgar* and anchor abreast of No. 6 and 7. The Glatton to pass the *Ardent* and anchor abreast of No. 9 a 64 gun ship hulk. The *Isis* to anchor abreast of No. 2 a 64 gun ship hulk. The *Agamemnon* to anchor abreast of No. 1.

Bellona
Elephant
Ganges
Monarch
Defiance
Russel
Polyphemus

To take their station and anchor as is prescribed by the following arrangement

The Memo. No. 1 begins with the Enemy's first ship at Southward.

No	Rate	Supposed no. of guns mounted on one side	Station of the line as they anchor and engage
1	74	28	*Agamemnon, Désirée* is to follow *Agamemnon*, and rake No. 2
2	64	26	*Isis*

3	Low floating	10	It is hoped that *Désirée*'s fire will not only rake No. 1, but also rake these two Floating Batteries. Capt. Rose is to place 6 gun brigs so as to rake them also.
4	batteries Ship rigged rather lay within the line	10	
5	64	27	*Edgar*
6	Pontoon	10	*Ardent*
7	Frigate Hulk	12	
8	Small – no guns visible		
9	64	20	*Glatton*
10	Ship Gun-boat of 22 guns	11	*Bellona* to give her attention to support the *Glatton*
11	Pontoons or	12	
12	Floating batteries	12	
13	74	36	*Elephant*
14	Pontoons or Floating batteries	12	*Ganges*
15		12	
16	64	30	*Monarch*
17	64	30	*Defiance*
18	64	30	*Russell*
19	64	30	*Polyphemus*
20	A small ship supposed a Bomb	11	

With the detailed planning completed, Nelson, in marked contrast to Parker, spoke to all his captains personally to ensure they were content with, and fully understood their orders. The fleet was anchored just to the north of the city and needed to sail around the small island and the Middle Ground sandbank, which would best be accomplished with a northerly breeze, followed by a southerly one to take them back up the channel against the current into Copenhagen harbour. Nelson's gods of war were with him for, at 2.30 p.m. on 1 April, the wind blew steadily from the north and he was able to take his division between the island of Saltholm and the Middle Ground to anchor that night just off the south-eastern point of the Middle Ground.

He used the brig HMS *Cruizer* commanded by Capt. James Brisbane to take soundings for the narrow channel between Saltholm and the Middle Ground and thus draw up charts for the approach to the battle as the fleet sailed southwards between the two shoals. As a further aid to navigation he had ordered Capt. Brisbane to anchor his brig at the entrance to the channel to serve as a navigational marker for the fleet.[17]

That evening Nelson invited the captains of the other ships to dine with him on HMS *Elephant*. Foley, Hardy, Fremantle, Riou, Inman, Graves and a few others sat down to a meal and drank to the prospect of a southerly wind and success. Nelson, as was his norm, was in high spirits now that the battle was so close. The anxieties and sheer frustration of Parker's indecisive behaviour was all behind him. He was, given a favourable breeze, master of his own fate. He spoke at length to each captain, making absolutely sure they understood what was required of them, and by early morning the operational order had been written out in sufficient numbers to distribute to all the captains involved.

On the morning of 2 April, incredibly, the wind had shifted through almost 180 degrees and blew south-south-easterly. From the British point of view this was ideal and at 9.30 a.m. the signal was given to weigh anchor. From the very start it became obvious that things were not going to go exactly as planned. Hardy's soundings from the previous night had shown there was deep water right up to the Danish line of vessels. Indeed, the further they pushed over to the westward side of the channel the better, both from the point of view of depth of water under the keel and also to bring the British gun crews as close as possible to the Danish fleet, maximising their superior gunnery drills. In the event the Baltic merchant pilots taken on by the Royal Navy were understandably loathe to risk their necks by taking the ships up close to the enemy. Nelson later remarked that he had:[18]

> ... experienced the misery of having the honour of our country entrusted to a set of pilots who had no other thought than to keep the ships clear of danger, and their own silly heads clear of shot.

Clearly, his habitual kindliness and thoughtfulness to his naval colleagues did not extend to the Merchant Navy!

Unfortunately, the plan started to go awry even before the ships had reached the mouth of the King's Reach. Nelson's old Mediterranean command, HMS *Agamemnon*, now skippered by Capt. Robert Fancourt,* failed to allow sufficient searoom around the southern edge of the Middle Ground and, despite signals from Nelson on HMS *Elephant*, she was forced to anchor to avoid getting irretrievably beached on the shoals. Although the crew made frantic efforts to haul her round the southern tip of the mudflats, the wind and currents conspired to leave her there, out of range of the battle.

The rest of the ships followed HMS *Edgar*, the lead vessel who was taken in by the Master of HMS *Bellona*, Alexander Briarly, who had volunteered and transferred to HMS *Edgar*. Fremantle followed Nelson in HMS *Elephant* up the line and, again, Nelson was forced to improvise as HMS *Bellona* and HMS *Russell*, in passing the line of ships already anchored, had both gone aground on the Middle Ground. HMS *Elephant* and *Ganges* passed between HMS *Bellona* and HMS *Edgar* to take their respective positions opposite the Danish ships, *Sjælland* and *Dannebroge*. As they moved up the channel the master on HMS *Ganges* was killed and the pilot was badly wounded and, as a result, Fremantle was forced to steer the ship himself. As would be expected of such a consummate seaman, he carried it out perfectly and was able to drop his stern anchor, bringing the ship into the precise spot indicated by Nelson.

By the time Fremantle anchored it had gone 10 a.m. and the battle was well and truly under way. The gun crews worked unceasingly as they battered the Danish ships opposite them. The slaughter was terrible on both sides of the channel as the Danish fought bravely against the superior gunnery of the British ships. The British ships, disadvantaged by their line being shorter than the Danish line, were required to engage with more than one Danish ship or gun battery, which also meant some of the British were being raked by Danish cannons.**

Parker, who was still some 4 miles north of the entrance to the King's Deep, with the smoke of battle blowing towards him, could see little of what was going on; what he could make out, however, were the signals

---

* After the battle, in his dispatch, Nelson generously recorded that 'not the smallest blame can be attached to Capt. Fancourt'. His fellow captains were far less kind and possibly more accurate in their judgements.

** A ship is described as being 'raked' when another vessel is able to fire its broadside into the stern or bow of its opponent who is therefore unable to reply. The stern of an eighteenth-century man-of-war was its most vulnerable area and cannonballs could enter the ship's hull and pass along the full length of a gun deck, doing terrible damage.

on the three grounded British ships. HMS *Bellona* and *Russell* were flying signals of distress and *Agamemnon* raised a signal of inability to proceed. He was in a dilemma and, with the fear that Nelson might be having the worst of the battle and be unable to retreat without orders (the Articles of War demanded that all ranks 'do their utmost' against the enemy in battle), at 1.30 p.m. Parker told his flag captain that he would signal number 39[19] to disengage and recall Nelson's division to save them from further damage. There remains debate as to Parker's motives for this signal. What is clear is that it was a general signal to the whole fleet and was therefore mandatory. It should have been obeyed but it was a signal made by a commander who was not in possession of the facts. It is entirely possible that Parker signalled through consideration of what he thought was Nelson's position but, if so, he was wrong. Nelson famously ignored the signal, ordering his signals officer to acknowledge it but not to repeat it to the rest of the ships. He turned to his flag captain, Thomas Foley, and said,[20] 'You know, Foley, I only have one eye – I have the right to be blind sometimes,' and then, holding his telescope to his blind eye, said, 'I really do not see the signal!'

Nelson's 'close action' signal continued to fly at his masthead and of the ships in the King's Deep only Riou's, who could not see Nelson's flagship, obeyed Parker's signal. Riou withdrew his force, which was then attacking the Trekroner fortress, thus exposing himself to heavy fire from the fortress and unfortunately he was killed before the frigates could get out of range.

What was actually happening, unseen by Parker, and despite the ad hoc rearrangements of the British line due to the running aground of two ships, was that the British were overwhelming the southern end of the Danish defence. More and more of the Danish ships struck their colours but unfortunately, and perhaps due to the fact that fresh gun crews were being ferried out from the city to take the place of their slaughtered colleagues, some of the ships fired after their colours had been hauled down, which quite naturally angered their British opponents.

Despite this, by 2 p.m., Nelson was able to hail Fremantle and invite him aboard the *Elephant*. Fremantle described it in a letter three days later to Betsey:[21]

As soon as the ships abreast of the *Elephant* and *Ganges* had struck he [Nelson] hailed and desired I would come on board. I found him talking with some Danes in his Cabin, and telling them how he longed to see the Russians down; at the same time he was sending an officer with a flag of truce on shore to tell the Prince that if he did not cease firing from the batteries he should be under the necessity of burning all the ships with the people in them. This produced a cessation to the very severe battle, which was certainly as convenient for *us* and the Enemy, as we had several ships on shore and most of the Ships engaged so completely crippled that it was with difficulty they could sail out.

The battle was hard fought and lasted for more than four hours, which is an extremely long time for two sides to batter each other with such heavy artillery. Shortly after 2 p.m., although the Trekroner fortress was still capable of carrying on the battle, the majority of the Danish ships down to the south of the channel had struck their colours. The British, while heavily mauled, were still capable of firing an almost continuous salvo of shot into the Danish lines with the threat of Parker bringing the really heavy ships in from the north and possibly pounding both the city and the Trekroner fortress. The superiority of the British gun crews and their discipline, honed by countless practice, meant that the battle had swung decisively in the British favour. The cessation of firing meant that the British bomb vessels with their heavy mortars were able to approach Copenhagen.

Two Danish ships, the *Nyborg* with *Aggershuus* in tow, tried to get away but both sank. The most northerly ship in the Danish line, the frigate *Hjælperen*, was more successful and managed to withdraw into Copenhagen harbour. The Danish commander, Cdr Olfert Fischer, moved from his flagship the *Dannebrog* to the *Holsteen* earlier on in the battle when *Dannebrog* caught fire but when the next in the line, the *Indfødsretten*, struck its colours at about 2.30 p.m., he moved yet again into the comparative safety of the Trekroner fortress. There he engaged three of Parker's ships, which had lost their manoeuvrability after being badly damaged and had drifted within range.

Although the *Indfødsretten* had already struck she resumed firing after Capt. Schrodersee was ferried to it and took command of the ship. Perhaps because of their inexperienced crews, many of whom were not seamen but volunteers from the city, several Danish ships fired on British boats sent out to them after their officers had signalled their surrender.

It was this last act that was to fire Nelson into sending his ultimatum to the Danes, saying that he 'must either send on shore and stop this irregular proceeding, or send in our fire ships and burn them', and went to his cabin to write a note to the Danes. He sent it with a Danish-speaking officer, Capt. Sir Frederick Thesiger, under a flag of truce to the Danish Regent, Crown Prince Frederik, who had been watching the battle from the ramparts of the Citadel. The note read:[22]

To the Brothers of Englishmen, the Danes
Lord Nelson has directions to spare Denmark, when she is no longer resisting; but if the firing is continued on the part of Denmark, Lord Nelson will be obliged to set on fire all of the Floating-batteries he has taken, without having the power of saving the brave Danes who have defended them.

Some British and Danish officers thought the offer of a truce a skilful ruse to enable Nelson to pull his much-battered ships out of the battle past the still fearsome Trekroner fortress for, although the British had lost no ships, most were severely damaged and three ships of the line were effectively aground and helpless. All the fighting ceased while the Crown Prince Frederick considered Nelson's note. He then sent his adjutant general, Hans Lindholm (a Danish Member of Parliament), to ask the reason for Nelson's letter. On arriving on HMS *Elephant*, Hans Lindholm asked Nelson for his reply in writing, while joking that if the British guns were not better pointed than their pens, they would make little impression on Copenhagen.

In reply, Nelson wrote a note:[23]

Lord Nelson's object in sending on shore the Flag of Truce is humanity; he, therefore consents that hostilities shall cease, till Lord Nelson can take his prisoners out of the Prizes, and he consents to land all the wounded Danes and to burn or remove his Prizes.

Lord Nelson, with humble duty to His Royal Highness, begs leave to say, that he will ever esteem it the greatest victory he ever gained, if this Flag of Truce may be the happy forerunner of a lasting and happy reunion between my most gracious Sovereign, and His Majesty the King of Denmark.

Subsequently, Nelson referred Hans Lindholm to the commander-in-chief and at 4 p.m. on HMS *London* a twenty-four-hour ceasefire was agreed.

Some half an hour after the truce was signed the peace was shattered by an enormous explosion when the Danish flagship *Dannebrog* exploded, killing a further 250 men. As the Danish ships had been partially manned by volunteers not listed on the ship's muster, it is not certain how many men were lost on the Danish side; estimates vary between 1,200 and 2,300 captured, killed or wounded. One official report estimated the Danish casualties to be between 1,600 and 1,800 captured, killed or wounded. According to the official returns recorded by each British ship, and repeated in dispatches from Nelson and forwarded by Parker to the Admiralty, British casualties were 875 killed or wounded.

The British fleet had sunk two Danish ships, one had exploded and twelve had been captured. With the constant fear of the Russians being able to clear their previously ice-bound ports and sailing their fleet out to meet the British, Parker felt unable to spare men for manning prizes. They burned eleven of the captured ships and only one, *Holsteen*, was sailed to England with the wounded under surgeon William Fergusson. *Holsteen* was then taken into service with the Royal Navy and renamed HMS *Holstein*.

On 4 April Fremantle wrote to the Marquess of Buckingham:[24]

For our action I shall refer you to Lord Nelson's letter, which, in confidence, he *dictated to me* on board the *St George* while I wrote it; but to make the business more clear, I inclose a draft of the situation of the Danish ships and ours as opposed to them. The fatigue of firing so long was great, but our unexampled good fortune in the *Ganges* is surprising. I felt much flattered at being appointed second to Lord Nelson, as well as to the Commander-in-chief. We followed the *Elephant*, and I dropt my anchor in the spot Lord Nelson desired me from the gangway of the *Elephant*. In passing the line, my master was killed, and my pilot had his arm shot off, so that I was obliged to carry the ship in myself, and I had full employment on my hands. The *Monarch* and *Defiance* are dreadfully cut up, as they were exposed to the Crown batteries; the *Bellona* got on shore on both sides the channel, and, notwithstanding all that may be said, never could fire a shot with effect. They, however, did fire, and the loss of her men was principally occasioned by the bursting of two guns on the lower deck, which hurt the ship much. I visited Sir Thomas Thompson with Lord Nelson this morning, and he is doing as well as can be expected.* The *Russel* got on shore and could do nothing; *Agamemnon* totally *hors de combat*; so that we were all but nine sail of two decked ships. I consider all this business as Nelson's, to whose ability and address we are certainly indebted for a conquest instead of a defeat.

The first mode of attack, I was attached to the command of the flat boats, but when I found a larger force was to go against the batteries, I begged Sir Hyde to allow the *Ganges* to go. After getting by the middle ground I dined with him; and at night with Riou, he planned the attack, a copy of which I received at eight next morning. At nine we weighed, and at ten we began. When the ships abreast of the *Elephant* and *Ganges* were completely silenced, Lord Nelson desired me to go to him. He was in his cabin talking to some Danish officers out of one of the ships captured, and saying how anxious he was to meet Russians, and wished it had been them, instead of Danes we had engaged, &c. At this time, he put into my hand a letter, which he meant to send immediately to the Prince in a flag of truce, threatening to burn every ship captured if the batteries did not cease firing. At this time he was aware that our ships were cut to pieces, and it would be difficult to get them out. We cut our cables and ran out. The ships were so surprised, they would not steer. The *Elephant* and *Defiance* both ran on shore. We ran on shore, and the *Monarch*; and at this period when the batteries had not ceased firing, we counted no less than six of the line, and the *Desiree* fast on shore. Luckily we had to contend with an enemy much beaten, and who did not take advantage of our situation; otherwise all those ships have been lost. They are not all off, with great exertion, but as you may imagine, what a state a ship must be in, with so many wounded people on board, and so much crippled. We are all fitting as if we were at Spithead, though within five miles of Copenhagen. The carnage on board the Danish vessels taken exceeds anything I ever heard of; the *Ca Ira* or Nile ships are not to be compared

---

* Sir Thomas Thompson served with both Nelson and Fremantle at Santa Cruz, where he was one of the first to storm the mole during the abortive third attempt on the town and also where he was wounded. He subsequently served with Nelson at the Battle of the Nile and afterwards, while taking the dispatches from Egypt to Gibraltar on HMS *Leander*, he fought the much larger and better armed French warship *Généreux* in a long-running engagement before eventually having to capitulate to the French ship. A court martial exonerated his behaviour. After Copenhagen, in which he lost a leg, he took only shore-based appointments, being made a baronet in December 1806 and awarded a KCB in 1822.

to the massacre on board them. The people generally were carpenters, labourers and some Norwegian seamen. Luckily we have been enabled to keep our flag of truce up until now that I am writing, which is of great advantage to us. The Danes are between two fires, and the difficulty is great for them to decide on. There are not *5000* troops in Copenhagen but I have no idea they can submit to the terms proposed to them. I have recommended stopping up the Sound with these hulks, and having no passage but through the Belt, in which case, a small force will depend that pass; and the Russians have not seamanship enough to get through such an intricate passage.

Our masts and rigging are cut to pieces, but I think in a few days I shall be as effective as the day I left Yarmouth. The *Monarch* is so bad, she must be sent home; one gun burst on board her, and another in the Isis. The frigates behaved most gallantly; poor Riou had just cut his cable, and was going off when he was killed. I was much pleased at Lord Nelson's manner on board the *Elephant,* after we ceased firing; he thanked me before everybody on the quarter-deck, for the support I had given him, &c. I have to attribute our good fortune in losing so few men to the bad gunnery of our opponents, and beating them most completely in less than an hour.

Lord Nelson, with whom I breakfasted this morning, has just been giving me an account of his reception on shore, when he went to treat with the Prince. He was hailed with cheers by the multitude, who came to receive him at the water-side, and 'Viva Nelson' resounded until he got to the palace, much to the annoyance, I believe, of his royal highness and his ministers. During dinner, the people were allowed to come in to look at him, and on going down to the boat, again he was saluted the same way. The populace are much in our favour and the merchants already feel the total want of commerce. I just received a letter from Otway, who is going on shore for a categorical answer, after which he will return to England; and as he is a particular friend of mine, he will, I am sure, give you any information you wish.* He will call on my brother William.

Fremantle's part in the battle had been considerable. The gunnery on HMS *Ganges* had been exemplary and had battered his opponent, the *Sjælland*, into submission with more than a third of her crew killed, her

---

* Otway was distantly related by marriage to Fremantle.

masts and rigging shot away, and her guns destroyed. The remaining crew left her in the ship's boats and she drifted, unmanned, out of the battle line. More importantly, Fremantle had demonstrated when he personally steered HMS *Ganges* into position, having lost her pilot and master, that he was the complete seaman. A captain at the peak of his powers; like the great sportsmen who are able to produce consummate moments of skill when the pressure and the occasion overwhelm lesser men, Fremantle demonstrated his greatest skill and calmness when the pressure and the dangers could have easily led to error. The last piece in the complex jigsaw that made a great sea-fighting captain was in place and Fremantle now knew that in a major sea battle, whatever happened, his nerve and skill would allow him to function effectively. Later events were to show this even more clearly.

The next few days were filled with negotiations as the Danish government tried to extricate itself without renewing hostilities. Parker seems to have abrogated almost all of the responsibility for the negotiations to Nelson and Fremantle was in attendance for most meetings. The two men dined together most nights when not with the Danes so that gradually the relationship between them grew as close as their difference in ranks allowed. On 8 April the Danes finally agreed to a lengthy armistice, mainly due to the fact that they were aware that Tsar Paul I had been murdered and that without him the League of Armed Neutrality was effectively at an end. Nelson had stuck to his brief and had, so far as the British fleet was concerned, negotiated a satisfactory armistice of sufficient length to allow them time to deal with the Russian fleet.

The aftermath of the battle was somewhat of an anti-climax. On 12 April Parker, together with Fremantle now extricated from the King's Deep, sailed to Karlskrona to threaten the Swedish fleet. The Swedish fleet immediately withdrew back to port as soon as the British were sighted, where they were surrounded with sufficient shore-based artillery to deter Parker from any attack. The British fleet therefore withdrew south to the Danish island of Bornholm, where Fremantle amused himself by going ashore on a small Danish island called Ertholmar[25] where he professed that the walk ashore had done him some good as he had been unwell with 'a cold and the bile'. It is perhaps this cold and bile that leads him later in his letter to Betsey to fulminate against the Methodists who had evidently moved into Swanbourne:

I am quite annoyed to hear you have got some Methodist preachers in the Village; I wish they were here for an hour or two. I shall make a point of bowling them out of line when I return.

By now, Parker had been informed of the death of Tsar Paul I, who had been assassinated in his own palace and was to be succeeded by his son, Alexander I, who's first action was to renounce the League of Armed Neutrality and begin to make peace overtures to Britain. The Baltic fleet's job was done. On returning to Copenhagen, Parker was presented with a dispatch from the Admiralty that announced that he was to be relieved of his command. On 5 May he was recalled and handed over command of the fleet to Nelson. Sadly this last voyage to the Baltic had been one command too many for Parker. At 61 and newly married, his vacillation and caution had nearly scuppered the task force's mission before it had begun. He had served his country for fifty years and his tragedy was that he simply went on too long.

In his absence, Nelson sailed eastwards again and, leaving six ships of the line at Karlskrona, he arrived at Revel on 14 May to find the ice had melted and the Russian fleet had departed for Kronstadt. He also found out that negotiations for ending the Armed Neutrality had started and so withdrew on 17 May.

Fremantle was now recognised as one of Nelson's favourite captains and one he could trust with difficult tasks. As soon as the diplomatic clearances were arranged with Russia, Fremantle was ordered to sail up the Baltic to St Petersburg to negotiate with the Russian authorities for the release of the British merchant sailors and their ships as quickly as possible. Fremantle soon found that the Russian Foreign Minister, Count Panin, was sympathetic to the British and that the new Tsar was eager to distance himself from his father's policies, so within a few weeks everything was arranged to the satisfaction of both parties. Later, Britain was to find Tsar Alexander I a far more untrustworthy ally but, for the time being, Fremantle found himself in the seductive world of international diplomacy and inevitably he found it exciting. The previous experience of negotiating with the Dey of Algiers faded into insignificance when compared to this experience, which involved him in a subject that was at the current heart of British politics.

While invited ashore he was able to carry out a little espionage, as his letter to Admiral Nelson explains:[26]

I had an opportunity of walking round the dock yard at Cronstadt. The Revel Squadron of 12 or 13 Sail of the Line are followed into Cronstadt the 7th inst. None of the ships appear to me to be in a good state for sea. None of them were completely rigged and out of the Mole back 3 three decked Ships and 5 two decked ships – 4 Block Ships for the defence of the port of 64 or 74 Guns are fitting two only on the 13th landed outside the Mole, their fleet generally are dismasted and they have little or no other in the Dock Yards. The English Merchant Ships Cargoes of Hemp has been made use of for the Russian men of war as they had <u>none</u>. The Mole of Cronstadt has been put in a state of Defence, 148 Large Guns and 12 large mortars face the entrance of the Road, beside the fort or citadel on the Larboard hand going in. Cronstadt has likewise been much strengthened and they have made embrasures by coiling large cables and filling them up 50 guns or more defend their port. They have likewise built in 15 ft. of water a fort something like the Crowns at Copenhagen – 48 guns are on it and it is on the South West side of Cronstadt. There is a large flotilla equipping 10 or 11 mountings 5 & 6 32 pounders are moored by the new fort built in the water. None of the English officers in the service of Russia were returned to Cronstadt the whole were at Moscow. The seamen belonging to the English Merchant ships had once been ordered to sail their respective ships but a second order detained all but 150 or 200 (who are at Petersburg and Cronstadt) at Novogorood. The sails of the English ships are quite decayed and unfit for use having been too long without air in the Vessels. They are all unloaded. There are in Russia 103 Sail at Petersburg, 88 at Riga and 10 others at other ports. No complaints of ill treatment from any of the Masters of the ships or seamen I saw.

The English Seamen at Petersburg and Cronstadt are maintained by the English Merchants.

These events made 1801 a significant year in Fremantle's naval career. It was not just the naval and political education, there was also the emotional switch from his most powerful and consistent mentor, Admiral Sir Hyde Parker, to Admiral Nelson. Some of the most important periods of his naval tutelage had been under Parker's guidance but from Copenhagen onwards his loyalty and his gaze turned firmly towards Horatio Nelson. It was an emotional shift of allegiance rather than a shrewd, calculating move away from someone whose stock then stood at an all-time low with the Admiralty hierarchy. Fremantle obviously felt that Parker had been extremely harshly dealt with by the Admiralty, as he stated in a letter to his wife from HMS *Ganges* on 21 May 1801:[27]

> In my opinion we must make our peace with Russia tho' they seem to stickle a great deal about this armed neutrality, I met Lord St Helens* in the *Latona* going to Petersburg and it is so much the interest of both countries to be at amity, he will I make no doubt make a treaty with them, none of the English ships or seamen were released when I left Petersburg. I can only add that I am well and satisfied with my trip to Petersburg, and the attention I received from Lord Nelson is flattering beyond what I can name. The insult of the Admiralty to my friend Sir Hyde is scarcely to be named without feeling detestation to the person who occasioned his recall in such a way as Treason only could have rendered necessary. God bless you.

The indignation over the sacking of Parker seemed real enough but significantly, his comments come right at the end of a long letter to his wife that is full of his own news. The comments on his disgust at Parker's treatment, together with their placement in the letter immediately after a rather gushing reference to his own delight at Nelson's compliments, seem to rob them of much of their emotional power. There is no doubt that Fremantle felt the man who he refers to as 'my friend' had been treated harshly but almost subconsciously he was already moving on. Complex negotiations with foreign, potentially hostile, governments were now to be part of his day-to-day duties and leading him was his revered Lord Nelson.

That he had reason to be grateful for Parker's patronage and support is incontrovertible. In a much earlier letter to his brother, William, from HMS *Inconstant* he writes:[28] 'My good friend Sir Hyde continues staunch, and has realy been the means of my getting this Ship.'

Neither did he shun the company of Parker. Subsequently, when back in Britain, there are references in his diary to dining with him in London and he was to name his third son after Parker and ask the retired admiral to be one of his godfathers. But whatever his private feelings, Fremantle

---

* Alleyne FitzHerbert, 1st Baron St Helens, was a distinguished diplomat who had previously served in Russia as envoy extraordinary to Empress Catherine of Russia and, subsequently, chief secretary to the Marquess of Buckingham in his role as Lord Lieutenant of Ireland. In April 1801 he had been sent back to Russia to agree a new treaty with Tsar Alexander I.

knew which way the wind lay and, with the system of appointments being so dependent on the whim of individual commissioners in a remote Admiralty, there was little to be gained, and potentially much to lose, by going out on a limb over someone whose career was now effectively over. From May 1801 he could no longer rely on the patronage of Parker, who was never again to hold a seagoing command.

Up until Copenhagen and the Baltic expedition Nelson's own star was not necessarily in the ascendancy so far as the Admiralty was concerned. With the British public he was Britain's most famous fighting admiral. The Battles of the Nile and St Vincent assured him of public adulation but with the Admiralty it was different. In its eyes this very adulation that Nelson so assiduously courted made him suspect. Added to that was his very public flaunting of his mistress, Emma Hamilton. In truth, this aspect of Nelson's character also worried Fremantle. It had been thus since he had first known him. It was not that Fremantle was a prude, he was very much a product of eighteenth-century naval morality that saw nothing wrong in enjoying the delights of female company when in a foreign city, but Nelson's dalliance was far, far more blatant than this.

Nevertheless, whatever his sense of moral outrage, it is hard not to escape the conclusion that Fremantle's feelings towards this complex little man who now dominated the news and who had become the public face of the Royal Navy were akin to hero worship. Lord Nelson reciprocated these feelings of close companionship, as witnessed in a jocular note he sent Fremantle three weeks after the Battle of Copenhagen:[29] 'If you don't come here on Sunday to celebrate the Birthday of Santa Emma, Damm me if I ever forgive you, so much from your affectionate Friend as you behave on this occasion.'

By midsummer the newly enthroned Tsar of Russia had signed a peace treaty with Britain. More importantly, Britain and France were also about to sign a peace treaty. The Austrians had already made their peace with the French at Lunéville. This treaty, signed on 9 February 1801 between the French Republic and the Holy Roman Emperor and Austria, effectively marked the end of the land-based coalition and now the British were beginning to signal their tiredness after eight years of warfare. Britain and France signed what became known as the Treaty of Amiens on 1 October 1801 and, although it was highly likely that none of the signatories to either of these treaties thought of them as a final settlement, for a short period Europe enjoyed a period of uneasy peace. Napoleon was unable to get his troops back from Egypt thanks to the efficiency of the Royal Navy's blockade of Toulon and the relatively new Grenville administration was far less hawkish than Pitt's government. Napoleon was also troubled by the new Tsar's attitude to France and it therefore suited all parties to have a ceasefire while they got their breath back.

On 2 August Troubridge, working with Earl St Vincent at the Admiralty, wrote to Betsey Fremantle to tell her that her husband was due back in Portsmouth any hour. Betsey was overjoyed and, on receiving a letter from Thomas on 7 August stating that he was back in Portsmouth but could not get home leave, she set off immediately in a chaise with her eldest son and her sister, Eugenia. They reached Reading on the first day and on the following day (8 August) Betsey was finally reunited with her husband after a twelve-month absence.

Despite the fact that Britain and France were now officially at peace, Fremantle's time ashore was yet again to be cut short. If nothing else, Fremantle was a fine advertisement for the cliché that a little sea air is good for the appetite for after this all too brief reunion, and nine months to the day of their first seeing each other again, at 8.30 a.m. on 8 May 1802, Betsey gave birth to the couple's third son, Henry Hyde Fremantle.

After just three months, on 5 November 1801 Betsey learned to her sadness that her husband had been ordered to sea again, albeit this time to a climate the complete opposite from the Baltic winter. Under secret orders Fremantle, on HMS *Ganges*, was to sail for the West Indies. Betsey was distraught but her emotional state was eased when just nine days later, back home in Swanbourne, she unexpectedly received a letter from the Fremantle's faithful mentor, the Marquess of Buckingham.[30] Having heard from Admiral Cornwallis of Fremantle's new assignment the Marquess of Buckingham used his influence with the Earl of St Vincent to get Fremantle ordered home.

He arrived home on the frigate HMS *Ambuscade* on 21 January 1802 and the very next day in Aylesbury the Fremantles were yet again reunited, albeit somewhat later in the day than planned as Thomas had been taken by his chaise to Woodford rather than Watford. The following day Fremantle was invited to Stowe to dine with Lord Buckingham, presumably to offer his profuse thanks. Reputedly Earl St Vincent, having agreed to the recall, was not happy to be used in such fashion and as a consequence Fremantle was advised to stay away from London temporarily until the incident could be glossed over.

His homecoming was shortly to be brought all too clearly to the attention of the Admiralty for that summer Fremantle received the first of what grew into a barrage of abusive letters. Lt Rice, whom Fremantle had sent home from HMS *Ganges* when she had first sailed to join the Channel Fleet, had obviously been quietly simmering on being left ashore and had convinced himself that his disgrace was entirely due to the personal animosity and malice of Fremantle.

The first letter from Rice arrived at Swanbourne on 16 July 1802.[31] It read:

> I have mentioned to all my friends, that your conduct to me when First Lieut., of HMS Ganges was unlike a <u>gentleman</u>, <u>unmanly</u>, <u>base</u>, and <u>dis</u>honourable.
> … You pledged your word and honour never to take an advantage of me.

The remainder becomes a meaningless rant but he was obviously challenging Fremantle to a duel. Fremantle was only too aware that he was dealing with someone who was not entirely rational and he sensibly referred the whole matter to the Admiralty.

Two weeks later Rice followed up with a further letter addressed to Capt. T.F. Fremantle at Swanbourne, Bucks. He wrote as follows:[32]

> I have been in hourly expectation of hearing from you since your letter of 24th inst and shall only observe that it will not be inconvenient to me to go two thirds of the way to any port of England or France.
> I am sir etc. etc.

The news that Fremantle had referred the whole matter to the Admiralty further provoked Rice into another outburst of colourful invective. A letter dated 20 August 1802 turned up in Swanbourne:

> Sir, Your claiming the protection of the Admiralty reminds me of a <u>little</u>, <u>dirty</u>, <u>snivelling</u> boy at School running to the Master, when threatened to be chastised for <u>low</u>, <u>mean</u> conduct – you know my opinion and you have not the <u>feelings</u> of a <u>gentleman</u>.

The Admiralty Board, having taken over the matter and concerned to ensure it did not escalate into a public farce, wrote back to Fremantle on 2 August 1802:[33]

Having laid before my Lords Commissioners of the Admiralty your letter to me of 27th of last month enclosing one which you had received from Lieut. Rice dated the 16th containing a challenge, I am commanded by their Lordships to acquaint you that they have directed their Solicitor to file an information against the said Lieutenant for his conduct on that occasion, and that he will apply to the court for that purpose as soon as the term begins, but that, if in the mean time you should think your person in danger you may apply to a magistrate who on such application will oblige him to find securities for his keeping of the peace.

Affidavits were sworn by various commanding officers who had commanded Rice in previous commissions to the effect that he was not quarrelsome or capricious and that another considered him: 'A Gentleman particularly beloved and esteemed by all such characters on board.'

It was all very messy but Rice had effectively condemned himself in his previous correspondence. Even his very handwriting had disintegrated as he poured his vitriolic feelings on to the paper. Anybody could see these were not the letters of someone who was anywhere near in control of himself. Nor was this someone to whom a battleship should, or could be, entrusted. Eventually, the matter was brought before the Court of the King's Bench in 1803, where Rice pleaded guilty.*

The whole experience must have been a trial for both Thomas and Betsey and although it only gets a passing mention in Betsey's diary it must have left a nasty taste. It was highly likely that Fremantle for once did not confide quite so closely with Betsey over Rice. If he confided his fears and frustrations with anyone it is likely that it was with Nelson, whom he met in London at this time. Luckily for Fremantle he did not have long to wallow in self-pity for on 18 May 1803 Britain yet again declared war on France; the false peace was over and once again Britain's navy prepared for war. Thomas's reappointment to command HMS *Ganges*, to become part of the Channel Fleet, arrived in July. He tentatively suggested to Betsey that his eldest son, Tom, should accompany him in one of the midshipman's berths; an idea that was quickly quashed by Betsey who enjoyed Tom's company far too much

---

* Lt Henry Rice died five years later aged just 31. He never served in another ship and died still a lieutenant. He is commemorated with a simple brass plaque in the chancel of Exeter Cathedral.

to let him accompany his father to sea. Understandably she considered him far too young: he was only 5![34]

From early August 1803, while waiting for HMS *Ganges* to be refitted, the Fremantles rented a house in Portsmouth. By late September the vessel was ready to put to sea and join the Channel Fleet. Fremantle's orders were to join a squadron off Ireland to form part of the guard against Napoleon's Armée de L'Angleterre, which it was thought might try to strike against Britain's underbelly through a landing on the west coast of Ireland.

While stationed off Bantry Bay, Fremantle was struck by one of the fearsome westerly gales that blew in off the Atlantic and was why this particular stretch of coast was so feared. During one critical phase of the storm he noted in his diary that he was on deck for a forty-eight-hour period with no rest or let up in the storm's ferocity. It was the sailors' old nightmare of a lee shore with precious little searoom in which to manoeuvre and keep off the waiting rocks. The problem was exacerbated by British warship design, which prioritised the carriage of guns over manoeuvrability and seaworthiness. Fremantle proved more than equal to the task but nevertheless the ferocity of the storms was worthy of a mention in his next letter to Nelson (see below).

In January 1804 Fremantle was reallocated to a squadron, commanded by Sir Edward Pellew, off Ferrol and again found himself on the endless blockade work that took up so much of the British seafarer's time. While sailing out to join the Ferrol blockade Fremantle wrote to Nelson and, for once, allowed his emotions to show in writing. Normally he was a very reticent writer who tried hard to conceal his true emotions but in this case with his friendship so strong, we get a glimpse of the sheer pleasure and the awe in which he holds Nelson:[35]

> My Dear Lord, I can't forego the satisfaction I always feel at having an opportunity of writing you a few lines. We are now on our way to join Sir Edwrd. Pellew off Ferrol ... The last fortnight the weather has been worse than can I recollect in my life. We are with one set of sails only left we however already begin to feel the difference between the Latt. Of 44 and 53. If reports are true you will have full occupation enough in the Mediterranean for the ships you have there, I hope you continue your health, your Spirits can never fail – I wish most heartily I had gone with you when you left England ... I shall therefore conclude with expressing

you of my sincere regard and attachment, as well as my gratitude for the many marks of favour you have shown me. Remember me to Murray, Hood Featherstone Adml. Campbell and believe me always ... etc. etc.

Nelson replied outlining his hopes that the French would eventually venture out of Toulon so that he could destroy their fleet. His letter to Fremantle of January 1804 reads as follows:[36]

I trust, my dear Fremantle, in God and in English valour. We are enough in England, if true to ourselves. He may by chance injure us, but can never conquer a determined people. It would be well if the generality of Englishmen would remember that they who know the whole machine can better keep it going than we who only see a very small part. Although I am naturally anxious for the issue of the attempt, yet I cannot doubt of the final attempt – it will be the ruin of that infamous Buonaparte,* and give us an honourable Peace. I should most assuredly rejoice to have you here, but we none of us see the inside of a Port: I have twice taken shelter under the Madalena Islands on the North end of Sardinia, which forms a very fine anchorage. The Village, I am told, for I have not set my foot out of the Victory, contains forty or fifty small houses. As to Malta, it is a perfectly useless place for Great Britain; and as a Naval Port to refit in, I would much sooner undertake to answer for the Toulon Fleet from St Helens, than from Malta; I never dare venture to carry the Fleet there. I know your friends think differently from me, but they talk of what they know nothing about in that respect, and I know it from dear-bought experience. During the winter, generally speaking I cannot get even a Frigate from Malta, the Westerly winds are so prevalent; and as they approach the Gulf of Lyons, they are blown to the South end of Sardinia. Perseverance has done much for us, but flesh and blood can hardly stand it. I have managed to get some fresh provisions from Rosas in Spain, which with onions and lemons have kept us remarkably healthy. We are longing for the French Fleet, which is to finish our hard fate. I am &c. Nelson and Bronte.

---

* Nelson appears to imply here that a defeat of the French fleet will signal the end of Bonaparte. However, he was by no means blind to the limits of sea power, having written to the Hon. John Trevor on 28 April 1796 stating, 'We English have to regret that we cannot always decide the fate of Empires on the sea.' The veracity of this statement was surely endorsed by the fact that the Napoleonic regime lasted a further ten years after the victory at Trafalgar.

By July Fremantle was getting bored with the constant blockade duties, and as he confessed to Betsey in a letter dated 25 July,[37] although he had managed to give up snuff, he had now taken up smoking cigars. The duties were not that onerous and they often got an opportunity to get ashore and eat a decent meal. When ashore Fremantle frequently dined with his French counterparts,* as he explained, having sat down to eat for two hours:[38]

> I was highly gratified and amused, and having vowed eternal friendship *privately,* and hatred professionally to the French Captains, I took my leave and in three hours rowing am safely landed again in my cabin.

It is during this phase of his life that, for the first time, the politically ambitious Fremantle came to the fore. Both Betsey and her husband shared a common drive of cementing their place in society and both were concerned in 'bettering themselves'. In the case of Betsey, this mostly manifested itself through her children, whom she pushed whenever and wherever possible, ensuring they received a good education. In Fremantle's case his ambition had now turned to politics, although whether he would be fitted to the duplicity and backbiting of the world of eighteenth-century politics remained to be seen.

So far as his brothers, John and William, were concerned, Thomas's infatuation with politics was mere hubris. His elder brother, John, wrote to William as follows:[39]

> I think he may stand some chance, but at present there is no assurance of success. I am sure your ideas respecting Tom's throwing away so much money for the mere gratification and vanity of being in Parliament, will meet mine, for should he be returned as the sitting Member, the expenses will be nearly £1,000, and being obliged to vote entirely with Lord Buckingham, there is nothing he can get or ask, to balance the flinging away so much money.

During the eighteenth and early nineteenth century it was by no means unusual for serving naval officers to become MPs, even those who spent the majority of their time at sea. A vote in the House of Commons, if wisely placed, could do much for a career and both Fremantle and

---

* Fremantle was a fluent French speaker.

Buckingham were well aware of this. Despite the fact that he was still at sea he volunteered his services to act as MP for Aylesbury, which should have been, in theory, within the marquess's gift. However, events did not turn out that way.

Perhaps to both his brothers joint satisfaction, Fremantle never did get the Aylesbury seat despite a petition lodged in his name that resulted in a by-election in 1804.[40] The Marquess of Buckingham had, by then, found himself another candidate to fight the seat. Fremantle seemed, however, while naturally disappointed, to take the news of his loss relatively calmly. He wrote to Betsey:[41] 'The loss of the Election at Aylesbury has given me real concern, and I am sure must have affected Lord B. very much. I shall not say one word to him on the subject.'

It was not until 31 October 1804 that HMS *Ganges* arrived back in Portsmouth, and yet again on returning to Britain Fremantle found himself in trouble. During his spell on blockade duties off Ferrol he had been under the command of RAdm. Sir Alexander Cochrane and for some unaccountable reason Fremantle had taken it into his head to defy the admiral and in doing so he had taken himself well beyond the line of acceptable conduct. The whole affair seems to have blown up over a junior captain and a possible letter of complaint from Adm. Cochrane as to his competence.

The admiral had shown the letter to both Fremantle and Capt. Bullen, presumably to get their views. Both had suggested to Cochrane that such letters often rebounded on the correspondent and that the Admiralty often 'took against' officers who they perceived as whining. Cochrane concurred with this view and the matter rested at that point.

The question came up again at a social gathering when Cochrane had invited Fremantle to dinner and for some reason best known only to Fremantle, he forcibly expressed the view that Cochrane was extremely harsh to all the officers, particularly to him (Fremantle). In a subsequent letter to the Admiralty, Cochrane described Fremantle's outburst:[42]

I received from captain Fremantle such a peal of invective against my conduct as I believe hardly has fallen to the share of the greatest tyrant that ever disgraced the Service – I was accused of being harsh, making it unpleasant to all the officers under my command (particularly to him) and that he need only refer to the Public Order Book as a proof.

Worse was to follow, for soon afterwards, when anchored off Ferrol in an adverse wind, Cochrane ordered the fleet to sail southwards to Ares Bay, just to the south of the entrance to Ferrol harbour. Cochrane gave orders for the fleet to anchor in a line. He described his order in his letter:

> I therefore made the signal to anchor in the line of bearing SSE and directed the Malta and the Ganges to anchor in the SSE and the *Illustrious* in the NNW. Observing that the Ganges did not proceed to her station I repeated her signal, notwithstanding which, and there was no impediment in the way of her complying with it he [Fremantle] wore round to the northwards and anchored from which situation I directed her to move into the prescribed station.

Cochrane continues:

> The day following I went onboard of the Malta, where I found Captain Fremantle, and received from him the most disrespectful and contemptuous treatment and language highly improper to pass between any Captain and his Commanding Officer. I was under the necessity of directing him to discontinue such a line of conduct.

To his credit, the captain of HMS *Malta*, Joseph Bullen, acted as a peacemaker between his fellow officer and the admiral and managed to smooth the admiral's feathers and got him to agree to forget the whole incident. Fremantle, however, refused to let the whole thing die, which would have been, by some considerable margin, the best course of action. Instead he raised it again at a social gathering that had been specially arranged in the great cabin of the flagship HMS *Northumberland* in order to facilitate normal relations. By now Cochrane was heartily fed up with Fremantle and had ample justification for such sentiments. Fremantle had acted throughout with a completely reckless lack of judgement that bordered on professional suicide; what motivated him is impossible to say and what he thought the outcome would be was equally unclear.

Cochrane wrote to Fremantle setting out in clear terms what he thought of his conduct and letting him know that the Admiralty would be notified formally:[43]

Upon duly considering the manner in which you have thought proper to conduct yourself to me since under my Command and the very extraordinary language you used in the cabin of this Ship on the Evening you returned from Corunna – in which conversation you again brought under review my Conduct as an Officer and having treated with harshness the Officers of this Squadron and appealed to the Public Order Book as a proof of the same in which it would appear how exceedingly ill I had treated you – and as you then pointed clearly to the occurrence which took place in this Bay, which was followed up by you with a behaviour to me in the presence of Captain Bullen on board the Malta, highly disrespectful on your part and Subversive of all that Good Order – which ought to exist in a fleet – which conduct I was induced to overlook at your request through the medium of Captain Bullen and on my part would have rested in Oblivion had you not thought proper to bring it again under review.

I therefore consider it as a justice I owe the Service to lay your Conduct before the Lords Commissioners of the Admiralty and to request of their Lordships that they will take such steps as to Them may seem proper for supporting my Authority in the Station I have had the Honour to be I appointed to.

I have further to inform you that in the same letter I have requested of their Lordships to cause my own Conduct to be inquired into How far the charges you have thought proper to bring against me are founded in fact will there be made to appear.

Cochrane's letter to the Admiralty sent via the commander-in-chief of the Channel Fleet, Admiral Cornwallis, was, in the circumstances, remarkably fair. Crucially it gave Fremantle a 'get out'. The letter detailed the whole sorry incident then paid tribute to Fremantle as an 'outstanding officer' and, to show that he was not motivated by revenge, Cochrane stated that he would be content with a public letter of apology. There is little doubt that in the circumstances Cochrane, with the backing of his commander-in-chief, could have insisted on a court martial and, given the direct disobedience to a lawful order from Fremantle, there could have been only one outcome.

The Admiralty followed the matter up and wrote to Fremantle at Swanbourne on 24 November:[44]

Admiral Cornwallis having transmitted to my Lords Commissioners of the Admiralty a letter he had received from Rear Adm Cochrane, complaining of your conduct to him, whilst you were under his command, I have their Lordships commands to send you herewith a copy of the said letter, and to signify to you their direction to you to let me know immediately, for their information, whether it is your intention to make the apology required by Rear Adm Cochrane, and if so, to transmit your letter unsealed to me for their Lordships inspection.

There was no other course of action open to Fremantle if he wished to resume his naval career and on 27 November 1804 he duly complied and issued a public letter through the Admiralty:[45]

In obedience to their Lordships commands I herewith enclose an apology to Rear Adml. Cochrane.

As I perceive that the Rear Adml. Has left the affair entirely to the decisions of their Lordships I trust they will be pleased to inform me whether it meets their approbation.

... Captain Fremantle having apologised to the Hon. Rear Adml. Cochrane, by a public letter as well as through the medium of Captain Bullen for what did occur in the Middle of Septr. Last, does not hesitate one moment in repeating in the most unqualified terms his distress and sorrow at what passed on that occasion.

Captain Fremantle is not aware, or conscious of having made use of invectives, or improper language to Adml. Cochrane on his return from Corunna, if he was – Captn. Fremantle is desirous and ready to make every possible concession.

Captn. Fremantle never thought Adml. Cochrane's conduct harsh or oppressive, and is apprehensive Adml. Cochrane must have mistaken his words, had Captn. Fremantle ever made such an assertion, it would become him, as it would be his inclination to retract so unfounded a charge.

Cochrane was as good as his word and accepted Fremantle's apology, leaving the somewhat discomforted captain free to pursue his naval career. However, the question surely remained as to what motivated Fremantle to such extraordinary lengths over matters that appeared, on the surface, to have such little substance. He had never been an easy subordinate officer to command except for Adms Parker and Nelson. With Adm. Hood, who he always thought unfair to him, Fremantle had obeyed each order scrupulously, thus avoiding any chance of the admiral being able to pick fault.

What precisely was the cause of Fremantle's behaviour is a mystery. Had Cochrane been one of the officers who signed an affidavit for Lt Rice or was there another grudge that Fremantle held? Perhaps the best clue to Fremantle's behaviour is contained in the words of Earl St Vincent, who reputedly said of the Cochranes:[46] 'The Cochranes are not to be trusted out of sight, they are all mad, romantic, money-getting and not truth-telling – and there is not a single exception in any part of the family.'

In short, Alexander Cochrane was the kind of man who could start a fight within a monastery and, unfortunately for both parties, Fremantle was not the type of man to back down. Although no specific actions are identified in the correspondence that provided the spark to this incident it is unlikely either party were totally innocent.

Did Fremantle, with his whiggish and relatively impoverished back-ground, take offence at the aristocratic Cochrane, whose elder brother was the 9th Earl of Dundonald? We will never know for sure and although Fremantle was never an easy officer to manage, this was the first and only time he refused to obey a lawful order. It was lucky for Fremantle that Cochrane accepted his apology.

That Christmas, with Thomas home for once, the Fremantles spent the festive season with their usual Christmas hosts, Lord and Lady Buckingham at Stowe. The 1804 Christmas was a particularly grand affair even by the Buckinghams' standards with some distinguished French nobility in attendance, including the future Charles X of France. Betsey refers to him as 'Monsieur' in her diary and on 1 January 1805 notes:[47]

Monsieur and his party went away after breakfast. He was particularly out of spirits today. I really regretted their departure as they made them-selves very pleasant. I believe Ld. Buckm. was much relieved, as waiting attendance must worry him much and he really shows him every atten-tion, which must gratify him.

7

PORTSMOUTH
TO TRAFALGAR

By 1805 Britain had been back at war for two years with its seemingly perennial enemy, France. In the circumstances, the Admiralty was not about to let one of its most experienced sea captains remain ashore for long and, on 7 May, Fremantle received a letter from their Lordships at the Admiralty informing him he had been appointed to HMS *Neptune*. For Thomas and Betsey an all too brief interlude of six months of togetherness came to an end on 14 May when Fremantle joined HMS *Neptune* at Spithead, just off Portsmouth.

The latest outbreak of war had started with the British declaration on 18 May 1803. Neither the French nor the British had any real intention of fulfilling the treaty conditions so painstakingly negotiated by the Addington government. The French would not accept withdrawal from Holland and Switzerland, and equally Britain was not about to vacate Malta. The declaration of war was a simple matter. What was not so clear was how either side could attack or seriously weaken the other. In typical fashion Napoleon seized the initiative and made the first move. Along the northern seaboard of France he assembled his Armée de l'Angleterre in order to threaten Britain with invasion.

In response Britain turned back to a political leader it knew and trusted, William Pitt. Initially, Pitt tried to convince King George III that what the country needed in a time of national peril was a widely based 'coalition' with a cabinet made up of the most talented politicians, irrespective of party. This would have included Grenville and Fox. After some regal reluctance, Pitt eventually got Royal assent to include Grenville but under no circumstances would the King countenance Fox. The exclusion of Fox so angered the Whigs that they withdrew from forming a coalition, leaving Pitt to form a government without the support of some of the most talented political minds in the country. Despite this, on 18 May 1804, the 45-year-old Pitt took on the job. He was a weakened man both politically and physically. Britain was back at war with a Prime Minister it trusted, albeit one they it was not to know was weakened by ill health and by the erratic support of a monarch increasingly prone to bouts of insanity and strange behaviour. To make matters worse his son, the Prince of Wales, was gathering opposition to him and Grenville, Fox, Grey and other prominent Whig politicians were meeting at Carlton House and providing a focal point for the opposition.

By contrast, the newly crowned Emperor Napoleon was unchallenged in his own country. He had demonstrated his ruthlessness when, in early March 1804, he suspected a relative of the Bourbon dynasty, the Duc d'Enghien, of plotting against him and arranged for him to be kidnapped from Baden. He was brought back to a chateau near Paris, hastily tried by a military commission and executed on 21 March. The message was clear. Napoleon's regime would allow no dissent or challenges to the status quo but, outside France, the action had the opposite effect of stirring up the dynastic rulers of Europe to oppose someone they believed was nothing more than a Corsican upstart. In particular, Tsar Alexander I of Russia was deeply concerned with Napoleon's cavalier treatment of Duc d'Enghien. The Russian ruler's view that Napoleon was a dangerous radical made him a natural ally for Britain, despite the ongoing grievance over Malta. It would ultimately lead to Napoleon's greatest military folly and the human disaster of the invasion of Russia.

Napoleon's problem was that, while a relatively prosperous Britain remained unconquered, there would never be a lack of opponents to his empire. British subsidies would ensure that armies would be raised to challenge his hegemony on the European mainland and his overseas trade would continue to be disrupted by the British navy. Early in 1805, he came up with a plan whereby the French and Spanish fleets block-aded in Brest, Rochefort and Toulon would break out and sail to the West Indies, where they would rendezvous and attack the rich British possessions in the Caribbean. Napoleon gambled that this would force the British fleet out of their positions guarding the Channel in order to protect their West Indian assets. Having achieved this, the combined French and Spanish fleet would race back to the Channel and hold it against the weakened Royal Navy while the huge flotilla of small ships, carefully amassed in the northern French ports, would transport the Armée de L'Angleterre over the water and Britain would fall.

Napoleon's grand strategy was far too complex and dependent on too many imponderable factors to have a realistic chance of success. Nevertheless, it partially worked but not sufficiently for him to launch his invasion. The Mediterranean Fleet under the command of Adm. Nelson did indeed chase after Adm. Villeneuve but the remainder of the British fleet, including Fremantle in HMS *Neptune*, withdrew northwards and were ready in sufficient numbers to defend the Channel should the need arise. On 22 July Villeneuve arrived back off Cape Finisterre, where he was met by a British fleet under Vice Adm. Sir Robert Calder. The result-ing action was indecisive with murky conditions hampering the fleets from getting properly to grips with each other. The British took two prizes and Villeneuve diverted his course southward to Vigo rather than Ferrol. Calder withdrew to join up with Cornwallis's fleet but met with nothing but opprobrium from both the British public and the Admiralty for his failure to draw the enemy fleet into a full-scale battle.

Fremantle was perhaps lucky in that his ship had been withdrawn from the fleet to go back to Cawsands to reprovision and pay the crew their backdated wages.* He therefore took no part in the fleet action, which did little to add to the reputation of those who participated. Subsequently, the Admiralty put Calder before a court martial resulting in Nelson writing to Fremantle to commiserate with him over the fate of a fellow officer:

> I could not last night sit down to thank you for your truly kind letter bewildered by the account of Sir Robert Calder's Victory, and the joy of the event; together with the hearing that *John Bull* was not content, which

---

* Cawsands Bay was the naval anchorage immediately to the south-west of Plymouth Hoe.

I am sorry for.* Who can, my dear Fremantle, command all the success which our Country may wish? We have fought together, and therefore well know what it is. I have the best disposed Fleet of friends, but who can say what will be the event of a Battle? And it most sincerely grieves me, that in any of the papers it should be insinuated, that Lord Nelson could have done better. I should have fought the Enemy, so did my friend Calder; but who can say that he will be more successful than another? I only wish to stand upon my own merits, and not by comparison, one way or the other, upon the conduct of a Brother Officer. You will forgive this dissertation, but I feel upon the occasion.

Is George Martin with you? If so remember me to him kindly. I have said all you wish to Admiral Murray, and to good Captain Hardy.

Dr Scott says you remember everybody but *him*.** I beg my best respects to Mrs. Fremantle, and with the most sincere wishes that you may have the Neptune close alongside a French three-decker.

Believe me as ever, my dear Fremantle, your most faithful and affectionate friend.

While the chase to the West Indies and the subsequent action off Cape Finisterre was taking place, Fremantle was quietly cruising off Ushant and Ferrol as part of the Channel Fleet, firstly under Adm. Lord Gardner and, subsequently, after July, Adm. Cornwallis. His thoughts, however, were now beginning to turn more than ever to politics. For the first time for many years the Whigs sensed weakness in Pitt. They gathered hungrily around the political table at Westminster to see if any pickings would be left by the Tories. For the first time Fremantle's letters contain political tittle tattle rather than pure navy talk. In his letter to Nelson on being appointed to HMS *Neptune* he referred to the political scene:

... the great joke in London is that Sir Peter Parker ought to have been first Lord of the Admiralty, he is a contemporary with Lord Barham. The fact

---

*   After the battle Calder was relieved of his command and brought home by the Admiralty to face a court martial, which severely reprimanded him for failing to renew the attack on Villeneuve's forces on 23 and 24 July. He never held a seagoing command again.

** The Revd John Scott, a naval chaplain who had acted as a translator while Nelson and Fremantle had negotiated with the Danes after the Battle of Copenhagen. He was subsequently by Nelson's side after his fatal wounding at Trafalgar.

is the place was *going abegging* as the Vulgar say, and unless You or some such person are at the head of that Department, we shall not be able to go on. The want of decision in the Naval Councils seems very apparent.

A letter to Betsey contains further political news: 'If I can at all guess from the debates in Parliament I should say that there was a prospect of union between the present Government and the Opposition.'

Despite this new interest in politics, his letters to Betsey are filled mainly with his feelings of loneliness; he seems to be depressed and always complaining of 'bilious attacks'. He professes himself quite happy with the ship but the thought of endless blockading duties, with seemingly no prospect of the enemy coming out of port to fight, had an effect on his spirits. On 23 May, just over a week after he sailed, he wrote to Betsey: 'My low spirits are excessive and I do nothing but take snuff and read Shakespeare, when I am off the deck.'

On 14 June, again to Betsey having just received one of her letters, he writes: 'You can have no idea how an arrival revives and comforts my spirits which are not so good as they used to be.'

He was, however, happy with his ship. HMS *Neptune* was a ninety-eight-gun three-decker and classified as a second-rate ship of the line.* The rating system, however, was somewhat misleading for she was in all but name, a 'first rate' line-of-battle ship. She had been built in 1797 so that she was, by the navy's standards, an extremely new ship. Because she was modern, HMS *Neptune* was big. Ship design had continued to evolve and generally ships were getting bigger and bigger. Although she was nominally rated a ninety-eight-gun three-decker, while the *Victory* was rated as a first-rate 104-gun three-decker, *Neptune* was almost exactly the same dimensions as the older flagship. She was also equipped with carronades, therefore her actual offensive armament greatly exceeded the nominal ninety-eight cannons.

She was one of the Neptune Class of ships and her sister-ships were HMS *Temeraire* and HMS *Dreadnought*. She was by some distance the largest but, more significantly, the most powerful ship that Fremantle

---

* The Royal Navy 'rated' ships from first down to sixth-rate vessels. First rates had three decks and more than 100 guns while second-rate ships had three decks with ninety to ninety-eight guns. At the Battle of Trafalgar HMS *Neptune* was carrying more than 100 guns, but as some of these were short-range carronades rather than the longer-range cannons they did not count towards the ship's rating, despite giving her far greater fire power than the older 'first rates'.

had commanded at this stage of his career. His previous line-of-battle ship had been HMS *Ganges* when he had been part of the Baltic fleet and she had been a third-rate seventy-four-gun, two-deck ship. At 169ft long with a beam of just under 48ft she was much smaller and lighter than HMS *Neptune*, whose vital statistics were a main gun deck of 185ft and a beam of 51½ft.

Fremantle, like most seamen, despite professing himself reasonably happy with HMS *Neptune*, could always find something that was not quite to his liking. In this case the source of his unease was First Lt George Arklom:

> I have no reason to complain of my ship which is in really perfect order but my temper naturally hasty is often put to the trial by my First Lieutenant, who has so long been in the habit of governing the Ship in his way that he cannot bear the smallest contradiction, which in turn obliges me to follow up my own System without benefiting by his assistance and advice, this added to the influence he has got in the Ship obliges me to be very circumspect.

On 31 August 1805 Fremantle wrote, as usual, to his brother, William, to report on the lethargy, which seemed to have overtaken the British fleet:

> I hope Lord Nelson will come out as he is the life and Soul of the Squadron he serves with. I am by no means comfortable, I have such severe fits of the bile I can't hold up my head. For my Ship I go on as usual but now that the Service appears to become more active I feel considerable annoyance at being in a heavy three decked Ship, if we were certain of coming to action immediately I should certainly prefer the *Neptune*, but in such a Ship it is very easy to be left entirely out, in short meeting with all my old Mediterranean friends with whom I have been formerly on such enterprising business has made me feel that I am not yet Old enough *in age* for a 90 gun ship … I conclude we shall remain here until the Ships fall to pieces or until the Enemy escape in a Gale of Wind, then probably we shall follow them to the West Indies again – do pray in charity write to me sometimes, Lord Garlies at the Admiralty will assist you in forwarding them if it should be necessary – remember me kindly to your Wife.

Fremantle was presumably hankering after the freedom of a frigate captain's life again. At 40 years of age, and now a senior post-captain, his career would never take him back to, what he perceived as, the rather more exciting and independent life of a frigate captain. For now it was the large battle ship, the humdrum life of blockade duty and just the vague promise that one day the combined fleet of the French and Spanish ships would come out of port and fight. His views on heavy battle ships were not, by any means unique. The second-rate, three-decked ships were notoriously bad sailors, being too short for their beam to sail well. Indeed HMS *Glory*, which was very similar to HMS *Neptune* in both size and armament, was reputedly the worst sailor in the navy and one of the jokes about her was that she would only bring to action an enemy ship that was willing to wait around for her to arrive!

Finally, on Saturday, 28 September, Lord Nelson arrived in HMS *Victory* to take over as commander-in-chief from Adm. Cuthbert Collingwood, who remained on station as his second in command. The feeling that now something was going to happen did not just lift Fremantle's spirits, for in some miraculous way the feelings ran right through the fleet. On HMS *Neptune* Able Seaman James Martin wrote:

> On the 28th of September was joined by HM Ship *Victory* Admrl Lord Nelson and the *Ajax* and the *Thunderer* it is imposeble to Discribe the Heartfelt Satifaction of the whole fleet upon this Occasion and the Confidance of Success with wich we ware inspired.

The excitement spread rapidly around the fleet and soon everyone was confident that Nelson's magic touch would ensure that this time, after years of fruitless blockades, the combined French and Spanish fleet would be tempted out of port to be destroyed. Whatever it took to accomplish the task, they were confident that the British fleet would be triumphant. Within a few short days Nelson had somehow managed to spread his influence throughout the fleet. He was not unaware of the feelings he inspired in all ranks and indeed he did everything he could to foster such a mood. He wrote to Emma Hamilton three days after arriving:

> I joined the Fleet late on the evening of the 28th of September, but could not communicate with them until the next morning. I believe my arrival was most welcome, not only to the Commander of the Fleet, but also to

every individual in it; and, when I came to explain to them the '*Nelson touch*' it was like an electric shock. Some shed tears, all approved – it was new – it was singular – it was simple! And, from Admirals downwards, it was repeated – It must succeed, if ever they will allow us to get at them!

Fremantle's spirits were lifted further when he managed to get three of his previous lieutenants transferred to the *Neptune*, one of whom was Lt Andrew Pelham Green, who was made flag lieutenant. Fremantle described him to Betsey in his letters as 'a famous good fellow and we shall then go on famously'. Just as important as the psychological lift to Fremantle was the fact that the three officers he brought on board were all battle hardened. Green had fought with Fremantle at Toulon, Corsica and Copenhagen and there was obviously a real friendship between the two men. Later, Lt Green, when promoted to post-captain, would serve as Fremantle's flag captain on HMS *Rochfort* and was with him right up to his death. For now, the introduction of Green to the ship's company was exactly the lift that Fremantle needed and, together with the three experienced lieutenants, it gave Fremantle an edge in imposing his own regime and procedures over the ship's company.

One of the main problems he had been battling with ever since leaving Portsmouth was that the crew had been paid in May with three years' wages. With no shore-side opportunities to spend it, the men were left with, what seemed to them, great wealth burning holes in their pockets and this led to several disciplinary problems involving gambling and thieving.

For a man who had a reputation as a strict disciplinarian, Fremantle was remarkably circumspect in his response. In all, between May and October, the ship's log records thirty-eight crew members being flogged, which was just over 5 per cent of the crew. This contrasts with, for example, Capt. Tyler of HMS *Tonnant*, a captain with a reputation of being extremely loathe to hand out floggings, ordering 14 per cent of his crew to be flogged in the same period and Capt. Thomas Hardy, of HMS *Victory*, a renowned flogger, handing out nearly four times as many punishments. Gradually, Fremantle was bringing the ship's company up to the state of readiness that he wanted. But if the morale of the British fleet was on the rise what of the combined French and Spanish fleet anchored in Cádiz?

Since his return from the West Indies, Adm. Villeneuve's fleet had been ravaged by sickness. Despite offloading some of his sick at Vigo he still needed to create field hospitals in Cádiz to cater for sick crew members and, at the end of September, there were more than 1,700 crew members unfit for service. The French tried to fill the numerous vacancies in their complements with soldiers, whereas Adm. Don Federico Carlos de Gravina, who commanded the Spanish fleet, tried to concentrate his fit crew members into fifteen ships. Despite his best efforts he was still seriously short of experienced men, especially gunners. In addition, Spain was in a financial crisis and, particularly in Cádiz, the situation was desperate.

Villeneuve's personal situation was worsened by the fact that he knew that he had lost the confidence of Napoleon. In France in 1805 those who were in positions of responsibility and had lost the confidence of the Emperor did not last long and Villeneuve knew that, barring a miracle, his time as admiral of the fleet was severely limited. On 14 September, Napoleon issued orders for the fleet to sail from Cádiz, through the Straits of Gibraltar to Italy to support St Cyr in his Italian campaign. Villeneuve did not receive these orders until 27 September and by then he was aware that Napoleon had appointed his successor, the exotically named Adm. François-Etienne Rosily-Mesros.

In addition to all his other woes, Villeneuve was also aware that Britain's premier admiral was waiting for him just over the horizon. Lookouts from Cádiz had spotted and reported back to him Nelson's arrival. On 8 October Villeneuve held a council of war on his flagship *Bucentaure* where the decision was taken to postpone sailing. Gales were forecast and there was always the hope that the weather would drive the British off their station, enabling the combined fleet to slip out of port when the gales abated and before the British could regain their positions. In the event, gales did blow almost continuously from 10 to 17 October but always from the west. Villeneuve's hopes were always something of a long shot as it was not easy to get out of Cádiz harbour unless there was a good easterly breeze blowing. The fleet would then need, ideally, a westerly wind to take them through the Straits of Gibraltar and into the Mediterranean. In other words, their fate was in the lap of the gods.

Villeneuve was further hampered by both the temperament and training of his commander-in-chief. Napoleon Bonaparte was an army man, an artillery officer who understood logistics and battles and movement of troops on land. He never tried, nor succeeded in understanding, the navy and its particular problems. These factors, when combined with his autocratic style and refusal to take advice, meant that Villeneuve was constantly looking over his shoulder fearful of the Emperor's wrath. Combined with his cautious nature, this was not an ideal mix in a commander of a bi-national fleet.

At midnight on Friday, 18 October the breeze shifted to an easterly wind and the following morning Adms Villeneuve and Gravinas began the laborious procedure of getting the ships out of port and on to the high seas. As they did so the British frigate, HMS *Sirius* commanded by Capt. William Prowse who was patrolling closest to the harbour entrance, spotted the movement and signalled to HMS *Euryalus*, skippered by the Hon. Henry Blackwood, that the enemy fleet was coming out.

Capt. Blackwood was the commodore of the frigate squadron whose job was to cruise just off the mouth of the harbour and signal to the main fleet as soon as they spotted any movement. Nelson was operating an open blockade system rather than the rigid closed blockade. The ships operating within sight of the coast were not there to intercept vessels, merely to report. Nelson was trying to lure the combined fleet out, not block them into port. His main battle fleet was over the horizon, some 50 miles off shore. In light of his recent experiences off Toulon, where the open blockade had allowed Villeneuve to slip out and escape the watching frigates to sail to the West Indies, it was a brave decision as he had come in for some criticism back in Britain for allowing Villeneuve out. This time, however, his tactics were spot on. He had implicit faith in Blackwood's abilities and he was rewarded amply. Within two and a half hours of the combined fleet hauling up their sails Nelson was receiving the news on HMS *Victory*, through a line of ships repeating the signal from HMS *Sirius* via several other ships strung out between the Sirius and the main battle fleet.

It was late afternoon on Sunday, 20 October before the combined fleet were all out of harbour and were able to steer a course south-easterly for the run down the coast to the straits. By this time, Nelson and the British fleet had moved east-south-east to the mouth of the Straits of Gibraltar and, having failed to spot Villeneuve's fleet, had partially retraced their course so that by 8.30 p.m. the fleets were only some 15 miles apart, albeit heading on opposite courses. Some two hours earlier the French ship *Achille* had spotted Nelson's fleet but the signal to Villeneuve took more than two hours to arrive at the flagship and, on receiving the news, the admiral took steps to try to organise his fleet into something that resembled a line of battle.

Due to the lack of trained seamen available to Villeneuve, even the simplest of manoeuvres took some time to accomplish and, although he continued on his course during the night, most of the vessels were still 'double banked' in two columns, meaning only one column could fire their guns without being a danger to their own ships. Blackwood's frigates stuck to their task throughout the night and trailed the combined fleet that, with their proliferation of lights and signals as they tried to form one line of battle, made his job easier. By 6 a.m. 21 October the two fleets heading in opposite directions were able to see each other some 10 miles apart.

In contrast to the combined fleet, every captain in the British fleet knew what was expected of him in the next twenty-four hours. Some days ago, on 9 October, in a letter to his second in command, Adm. Collingwood, Nelson had set out his final thoughts on how they would fight a decisive battle:

> Thinking it almost impossible to bring a Fleet of forty Sail of the Line into a Line of Battle in variable winds, thick weather, and other circumstances which must occur, without such a loss of time that the opportunity would probably be lost of bringing the Enemy to Battle in such a manner as to make the business decisive, I have therefore made up my mind to keep the Fleet in that position of sailing (with the exception of the First and Second in Command) that the Order of Sailing is to be the Order of Battle, placing the Fleet in two Lines of sixteen Ships each, with an Advanced Squadron of eight of the fastest sailing Two-decked Ships, which will always make, if wanted, a Line of twenty-four Sail, on whichever Line the Commander-in-Chief may direct.

He went on to stress that Collingwood would have discretion to react to the situation as he saw fit, once battle was joined, but that he ideally should cut the enemy's line some twelve ships from the rear, whereas he Nelson would aim to cut through the enemy line in the centre. Crucially, he recognised that chance would always play a part in something as complex as a sea battle, especially when the battle was joined and the

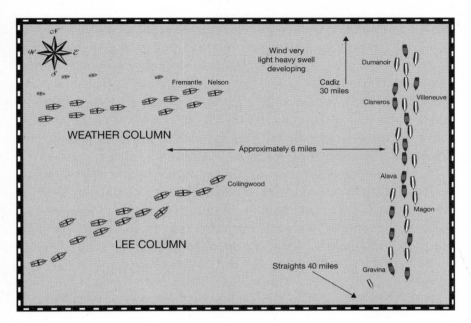

The British fleet divided into two columns prior to attacking the combined French–Spanish fleet at Trafalgar, immediately before the fleet turned towards Cadiz.

black powder used as the propellant in the cannons had spread its thick acrid smoke, obscuring individuals from seeing their commander's signals. He concluded this section of his memorandum with his famous mantra: 'But, in case Signals can neither be seen or perfectly understood, no Captain can do very wrong if he places his Ship alongside that of an Enemy.'

The Approach to Battle

By 6 a.m. on 21 October 1805, Fremantle would have been almost certain that there was to be a battle. From the moment that HMS *Sirius* had first spotted the combined fleet leaving harbour on 19 October until the morning of the 21st he would have been wondering nervously whether there was to be the decisive battle that Nelson had always promised. But, from this moment onwards, the respective positions of the two fleets made a major conflict as certain as anything could be in an uncertain maritime environment. This time, Nelson's plans for a decisive action, designed to crush the naval spirits of France and Spain, were to happen; the die was cast. Fremantle rose early that morning, in time to reach the quarterdeck as first light was breaking. At that time of the year, off the coast of south-west Spain, the sun rises at around 6.30 a.m. No doubt he had spent some time in his cabin prior to going on deck, putting his paperwork in order, perhaps writing a letter to Betsey, there being no guarantee that by sunset he would still be alive.

The crew responsible for getting things shipshape down below would have probably breathed a sigh of relief once the captain vacated his cabin; his steward would have packed his things away immediately allowing the crew to dismantle the bulkheads, thus clearing the main gun deck, allowing free access to the full length of the deck. Animals would be slaughtered so that they did not become crazed in the ensuing melee and run amok. This included the ship's goat that faithfully provided Fremantle with milk for the duration of the blockade. Now, in accordance with navy custom, she unwittingly became one of the first casualties sustained on HMS *Neptune*. Midshipman Badcock was on watch on the forecastle and was reckoned to be the first on *Neptune* to sight the enemy. He remembered:

> The sun looked hazy and watery, as it smiled in tears on many brave hearts which fate had decreed should never see it set ... I ran aft and informed the officer of the watch. The Captain was on deck in a moment and ere it was well light, the signals were flying through the fleet to bear up and form the order of sailing in two columns.

Lt Paul Harris Nicholas also remembers his sighting of the enemy fleet from HMS *Belleisle*, where he was serving as a Royal Marine:

> As the day dawned the horizon appeared covered with ships. The whole force of the enemy was discovered standing to the southward, distant about nine miles, between us and the coast near Trafalgar. I was awakened by the cheers of the crew and by their rushing up the hatchways to get a glimpse of the hostile fleet. The delight manifested exceeded anything I ever witnessed, surpassing even those gratulations when our native cliffs are descried after a long period of distant service.

At approximately 7 a.m., Villeneuve took a fateful decision when he ordered his ships to 'wear' together and to sail back towards Cádiz.*
It had always been Nelson's worst fear that the combined fleet would escape back to port without facing battle and it looked as if that was Villeneuve's intention. In fact, due to the lack of skilled seamen in the combined fleet, the whole manoeuvre took some two hours and left the fleet in a ragged crescent shape rather than in one neat battle line that would have maximised its firepower. By 9 a.m., when the combined fleet had completed its turn, the British fleet had already altered course, split into two columns, the weather column under Nelson and the lee column under Collingwood. They were some 6 miles off the port side of Villeneuve's fleet with the wind in their favour. The opening moves of the forthcoming battle were now completed and Villeneuve's indecision, and the untrained nature of many of the crews, meant that the French–Spanish fleet was now in the worst possible position with the British fleet able to dictate tactics. Nelson had gone below to his cabin to write a codicil to his will, satisfied that nothing short of a traumatic change in weather conditions could affect the interception of the enemy fleet.

Nelson had issued his orders to the captains on 10 October and had allocated Fremantle and the *Neptune* second place in the weather column behind HMS *Victory*. This was a considerable compliment to Fremantle and was clear, public recognition of the place he held in Nelson's affections. The rest of the fleet was then ordered into line based on the hitting power of those who would first break the combined fleet's line, their likely sailing speeds and the seniority and how much Nelson trusted the respective captains. HMS *Neptune*, despite being in theory exactly the same as HMS *Temeraire*, was a notoriously slow sailer. On this day, however, she seemed to have the scent of battle in her nostrils for again Midshipman Badcock reports: 'Old Neptune which never was a good sailer took it into her head to sail better that morning than I ever remembered.'

Indeed so much so that even in the light breeze which was blowing that day she had come up alongside HMS *Victory* by 10 a.m. At that time Nelson was taking the air on the stern walk of HMS *Victory* and shouted across to HMS *Neptune* to: 'Take in your studding-sails and drop astern; I shall break the line myself.'

---

*   See footnote on page 25.

It was to be the last time Fremantle saw Nelson alive. As *Neptune* obeyed the admiral's order, the *Temeraire* caught up with her sister-ship and overtook her. The progress was extremely slow for there was almost no breeze but there was a heavy swell. The British fleet, now clearly separated into two columns, was approaching the combined fleet at no more than walking pace. The main concerns for the British were the shortness of daylight in October and the impending storm, which was imminent and might possibly deprive them of the complete victory the country craved so desperately.

On HMS *Neptune*, Fremantle allowed the men to leave their battle stations to take their breakfast. James Martin, the able seaman, commented: 'Captain Fremantle allowed us the same Rest nearley as was ushall.'

Just before 11 a.m. Fremantle mustered the crew to their quarters just as he did every Monday at sea and addressed them. Again, James Martin records:

He addressed us at our Diffrent Quarters in words few but Intimated that we ware all alike Sensable of our Condition our Native Land and all that was Dear to us Hung upon a Balance and their Happyness depended upon us and their Safty also Happy the Man who Boldly Venture his Life in such a Cause if he shold Survive the Battle how Sweet will be the Recolection be and if he fall he fall Covred with Glory and Honnor and Morned By a Greatfull Country the Brave Live Gloryous and Lemented Die.

Just after 11 a.m. Nelson hoisted his famous message, 'England expects every man will do his duty' and, as Fremantle completed his last tour of inspection around his ship, he took the opportunity to inform the crew of the admiral's signal and his progress around the vessel could be charted by the loud cheers accompanying his message.

In truth, there was little that Fremantle could now do other than to appeal to the loyalty and patriotism of the crew. For them the battle and the killing were about to begin and success would depend on simple seamen, such as James Martin, sticking to the place of duty in conditions so terrible that it is difficult for twenty-first century readers to comprehend. The crews allocated to the guns would have stripped down, many discarding their shirts to fight bare-chested as, during the next few hours, it would become unbearably hot between decks, not to mention the immense physical strain of working the guns, hauling them out after each firing. Most would also fight barefoot to give them the best possible grip on the newly sanded decks. Those with experience from previous battles would tie neckerchiefs around their heads to stop the sweat running into their eyes but, more importantly, to try to protect their ears from the earth-shattering and repeated percussion of the guns. Despite this precaution, most of them would have bleeding eardrums at the end of the day and be partially deaf for several days afterwards.

Midshipmen and junior lieutenants would take up their stations in command of six to eight guns each. A gun captain controlled each gun responsible for aiming and firing, the rest of the gun crew mustered around him. One major difference between the combined fleet of the French and Spanish fleets and the Royal Navy was the methods employed in sea battles. Traditionally, French and Spanish fleets aimed at the enemy rigging in an effort to disable their opponents and thus allow them to manoeuvre alongside, where they would sweep the enemy decks with sharpshooters stationed in the rigging. This would be the precursor to boarding and thus seizing control of the vessel.

The Royal Navy, in stark contrast, aimed low. It aimed to kill. Like the boxer who likes to get in close and directs his killer blows at his opponent's body and ribs, the Royal Navy tried, as quickly as possible, to get close to enemy vessels and then fire on the downward roll of the vessel so that the majority of the broadside would hit the enemy vessel in the hull, preferably entering the main gun deck. Even better was to try to get into position at right angles to the enemy's stern so the attacking ship could pack a broadside with double shot and rake the enemy's main gun deck, killing and maiming as many men as possible.* The stern of these vessels were mainly composed of large windows to let in as much light as possible into the captain's quarters, and, once the wooden partitions were down, into the gun deck. This made them vulnerable and a rolling broadside from a ship sailing across the wake could wreak terrible damage along the length of the main gun deck.

An eighteenth- and early nineteenth-century sea battle was probably the most brutal and mind-numbing form of warfare known to mankind.

---

* When fighting at close range, where muzzle velocity was not a critical factor, the Royal Navy frequently inserted two cannonballs in the muzzle, thus doubling the effect of a broadside.

Only the earth-shattering artillery bombardments that rained down on men in trenches in the Great War some 100 years later could approach the terror of a broadside at sea. In 1815 at the Battle of Waterloo, the British had 174 cannons while, at the Battle of Trafalgar, they were sailing towards the combined French and Spanish fleet with more than 2,000 cannons at their disposal, most of which were of far greater calibre than the army's artillery.

British tactics were simple. By dint of discipline, hours of endless practice and the close proximity to the enemy, they backed themselves to fire more accurately and more often than the opposition and, as they progressively killed and incapacitated enemy gun crews, the enemy fire would inevitably lessen until eventually the ship would be forced 'to strike their colours'. Only then would the slaughter cease.

There was some debate within naval circles as to what was the best range for ensuring maximum damage to an enemy vessel. Some argued that a slightly longer range was preferable because, by the time the ball hit the wooden sides of its target, it was travelling slightly slower. Therefore it created a more ragged hole with a greater amount of wooden splinters, which were often the greatest killers of men as they sheared off at great speed from the vessel's hull and masts. Others experimented with slightly lower amounts of gun powder in order to achieve the same effect. Nelson had no doubts and much preferred being as close as possible to the enemy. That way it was impossible to miss and he would then rely on the British seamen's discipline and better rates of fire to carry the day.

As the two fleets closed for action the numerical odds were stacked against the British fleet, which consisted of:

3 × 100-gun first rates
4 × 98-gun second rates
1 × 80-gun third rate
16 × 74-gun third rates
3 × 64-gun third rates

Combined against this fleet of twenty-seven line-of-battle ships was a combined French–Spanish fleet of:

4 × 100–136-gun first rates
6 × 80-gun third rates
22 × 74-gun third rates
1 × 64-gun third rate

A total of thirty-three line-of-battle ships.

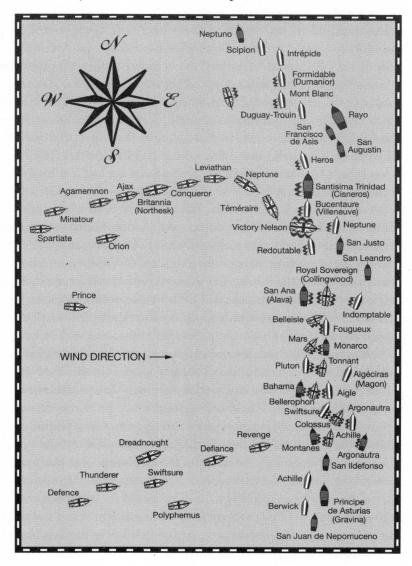

The opening stages of the Battle of Trafalgar.

The Battle

Fremantle and the other captains who served with Nelson that day were under no illusions about what was to be required of them during the following hours of daylight. They were to sail right into the midst of the enemy fleet, break up their line of battle and reduce the whole thing to a vicious dogfight, one without form or pattern. Nelson had frequently referred to wanting a 'pell mell battle'. There would be no backing down, no real tactics or complex manoeuvring. This day was to be decided by British gunnery and discipline. Nothing else mattered.

The first ship to join the battle was Collingwood's flagship, HMS *Royal Sovereign*, who came under fire at approximately 11.30 a.m. By 12.15 p.m., the *Héros*, *Santissima Trinidad*, *Bucentaure* and *Redoubtable* were all firing broadsides at HMS *Victory*, aimed at the oncoming bows of the British flagship. At around this time Nelson's secretary, John Scott, was ripped apart by a cannonball, the blood from the luckless man spraying on to Nelson's coat. A further shot killed eight of the marines standing on the poop deck and it was around this time that Nelson also made his famed remark to his captain: 'This is too warm work, Hardy, to last long.'

As HMS *Victory* broke into the combined fleet's line she was heading almost south-east, having turned when the flag of Villeneuve was raised to ensure that it was the enemy's command and control centre against which Nelson launched his attack. HMS *Victory* was unable to break through the line but became entrapped in the midst of several enemy vessels having come in across the stern of the *Bucentaure*. In fact, the enemy line at this point was several ships deep. So disorganised was the combined fleet that it had failed to form a single battle line but was, in several places, in lines of two and sometimes three ships all sailing broadly parallel courses. The disadvantage was that the most easterly ships could not fire their guns for fear of hitting their own ships on their port beam. The inadvertent advantage was that it made it impossible in most cases for the British ships to 'break the line' and come up alongside the French and Spanish on the leeward side to fire their broadsides.

Midshipman Badcock had been on deck as the *Neptune* approached on the same course as HMS *Victory* and could plainly see the *Santissima Trinidad* through the smoke. As he returned to his post on the gun deck, Fremantle ordered the crew to lie down to avoid any raking shots that the ship might take. Midshipman Badcock commented:

During the time we were going into action, and being raked by the enemy, the whole of the crew, with the exception of the officers, were made to lie flat on the deck, to secure them from raking shots, some of which came in at the bows and went out at the stern. Had it not been for the above precaution, many lives must have been sacrificed.

HMS *Victory* broke into the French line between the *Bucentaure* and the *Redoubtable*. As she moved laboriously into the gap she fired her 68-pounder carronade loaded with round shot and a keg of some 500 musket balls straight through the vunerable window lights of the stern of the *Bucentaure*. The damage was devastating and before the French crew could recover from that shock the main guns of HMS *Victory's* fearsome broadside were pounding into her hull causing further death and mutilation amongst her crew. As HMS *Victory* swung into the French line the *Redoubtable* had been trying to close up the gap between her and the French admiral's flagship. Hardy, seeing that in order to break the line he would need to run aboard one of the enemy's ships, turned to Nelson to offer him the choice. He was informed by his commander-in-chief that he should make his own choice and accordingly swung his rudder over to thud into the port side of the *Redoubtable*. Momentarily the two ships bounced apart but their rigging became intertwined and held the two ships together in a deathly embrace.

HMS *Temeraire* was by now slightly to the starboard of HMS *Victory* and Capt. Harvey lost sight of the *Victory* in the heavy smoke that was beginning to envelop the battle. He turned in and passed to the stern of the *Redoubtable* just ahead of the French *Neptune*. As she went through the gap she was so severely mauled by the *Neptune* that she lost control and she too became entangled with the *Redoubtable*, this time on her starboard beam.

HMS *Neptune* was now only 100 yards behind HMS *Victory*. The sheer bulk and momentum of HMS *Victory* hitting the *Redoubtable* had opened up the gap between her and *Bucentaure* and Fremantle took his opportunity to break into the French line through the widening gap that had developed. As she passed through the line she fired a double-shotted broadside, raking the stern of the French flagship, *Bucentaure*. The fire from the carronades of both *Temeraire* and *Neptune* cleared the French decks on *Bucentaure* and effectively stopped any potential boarding of HMS *Victory*.

Ahead of the *Bucentaure* was the largest ship in the world, the Spanish vessel *Santissima Trinidad*. As HMS *Neptune* sailed up the leeward side of the *Bucentaure* she engaged the Spanish ship by luffing up under her stern,* thus allowing her starboard gun crews the best possible shot without taking the broadside from the massive Spanish flagship. Yet again, in the heat of the most violent action that Fremantle had ever been involved in, and with scarcely any room to manoeuvre, he had demonstrated consummate seamanship and had brought his vessel into the ideal position to inflict damage on the enemy without allowing them to retaliate. HMS *Neptune* was however, despite Fremantle's best efforts, still badly shot up. She had taken broadsides from both the *Héros* and the *San Augustín* but, despite the heavy damage sustained, thanks to Fremantle's care of the crew in making them lie down, casualties were remarkably light.**

Sir Hercules Robinson was a midshipman on HMS *Euryalus*, a frigate positioned just to the north of the windward column. As a frigate she had no part to play in the actual battle but positioned herself in the ideal place to keep an eye out for the admiral's signals while remaining out of trouble. She therefore had an ideal view of the opening exchanges. Midshipman Robinson commented on HMS *Neptune*:

> If I were to select the most seamanlike act I witnessed, I should name the Neptune rounding to on the quarters of the Santissima Trinidada and keeping the ship in command till she brought down her huge opponent's three masts altogether.

In contrast to HMS *Neptune*, the situation on Villeneuve's flagship, the *Bucentaure*, was almost indescribable. After just one hour of the battle she had taken broadsides, and had been raked by at least five of the most heavily armed ships in the British fleet. *Bucentaure* was a shattered charnel house, incapable of hitting back at her enemies because of

---

* To luff up on a sailing vessel is to deliberately turn into the wind to cause the front edge of the sails (the luff) to start to shake, thus immediately losing forward momentum. An easy move to do inadvertently but extremely difficult to do when attempted deliberately.

** Casualties on HMS *Neptune* at the end of the battle were ten killed and thirty-four injured. In contrast, the equivalent figures on HMS *Victory* were fifty-seven killed and 102 injured and on HMS *Temeraire* forty-seven killed and seventy-six injured – figures that amply justify Fremantle's policy of having the men lie down prior to entering battle.

rigging and masts hanging over the sides of the ship that were preventing the guns being fired. Even it had been possible to run the guns out there was precious few crew left to fire them as an astonishing 450 out of her crew of 770 were either killed or seriously wounded.

Lt Green, the flag lieutenant on HMS *Neptune* and therefore alongside Fremantle on the quarterdeck at all stages of the battle, wrote the following account of the opening stages that Fremantle subsequently included in a letter to Betsey:

> Minutes kept on board H.M. Ship *Neptune* by Lieutenant Andrew Green Signal Officer, the 21ˢᵗ of Octr. 1805:-
>
> At day light discovered the Enemy's Fleet on the Lee Beam keeping their wind on the Larboard Tack, consisting of 33 Sail of the Line Four frigates and two Briggs. The English Fleet 27 of the Line four Frigates and one Schooner and one Cutter.
>
> A.M.
>
> 6.15 The Admiral made the Signal to form in two divisions.
>
> 6.30 To bear up for the Enemy.
>
> 6.32 To prepare for Battle.
>
> 6.40 To Steer East.
>
> 7.25 For the *Brittannia*, *Prince* and *Dreadnought* to take their Station as most convenient.
>
> 7.35 For the Captains of the Frigates to go on board the *Victory*.
>
> 9.45 Was haild by the *Victory* and desired not to keep quite so close.
>
> 10.00 The *Mars* Signal to lead the Larbd. Division.
>
> 10.50 Telegraph to *Royal Sovereign* from Lord Nelson. It is my intention to pass through the Enemy's line and prevent them getting into Cadiz.
>
> 11.40. Telegraph to the whole Fleet. England expects every man will do his duty.
>
> 11.46. Prepare to Anchor during the ensuing night.
>
> 11.50. Temeraire to take station astern of *Victory*. Captain Blackwood of the *Euryalus* came alongside and acquainted Captain Fremantle it was the Commander-in-Chiefs intention to cut through the Enemy's line about their 13 or 14 Ship, then to make sail on the Larbd. Tack for their Van.
>
> 11.55. Engage the Enemy quite close.
>
> 11.56. The Enemy open'd their fire on the *Royal Sovereign* and in a few minutes after on the *Victory*.

P.M.

12.5. The *Royal Sovereign* most nobly began to fire and passed through the Enemy's line under the stern of *Santa Ana,* a Spanish Ship on three Decks. On the smoke clearing away saw the *Royal Sovereign* closely engaged with the *Santa Ana,* and several of the Enemy's Ships firing into her, the Tonnant in her Rear with a two Deck Ship on board her.

12.10. The *Victory* open'd her fire and endeavouring to pass under the Stern of the French Admiral in the *Bucentaur,* the *Redoubtable,* closed so near the *Bucentaur,* to support his Commander-in-Chief, that the *Victory* was obliged to lay that Ship on board, when both Ships paid off before the wind. The *Temeraire* in following gallantly Lord Nelson's Ship, fell on the opposite side the *Redoubtable,* from the same cause and the *Intrepide* alongside the *Temeraire,* the four Ships lock'd in and on board each other, and their Sterns to us. We put the Ship's helm a Starboard and the *Neptune* passed between the *Victory* and *Bucentaur* with which Ship we were warmly engaged (The *Conqueror*'s Jib Boom nearly touching our taff rail) we passed on to the Santissima Trinidad whose stern was entirely exposed to our fire without her being able to return a single shot with effect. At 50 minutes past one observed her Main and Mizen Masts fall overboard, *gave three cheers,* she then paid off and brought us nearly on her lee Beam, in about a quarter of an hour more, her Fore Mast fell over her Stern, and shortly after an Officer threw a Union Jack over her Starboard Quarter, hailed the *Neptune* and said they had struck.

For close on two hours HMS *Neptune*'s gun crews had pounded the Spanish giant, probably firing nearly fifty broadsides of double shot into the vessel. When the gallant Spanish crew finally surrendered it was because there were simply insufficient men to man her guns and she had been completely de-masted and was drifting helplessly. Later, when Midshipman Badcock went on board her to claim the prize, he was sickened by the damage wrought by the British guns. More than 200 of the crew were killed, and more than 100 wounded, many of them seriously. He described a scene that was like a vision of hell with bodies and parts of bodies strewn across the deck, which were swimming in blood:

I was on board our prize the *Trinidada,* getting the prisoners out of her. She had between three and four hundred killed and wounded; her beams were covered with blood, brains and pieces of flesh and the after part of her decks with wounded, some without legs and some without an arm.

The Spanish ship had fought bravely but had been fatally hindered by her lack of manoeuvrability and her lack of trained crew. She was no longer able to work her guns because of the sheer numbers of the crew who were killed and wounded and because many of the guns were useless being fouled by the mass of wreckage across her decks and hanging over the sides, blocking the gun ports. Her admiral, two lieutenants and more than twenty other officers had all been severely wounded and many of them would die subsequently.

The situation between the *Santissima Trinidad* and HMS *Neptune* was being mirrored all over this small stretch of sea as the superior British gunnery began to pound, and then overpower, their French and Spanish adversaries. It was not that the French or Spanish fought badly or lacked spirit. On the contrary, they fought with almost suicidal bravery but the lack of trained crews and the traditional French tactics of firing into the rigging, prior to boarding, worked against them.

Some of the sheer horror of what the sailors on both sides of the battle had to endure is contained in the laconic account given by Lt L.B. Halloran on board HMS *Britannia*:

Between one and two o'clock, a shot struck the muzzle of the gun at which I was stationed (the aftermost gun on the larboard side of the lower deck), and killed or wounded everyone there stationed myself and Midshipman Tompkins only excepted. The shot was a very large one, and split into a number of pieces, each of which took its victim. We threw the mangled body of John Jolley, a marine, out of the stern port, his stomach being shot away; the other sufferers we left to be examined.

He continues later in the same vein:

Amongst the wounded who suffered at my gun was a man named Pilgrim, an Italian, who was stooping to take up a shot for the gun, when it was split, and both his arms were blown off. He afterwards had a pension allowed him, and I have since heard he adds to his little income by travelling the country with his wife, who turns a hand organ.

The small extracts from one man's account of the battle illustrate the terrors that the participants faced, also the cosmopolitan nature of the average ship's crew. Lt Halloran refers to an Italian but the muster log for HMS *Neptune* includes some twenty different nationalities among her crew at the time of Trafalgar. The second point worth making from the above account is the fact that the wounded sailor was forced to rely on begging to supplement his meagre pension following the battle. For many men the battle proved to be worthless so far as their income was concerned. No prizes means no prize money and sadly for all concerned, although the British initially had within their custody nearly twenty vessels many would be subsequently lost in the following storm.

The final act of the battle was when Adm. Pierre Etienne René Marie Dumanoir de Pelley on the *Formidable* led four French ships from the rear of the French line but managed to stay well to the windward. Rather than coming to Villeneuve's assistance he fired off several ineffective broadsides before making his escape to Cádiz. Later he was to face a court of inquiry and a subsequent court martial, where the charges lain against him were dismissed, much to the dismay of both Napoleon and some of his fellow sea captains.

By the closing stages of the battle, the earliest British ships to go into action such as HMS *Victory*, *Temeraire*, *Neptune*, *Royal Sovereign*, *Belleisle* and *Mars* had been almost pounded to floating hulks, although ultimately, the British did not lose any of their vessels. As the French and Spanish vessels that had not been involved in the initial melee tried to intervene, they were held off and some taken by the slower arriving British vessels. Again Lt Green takes up the story:

The Van of the enemy had now Wore and were crossing us apparently with an intent to support their Admirals, the Conqueror at this time passed over to windward to engage them, put our helm a port and fired successfully going to leeward of all, observed the *Leviathan* and another Ship who had passed on closely engaged with two of the Enemy's Ships, who had bore up and soon after struck. The *Victory* and *Royal Sovereign*, keeping up a brisk fire on the Squadron passing to Windward, at about ½ past 4 the firing ceased on both sides when the Signal was made to haul to the Wind on the Larboard tack. A French Ship in the rear L'Achille was on fire and soon blew up. Of the 6 sail which passed to windward on the Starboard tack, 5 stood on to the Southward, one was taken, the remaining part of the Enemy's fleet to leeward consisting of 16 sail of which we supposed 3 or 4 to be Frigates, were apparently forming to support their disabled Ships. At Sun-set the Enemy's Squadron to leeward with their heads in shore.

The melancholy Account which we at this time received of the loss of our much beloved, honoured, and respected Commander-in-Chief threw a damp on our Spirits which we were by no means prepared for after so decisive a Victory.

The official log for HMS *Neptune* for 21 October 1805 was obviously written up sometime on 22 October and gives no inkling that the ship, her officers and crew have just been through the most traumatic experience of their lives. The dry official entry gives no clue as to their states of mind. It reads as follows:

A.M., moderate and fine weather; at daylight discovered 39 strange ships to leeward. At 6, answered the signal from the *Victory*, Lord Nelson's flag-ship, No 76, to form the order of sailing in two lines; bore up and made all sail, the fleet consisting of twenty-seven ships of the line, four frigates, a cutter, and schooner, in company; cleared ship for action. At 11, answered the general telegraph signal, 'England expects every man will do his duty'; Captain Fremantle inspected the different decks, and made known the above signal, which was received with cheers. At 11.30, the signal to break the enemy's line, and engage to leeward.

At 12, the *Royal Sovereign* (110), Vice-Admiral Collingwood, most nobly broke the enemy's line and engaged the Spanish Admiral Gravina, whose flag was flying in the *Santa Anna* (112), cutting off the 19th ship from their rear; the French and Spanish fleet of 33 sail of the line, 4 frigates, and 2 brigs, lying-to for us to leeward, with their heads to the northward.

At 12.15, the *Victory* (100), Vice-Admiral Lord Nelson, followed by the *Temeraire* (98), Captain Eliab Hervey and *Neptune* (98), Captain Fremantle, broke the line of the enemy by the French Commander-in-Chief's ship, Admiral Villeneuve, in the *Bucentaure* (84), and *Santissima Trinidad* (138), of four decks, bearing the flag of Rear-Admiral Don Cisneros Baltazar, the eleventh ship from the van.

At 12.25, three of the enemy's ships of the line opened their fire upon us, raking us fore and aft. At 12.35, we broke their line, passed between, and opened our broadside and raked them on both sides. At 12.47, we

engaged a two deck ship, with a flag at her mizzen. At 1.30, entirely dismasted her, she struck her colours; but before that, the *Leviathan* (74),
also opened her broadside upon her, we passed on (first giving her three
hearty cheers) and bore down and attacked the *Santissima Trinidada*, a
Spanish four-decker of 140 guns, with a flag at her mizzen; raked her as
we passed under her stern; and at 1.50 opened our fire on her starboard
quarter. At 2.40, shot away her main and mizzen masts; at 2.50, her
foremast; at 3, she cried for quarter, and hailed us to say they had surrendered, she then stuck English colours to the stump of her mainmast;
gave her three cheers. At this time the *Leviathan* and *Conqueror* (74's),
on our starboard quarter firing on some of the enemy's ships. Our standing and running rigging much cut; foretop-gallant and royal-yard shot
away; the foremast and foretop-mast very badly wounded; three shot in
the main-mast; one cheek of the mizzen mast shot away, and wounded
in other places; foreyard nearly shot in two, and ship pulled in several
places; sent down men to get up more shot, having nearly fired all away
that was on deck.

When the smoke cleared away, observed the *Victory*, *Royal Sovereign*,
and *Téméraire* warmly engaged, and the six van ships of the enemy who
had not been engaged had tacked, and were bearing down to attack
us. At 3.30, opened our fire on them, assisted by the *Leviathan* and
Conqueror; observed one of them to have all her masts shot away by
our united fire; the rest then hauled their wind (we learned afterwards
it was Rear-Admiral Dumanoir) and making off to the southward, and
we were not in a condition to follow them, our sails being nearly shot
from the yards, and, in addition to other defects, not a brace or bowline
left. Turned the hands up to knot and splice, and bend new sails. At
5, observed 18 sail of the enemy making off, viz., 13 sail of the line,
3 frigates, and 2 brigs leaving to us 20 ships of the line, 2 of which were
first rates, viz., *Santissima Trinidada* and *Santa Anna*. At 5.15, a French
ship of the line *L'Achille* blew up with nearly all her crew. Observed the
Victory with her mizzen-mast and all her topmasts shot away; the *Royal
Sovereign* with only her fore-mast standing; unable to see the condition
of the rest of the fleet. At 6, we hailed the *Ajax* (74), and told her to
go and take possession of a French ship of the line dismasted; saw the
Prince (98) take the *Santissima Trinidada* (138) in tow, which had struck
to us. Found we had 10 men killed, and 35 wounded, 4 of whom shortly
after died of their wounds.

At midnight, having repaired what damages we could, made sail. At 4 in the morning of the 22nd, we were spoke to by the *Pickle* schooner who told us it was Admiral Collingwood's orders. We took some ship in tow. At daylight, observed Admiral C.'s flag in the *Euryalus* frigate with the *Royal Sovereign* in tow, who made our signal to take her in tow, which we did.

A more poetic and succinct precis of the battle was given by one of the British sailors present, who wrote the following lines concerning the coincidence of three vessels named 'Neptune' all being present at the battle: 'The British Neptune, as of yore, Proved master of the day; the Spanish Neptune is no more, the French one ran away.'

A marine named Smith was stationed on HMS *Neptune*. He was far more ambitious in his poetic efforts and the following is an extract from his mini poetic epic on HMS *Neptune*'s role in the battle:

> The *Neptune* she kept pressing on, willing to know her fate
> Her officers like heroes bold, their men did animate
> Each man stood to his quarters, with lionlike desire.
> When she discharged her weighty shot, you would think she was on fire.
>
> The first ship she engaged it was an eighty four.
> Well manned she was with Frenchmen, nine hundred and more.
> We drove them in confusion, our shot told home so true.
> At each broadside she did receive, the French cryed morvelew.
>
> The next that she engaged, was the *Trinidad* of Spain.
> One hundred and forty guns, upon her decks lay plain.
> We beat them from her quarters, they could no longer stay.
> They had their choice to strike my boys, or jump into the sea.
>
> The *Conqueror* she cheered us, and gave us loud applause.
> Fight on you warlike *Neptune*, maintain your Country's cause.
> The enemy are vanquished, fight on they all did say,
> for they have hauled down their colours and their masts are shot away.
>
> The Spanish Don a signal made, all in the time of need.
> For seven of their ablest ships, to sink us with all speed.

Captain Fremantle bravely said as stout as Hannibal.
I'll fight my way throughout their fleet, in defiance of them all.

It would be wrong to assume from the magnitude or, indeed, the fame of the British victory at Trafalgar, that everything went according to plan, or indeed that there was a carefully written plan at all. The differences between Nelson's battle orders for Copenhagen and that for Trafalgar are illustrative of the fact that what he wished to achieve at Trafalgar was totally different to his overall objectives at Copenhagen. Trafalgar was planned to be a massacre, a single, traumatic blow to the combined fleet such as to remove the threat of it ever putting to sea again as a credible offensive force. It was to destroy its morale as well as its ships and to achieve this, with a foe that was not overly keen to fight, meant the British fleet would be forced to seize whatever chance it had.

To this end, Nelson talked endlessly to his captains and his subordinates. He wanted them to understand his thinking and his tactics. He frequently referred to the concept of a 'pell mell' battle and what he meant by this was something more akin to a street brawl rather than a pugilistic match. He wished for a battle with no rules and manoeuvres in which his subordinates took the initiative and acted, if necessary, independently.

The 'Nelson touch', referred to by Nelson himself and by historians, was not a set of tactics or battle plans; rather it was the imbuing of Nelson's spirit, his aggression and his thoughts into each one of his captains. Fremantle understood this and acted accordingly. His handling of HMS *Neptune* prior to and during the battle was masterly and Nelson could have demanded no more of him. The same is true of Collingwood and Capts Harvey and Tyler and Cooke. But it could not be said of all.

Capt. Sir Edward Berry on HMS *Agamemnon* plainly did not grasp what was required of him. When he had accompanied Lord Nelson to court, the King had commented on the loss of Nelson's right arm and Nelson had reputedly introduced Berry as his right arm. Whether this was a compliment or an example of Nelson's wit is open to question as Berry was far more renowned as a 'jolly good chap', extremely brave but not a particularly bright or skilled seaman. Perhaps a greater indication of Berry's worth was Nelson's comments when he belatedly joined the fleet: 'Here comes that damned fool Berry, now we shall have a battle.'

Berry never managed to get into the battle properly and, although he fired off nearly 6,500lb of gunpowder and nearly 1,200 shot,[1] there is no record of HMS *Agamemnon* having much effect on the battle. Indeed, his casualty figures would support this.

Adm. Lord Northesk was another who failed to grasp Nelson's principles. As the ships in the windward column made their way into the enemy fleet, Northesk was busy arguing with his captain on HMS *Britannia* about reducing sail so as to preserve their place in the line. In contrast, Nelson would have wholly approved of Capt. Charles Bullen's attempts to get his ship 'alongside a Frenchman as soon as possible' and would not overly worry about keeping strict station in the column.

The final death toll, however, demonstrates in the most melancholy way possible, the size of the British victory. The combined French and Spanish losses were approximately 8,000 dead, wounded and drowned while equivalent British losses were 1,600. In ships lost the difference is even more marked with the combined fleet losing eighteen ships, more than half its strength of line-of-battle ships and the British losing none.

The Aftermath of the Battle

With the death of Lord Nelson, Adm. Collingwood took over as commander-in-chief. His first job was to transfer his flag from HMS *Royal Sovereign*, which was now a floating hulk, to the frigate, HMS *Euryalus*. It was from the frigate that he sent via HMS *Pickle* his dispatch to the Admiralty:

HMS Euryalus, off Cape Trafalgar Oct 22 1805[2]
The ever-to-be-lamented death of vice-Admiral Lord Viscount Nelson, who, in the late conflict with the enemy, fell in the hour of the victory, leaves to me the duty of informing My Lords Commissioners of the Admiralty, that on the 19th instant, it was communicated to the Commander-in-Chief, from the ships watching the motions of the enemy in Cadiz, that the Combined fleets had put to sea; as they sailed with light winds westerly, His Lordship concluded their destination was the Mediterranean, and immediately made all sail for the Straits' entrance, with the British squadron, consisting of twenty seven ships, three of them sixty-fours, where his Lordship was informed by Captain Blackwood (whose vigilance in watching, and in giving notice of the enemy's movements, has been highly meritorious), that they had not yet passed the Straits.

On Monday 21st instant, at daylight when Cape Trafalgar bore E. by S. about seven leagues, the enemy was discovered six or seven miles to the eastward; the wind was west, and very light; the Commander-in-Chief immediately made the signal for the fleet to bear up in two columns, as they are formed in order of sailing; a mode of attack His Lordship had previously directed, to avoid the inconvenience and delay in forming a line of battle in the usual manner.

The enemy's line consisted of thirty-three ships (of which eighteen were French, and fifteen Spanish), commanded-in-chief by Admiral Villeneuve: the Spaniards, under the direction of Gravina, wore, with their heads to northwards, and formed their line of battle with great closeness and correctness; but as the mode of attack was unusual, so that, in leading down to their centre, I had both their van and rear abaft the beam; before the fire opened, every alternative ship was about a cable's length to windward of her second ahead and astern, forming a kind of double line, and appeared, when on their beam, to leave a very little interval between them; and this without crowding their ships. Admiral Villeneuve was in the *Bucentaure*, in the centre, and the Principe de Asturias bore Gravina's flag in their rear, but the French and the Spanish ships were mixed without any apparent regard to order of national squadron.

As the mode of our attack had been previously determined on, and communicated to flag officers, and captains, few signals were necessary, and none were made, except to direct the close order as the lines bore down. The Commander-in-Chief, in the *VICTORY*, led the weather column, and *ROYAL SOVEREIGN*, which bore my flag, the lee. The action began at twelve o'clock, by the leading ships of the columns breaking through the enemy's line, the Commander-in-Chief about the tenth ship from the van, the Second-in-Command about the twelfth from the rear, leaving the van of the enemy unoccupied; the succeeding ships breaking through in all parts, astern of their leaders, and engaging the enemy at the muzzle of their guns; the conflict was severe; the enemy's ships were fought with a gallantry highly honourable to their officers; but the attack on them was irresistible, and it pleased the Almighty Disposer of all events to grant His Majesty's arms a complete and glorious victory. About three p.m. many of the enemy's ships having struck their colours, their line gave way; Admiral Gravina, with ten ships joining their frigates to leeward stood towards Cadiz. The five headmost ships in their van tacked, and standing to the southward, to windward of the British line, were engaged and the sternmost of them taken; the others went off, leaving to His Majesty's squadron nineteen ships of the line (of which two are first rates, the *Santissima Trinidad* and the *Santa Ana*), with three flag officers, viz. Admiral Villeneuve, the Commander-in-Chief, Don Ignatio Maria D'Alava, Vice-Admiral; and the Spanish Rear-Admiral, Don Baltazar Hidalgo Cisneros.

After such a victory it may appear unnecessary to enter into encomiums on the particular parts taken by the several commanders; the conclusion says more than I have language to express; the spirit which animated all in their country's service, all deserve that their high merits should stand recorded; and never was high merit more conspicuous than in the battle I have described.

The *Achille* (a French 74) after having surrendered, by some mismanagement of the Frenchmen, took fire and blew up; two hundred of her men were saved by the tenders.

A circumstance occurred during the action, which so strongly marks the invincible spirit of British seamen, when engaging the enemies of their country, that I cannot resist the pleasure I have in making it known to Their Lordships; the *TEMERAIRE* was boarded by accident or design, by a French ship on one side, and a Spaniard on the other; the contest was vigorous, but, in the end, the combined ensigns were torn from the poop, and the British hoisted in their places.

Such a battle could not be fought without sustaining a great loss of men. I have not only to lament, in common with the British navy, and the British Nation, in the fall of the Commander-in-Chief, the loss of a hero, whose name will be immortal, and his memory ever dear to his country; but my heart is rent with the most poignant grief for the death of a friend, to whom, by many years intimacy, and a perfect knowledge of the virtues of his mind, which inspired ideas superior to the common race of men, I was bound by the strongest ties of affection; grief to which even the glorious occasion in which he fell, dos not bring the consolation which, perhaps, it ought; His Lordship received a musket ball in his left breast, about the middle of the action, and sent an officer to me immediately with his last farewell; and soon expired. I have also to lament the loss of those excellent officers, Captains Duff on the *MARS*, and Cooke, of the *BELLEPHERON*; I have yet heard of none others.

I fear that the numbers that have fallen will be found very great, when the returns come to me; but it having blown a gale of wind ever since the action, I have not yet had it in my power to collect any reports from the ships.

The *ROYAL SOVEREIGN* having lost her masts, except the tottering foremast, I called the *EURYALUS* to me, while the action continued, which ship lying within hail, made my signals – a service Captain Blackwood performed with great attention; after the action, I shifted my flag to her, that I might more easily communicate any orders to, and collect the ships, and towed the *ROYAL SOVEREIGN* out to Seaward. The whole fleet was now in a very perilous situation, many dismasted, all shattered, in thirteen fathoms of water, off the shoals of Trafalgar, and when I made the signal to prepare to anchor, few of the ships had an anchor to let go, their cables being shot through; but the same good Providence which aided us through such a day preserved us in the night, by the wind shifting a few points, and drifting the ships off the land, except four of the captured dismasted ships, which are now at anchor off Trafalgar, and I hope will ride safe until those gales are over.

Having thus detailed the proceedings of the fleet on this occasion, I beg to congratulate Their Lordships on a victory which, I hope, will add a ray to the glory of his Majesty's crown and be attended with public benefit to our country.

With the official dispatch on its way to London the fleet prepared to weather the storm that was gathering. By 5 p.m. that evening Lt Senhouse of HMS *Conqueror* was able to look out over 4 miles of ocean littered with wreckage. Where once there had been two of the greatest maritime fleets in history was now a scene of dismasted ships:[3]

For a distance of about four miles around covered with about thirty ships dismasted, lying like logs on the water, the surface of which was strewed with wreck from various vessels and their hulks interspersed with the remaining part of the fleet in a most shattered state, many slowly aroused to grant assistance where it was most needed. The principal feature at six o'clock was the French ship *ACHILLE* (of 74 guns) in flames which filled up the measure of the havoc the day had occasioned. About six she blew up, and closed the memorable battle with one of the grandest spectacles to be met with in nature.

For Fremantle the battle would place him among the foremost of the twenty-seven officers who had captained a line-of-battle ship at Trafalgar. These men would form an elite within the Royal Navy and could justifiably claim that they were there, alongside Nelson, on the day of the greatest sea battle in history. And not only was Fremantle there but he captained one of the eight or nine ships who took the majority of the hammering from the enemy and were most responsible for the ultimate victory. In the evening of 21 October, for most of the officers who afterwards recorded their feelings, it was hours of terrible tiredness and lassitude. Although contemporary medicine had no idea of such conditions, they were all probably suffering a form of post-traumatic shock for they had been through some five hours of the most horrific hammering imaginable and, tough as these men undoubtedly were, it must have had some effect on their mental well-being.

However, whatever their mental condition, there was to be little time to rest because the seventeen captured ships and many thousand prisoners of war all needed to be dealt with. They represented a possible fortune for the British fleet in prize money and there was an understandable reluctance to lose them. One of Nelson's dying reminders to Capt. Thomas Hardy had been to anchor. However Adm. Collingwood, in light of the fact that several of his ships had lost their anchors and cables in the battle, decided to run for Gibraltar. However, the morning after the battle the threatened storm broke and the fleet found itself in that most dangerous of situations of being just off a rocky treacherous coast with an onshore wind blowing. To make matters worse it had precious little sea room to manoeuvre in and many ships were operating with jury rigs following the immense battle damage.

The result was inevitable. The precious prizes under tow had to be cut loose and scuttled (deliberately sunk), meaning yet more prisoners of war evacuated off the prizes to be housed on the British ships. Midshipman W.S. Badcock from HMS *Neptune* describes the situation with the *Santissima Trinidad*:[4]

I was sent on board the Santissima Trinidad a few days after the action to assist in getting out the wounded men previous to destroying her. She was a magnificent ship, and ought now to be in Portsmouth harbour. Her top sides it is true were perfectly riddled by our firing, and she had, if I recollect right, 550 killed and wounded, but from the lower part of the sills of the lower-deck ports to the water's edge, a few shot of consequence had hurt her between wind and water, and those were all plugged up. She was built of cedar and would have lasted for ages, a glorious trophy of the battle, but 'sink, burn and destroy' were the order of the day, and after a great deal of trouble, scuttling her in many places, hauling up her lower deck ports – that when she rolled a heavy sea might fill her decks she did at last unwillingly go to the bottom.

After getting the prisoners off the *Santissima Trinidad*, plus some booty including a pug dog, Fremantle had a full ship with more than 1,200 people on board. She finally struggled into Gibraltar towing HMS *Victory* with her precious cargo of Nelson's body. Fremantle and the *Neptune* were to spend several weeks in Gibraltar while new masts were stepped and new rigging fixed. From Gibraltar Fremantle wrote to Betsey:[5]

If I know your heart, or your sentiments I think I may depend that you will be truly happy to hear that I am well after the very severe action we have had, – This last Week has been a scene of Anxiety and fatigue beyond any, I ever experienced but I trust I God that I have gained considerable credit, and that it will ultimately tend to the benefit of you and my dear little Children for when – alone [as] I am now here, – I am at present towing the Victory and the Admiral has just made the signal for me to go with her to Gibraltar, which is a satisfactory proof to my mind that he is perfectly satisfied with Old Neptune who behaves as well as I could wish. The loss of Nelson is a death blow to my future prospects here, he knew well how to appreciate Abilities and Zeal, and I am aware that I shall never cease to lament his loss whilst I live. We have ten Men killed and 37 Wounded, which is very trifling when compared to some other Ships, however we alone have certainly the whole credit of taking the *Santissima Trinidada*, who struck to us alone. Adml. Villeneuve was with me on board the *Neptune* over two days, I found him a very pleasant and Gentlemanlike man, the poor man was very low!

Yesterday I put him on board the Euryalus with Admiral Collingwood, but I still have the pleasure of feeding and accommodating his Captain and his 2 Aid du Camps and his Adjutant General, who are true Frenchmen, but with whom I am much amused, I have also 450 poor Spaniards from the *Santissima Trinidada*, with a true Italian priest born at Malta, – I have found also an excellent French cook and a true Spanish pug dog – This fatigue and employment has entirely drove away the bile and if poor Nelson had not been among the slain I should be most completely satisfied, would you believe that Old Collingwood has now made the Signal for me to go off Cape Espartel instead of Gibraltar, the poor man does not know his own mind 5 minutes together. I am afraid this brilliant Action will not put money in my pocket, but I think much may arise out of it ultimately, I shall with this send you a copy of the Minutes kept by my old Lieut. Mr. Green, I hope with the Line of battle and the drawing you will be enabled to make it out, you may give the Ringers 1 guinea on the occasion to save your credit to my brother William I send one also that you may show your plan over Buckinghamshire as much as you please, – My Cabin that was so elegant and neat is as dirty as a pig style and many parts of the bulk head are thrown overboard, however I shall find amusement and indeed employment in having them fitted in some new way – These Frenchmen make me laugh at the gasonade as well as at their accounts of Buonaparte the Palais Royal Paris etc. – I hope you have ere this received my letter for Wyatt [the letter is torn here]. The French Captain drinks your health regularly every day at dinner. The poor man is married and laments his lot, one of the younger ones is desperately in love with a lady at Cadiz and Frenchman like carries her picture in his pocket.

Betsey's diary entry for Sunday, 1 December 1805:[6]

Sunday 1st December. At length, my long wished for Dispatch arrived & I had inexpressible joy, in hearing from *Fremantle himself* he was quite well and safe after the action. He mentions the week succeeding their Victory as a scene of fatigue & anxiety not to be described. He sends me a plan of the action from which it appears it was not *Victory* but the *Neptune* who engaged the *Santissima Trinidada*, who struck to the *Neptune* alone, by placing the Ship against the stern of the gigantic four decker, he succeeded in dismasting her without scarcely receiving a shot – he had only ten killed & 37 wounded – he was likewise at one time engaged with the *Bucentaure*. Admiral Villeneuve had spent two days on board the *Neptune* with all his etat major. They had 450 Spanish prisoners. Lord Buckingham sent me in the evening the long & interesting account he received from Fremantle from which it appears poor Nelson was killed by a musquetry shot from the *Redoubtable*, the ship he was engaged with, which must have been aimed at the Stars on the coat he wore – he preserved his coolness to the last, & expressed a wish he could once more have come to London after so brilliant a victory. Collingwood appears not to know his own mind, *& I think* he is not equal to the command of a large fleet. Poor Nelson! is indeed a loss & to Fremantle particularly great. He seems to have felt it very severely indeed.

As usual it is to his younger brother, William, that Fremantle more truly unburdens himself in a letter written on 19 November: [7]

I have so much to say that I scarcely know where to begin, long before you receive this you will probably tho' imperfectly have received some account of our action off Cadiz where poor Nelson lost his life. The engagement was bloody and lasting, and if it had not been for the very severe gales from the Southward which we have had ever since the 21st our triumph must have been complete, as it is I don't believe we shall save a single Ship captured from the Enemy altho' 14 at least were fairly captured. The loss of Lord Nelson is the loss of everything and no man now knows which way he is to look for the common and necessary qualities for the command of a fleet of such magnitude as there is now here, at this instant that I am writing the Whole fleet are upon a Lee shore and more than half crippled. We have got the *Victory* in tow, and endeavouring to get her into the Straits mouth. Our Admiral is never of the same opinion 4 hours together consequently little can be expected from a man, of so undecided a Character. I am already heartily tired of the change, and if any favourable opportunity presents itself of going into a three decked Ship going to England I shall avail myself of it.

With respect to myself and my Ship nothing can be more satisfactory to my mind than all we have done, and altho' our loss has not been very great, I trust we broke through the line at the best place and certainly carried the Spanish Ship with four decks without assistance, – here it is quite impossible to receive a fair reward for exertion of any sort, everything is conducted by Violence, and an ungentlemanlike order, such a fleet ought not to be in such hands.

I shall with this send you a list of our Line of battle, as also of that of the French and Spanish ships Corrected by the French Captain of the *Bucentaure* who is now sitting by my side on board the *Neptune*. I found Adml. Villeneuve with all his suite onboard the *Mars* and as the Captain of that Ship was killed* and there was no sort of accommoda-

---

*   Captain George Duff.

tion for them, I offered them my ship, which they readily accepted. Yesterday Adm. Collingwood took Villeneuve on board the *Euryalus* refusing to take with him *any one person* consequently the poor man is quite by himself, whilst his Captain his two Aid du Camps and Adjutant General are on board the *Neptune*. The act in itself is so savage and unfeeling independent of the impropriety of it that I am quite angry and the people here don't fail crying out on the cruelty of the measure. On this as on all occasions of the sort many have in my opinion behaved improperly; had all gone into action with the determination Lord Nelson did, it is probable few only could have escaped, as it was I apprehend 14 or 15 struck, god knows how many have sunk or how many have escaped.

The heat of the action was excessive, and ten Ships were totally dismasted in an hour. We got in so favourable a position by the *Santissima Trinidad* that I believe we did not suffer at all from her, our loss was occasioned by the Ships in the Van who doubled on us, but without effect as you will perceive by the plan. My Masts are all much damaged, but I have never made a complaint, and got my Ship entirely refitted as well as circumstances would admit the Night of the action, at this time we have at least a dozen Ships at Anchor dismasted in some degree off Cadiz and until the Wind shifts which there is no great probability of just now none of them can move, they are certainly in a very precarious situation, from the day of the action until this instant I have not put pen to paper and the Anxiety of Mind, as well as fatigue I have undergone, continually on a Lee Shore.*

There must have been a welter of such letters going home to Britain assuring relatives of the writer's well-being and proudly describing their part in the battle. One such letter was from Lt George Hooper on HMS *Neptune*, who wrote to his favourite girl, Miss Sybilla Shanach, on 31 October 1805:[8]

My Dear Girl I imagine before this reaches you, you will have heard of the action of the 21st of October, a most glorious though dismal day. Having a day or two known the combined fleet had put to sea we stood for Cadiz

---

* A lee shore is one where the ship is continually being driven towards the coastline by an onshore wind.

and on the morning of Monday 21st October at day light observed the combined fleets to leeward consisting of thirty three sail of the line and four frigates, our fleet twenty seven sail of the line and four frigates. The Admiral made the signal to bear up and engage by breaking their line, but having little wind it was twelve o' clock before the *ROYAL SOVEREIGN* got into the middle of the enemy's fleet when every ship began to engage her. At half past observed the *VICTORY*, Lord Nelson's ship run on board a French seventy four, immediately afterwards the *TEMERAIRE* ran on board the other side and directly a Spaniard run on board the *TEMERAIRE* so there were four ships alongside of each other. We being next to Lord Nelson he hailed us to keep farther off. We immediately ran alongside of the *BUCENTAUR*, Admiral Villeneuve's ship of eighty guns and in about three quarters of an hour had the pleasure of seeing all of his mast shot away. He struck. Afterwards we ran alongside the *SANTISSIMA TRINIDAD* and engaged her so smartly that all her people ran from their quarters and in a short time carried away all his mast, when they wove their hats to say they had struck, but one of his guns going off we began until such time as he hoisted an English flag. She is the largest ship in the world having four tiers of guns, one hundred and forty guns and one thousand and eighty men. When Lord Nelson was told she had struck he was quite contented.

We were not then so much disabled but we began to engage the Spanish *NEPTUNE* till some other ships came up and took her. One ship of the enemy caught fire in the action and blew up afterwards and I believe one sunk. Another sunk the night after the action with most of the people. There was sixteen struck. How many we shall save is impossible to tell as we have a gale of wind ever since on the shore and many of our ships dismasted and obliged to come into an anchorage off Cadiz. The *SANTISSIMA TRINIDAD* we blew up the other night, after taking out all of the people, being close in shore and a foul wind to get off.

Everyone is sorry for Lord Nelson. He was killed with a musket ball almost close to his heart. He lived two hours and was sensible of his death. In going into action he made the telegraph signal to say England expects that every man will do his duty that day, a most noble speech and when told to our people, they seemed rejoiced and that they would do theirs, none could behave better.

We have Admiral Villeneuve and suite on board of us,* but Admiral Collingwood sent for him on board his ship, having his captain and other officers on board who acknowledged to me that they had three hundred killed and wounded. On board the *SANTISSIMA TRINIDAD* they had one hundred and fifty killed, but I believe many more. We have been very fortunate, more so than any one in the action would believe. We had about eighty killed and thirty wounded, not a single officer hurt. The *VICTORY* had fifty killed and eighty wounded and some of our ships must have lost a great number of both officers and men among whom as Captain Duff of the MARS and Captain Cook of the *BELLEROPHON*. We have at present four hundred prisoners on board which we took out of the *SANTISSIMA TRINIDAD*. The *VICTORY*, Lord Nelson's ship is gone to Gibraltar and I believe some others. I shall thank you to keep the newspaper with Admiral Collingwood's letter also the French account of it till I come home which I hope will be soon as all our masts are wounded.

I shall thank you to show your brother this letter and any one you please. We are constantly employed repairing the damage and getting the ship ready for another action. When we arrive in port I will give you a full account. Pray acquaint my relations you have heard from me, and remain yours sincerely and truly

George W. Hooper.

Fremantle provided his last melancholy footnote to the Battle of Trafalgar when he wrote to Betsey on Boxing Day 1805:[9] 'I forgot to tell you that I have a lock of poor Nelson's hair and his best spying glass which I shall retain as long as I live, as a precious relic of a very sincere friend.'

Fremantle was true to his word and did indeed retain the keepsake until he died. It was passed down the family until his great-grandson, Adm. Sir Sydney Fremantle, took it to sea with him some 110 years later. Unfortunately, whilst serving on HMS *Russell*, the ship struck a mine just outside Valletta harbour in Malta, where she sank. Adm. Fremantle,

---

* Later in May 1806, Fremantle was to receive the news of Villeneuve's death and assumed, along with the British press, that he had been assassinated by Napoleon. On 22 April 1806, he was found dead at the Hôtel de la Patrie in Rennes with several stab wounds to the chest, including one to the heart. Bizarrely, the coroner's verdict was suicide; however, the nature of the death meant that the British press mocked the official verdict and the consensus was that Napoleon had ordered Villeneuve's death as a reprisal for losing the Battle of Trafalgar.

standing on the forecastle at the time, was rescued, albeit with minor foot injuries, but the precious Nelson relic went down with the ship.

The Battle of Trafalgar defined the Royal Navy in the eyes of the public. Not only did it ensure and make clear that Britain would never be invaded by France, it also ensured that Britain's martial reputation remained intact. It did not make much difference to the defeat of Napoleon, at least not immediately. What it did was ensure that Napoleon could not defeat Britain and that, with the world's oceans even more firmly in Britain's control, it could continue to trade and to build the wealth that would ensure Napoleon's military hold over Europe could never be assured. Britain's trading wealth would keep armies in the field and, ultimately, lead Napoleon to his greatest mistake when he tried to knock Russia out of the coalition by invading the country and in the process losing his army and his reputation of invincibility.

That was for the future. Now, after refitting HMS *Neptune* and making her ready for sea, Fremantle began the endless routine of blockading the fleet with the addition of knowing that now it was extremely unlikely that the French would venture out of port. The endless cruising up and down outside the main French ports would continue until eventually Britain could find a way to defeat Napoleon's army on land. In 1805 this appeared a forlorn hope.

HMS *Neptune* stayed in the Mediterranean on blockade duty for a further twelve months following the Battle of Trafalgar and it was to be early November 1806 before Betsey and her husband were reunited.

8

POLITICS AND PROMOTION, 1806–1810

At 4.30 a.m. on 23 January 1806,[1] William Pitt died; he was aged a mere 46 and his death was probably caused by a duodenal ulcer, certainly overwork and possibly excessive drinking. He had first served as Prime Minister aged 24 and since first coming to office had been in power for almost nineteen years. A more modern politician, Enoch Powell, once remarked that all Prime Ministers end their days in failure and Pitt, despite his undoubted brilliance, was no exception. Just weeks before his death on 2 December 1805 Napoleon had destroyed the Russian and Austrian armies at the Battle of Austerlitz. The reports of the military disaster that was to spell the end of Pitt's carefully assembled third coalition appeared in London newspapers during the last few days of 1805.

Pitt had been a great war leader and his death was a tragedy for Britain, but politics is an unsentimental business and his death opened opportunities for the Whigs, which in turn could be expected to favour Fremantle's career. It was a fact to which Fremantle was not blind because the Granville family was now in a position to grant favours. The 'ministry of all talents', as it became known, was, at least in theory, to be formed from among Lord Buckingham's circle. The administration was headed up by the Right Honourable William Wyndham Grenville, the First Lord Grenville. His brother, Tom Grenville MP, was initially president of the Board of Trade and by July William Fremantle had been brought into government as one of the secretaries to the Treasury. Things could have hardly looked more favourable for Fremantle. Rather more surprisingly was that King George III, in the interests of national unity, finally agreed to the inclusion of Charles James Fox. For the first time, Fremantle could look forward realistically to a political appointment, if only a suitable constituency could be found. The other possible hitch was that the Prince of Wales, who as an unofficial focal point of Whig opposition, naturally expected many nominees of his own to be granted suitable posts before Fremantle could expect his ambitions for office to be granted.

The ministry was intended as a national government expected to pull the country together at what was still, despite the victory at Trafalgar, a time of danger. The threat of invasion had faded both in reality and in people's perception but Napoleon was still there, just over the Channel, and still, militarily, in the ascendancy. The government came into power on 1 February 1806[1] but it would be some time before Fremantle would be supplied with all the details for, on 22 February, he wrote to his brother William:

> The day before yesterday the *Apollo* with her convoy arrived and brought us the first letters we have received since October … The changes that must have taken place in consequence of Pitt's death will I trust not give me apprehension should another promotion take place.

He was to wait impatiently for many months at sea feeling helpless and unable to press his case until, in early October, Sir Charles Pole vacated his post as one of the junior Lords of the Admiralty. This was exactly the type of opening that Fremantle was seeking and even more favourably from his viewpoint, Tom Grenville had been moved from the Board of Trade into the Admiralty following a reshuffle caused by the death of Fox. Now the way really was opening up for him and to add to the possibilities the Marquess of Buckingham was now cultivating an interest in the parliamentary constituency of Saltash. After the October dissolution of Parliament, William would stand as one of the MPs for Saltash, albeit only winning the seat after a petition.

Fremantle was not privy to all that was going on, which only served to exacerbate his nervousness and feelings of helplessness. In his letters home to Betsey he was complaining constantly of feeling bilious or of seasickness, which were his usual complaints when feeling stressed or isolated. However, unbeknown to him, events were beginning to move in his favour for, on 17 July 1806, Tom Grenville wrote to the Marquess of Buckingham:[2]

> I have almost persuaded Lord Grenville to take Fremantle instead of King*
> and I believe Lord Grenville will write to you about it as an experiment
> that he will try. If Fremantle will set to work thoroughly he may do it
> well. I am inclined to think it best and that it will be tried. It is no small
> inducement, in addition that you will naturally wish it, and I now hope
> it will be done.

The marquess received, as promised, on the same day a letter from Lord Grenville:[3]

> I have taken the resolve today to send to Fremantle to offer him that he
> shall take King's situation upon an understanding that he takes it upon
> trial, and that he is not to be hurt if I should at any time hereafter be
> obliged to say to him frankly that I find it does not go on satisfactorily.
> This reserve I feel necessary because I cannot help doubting, when the
> novelty of the thing is once over, he will be able to bring his mind to so
> much unpleasant drudgery as the situation must necessarily require.

Betsey, at home in Swanbourne on Friday, 10 October 1806, recorded in her diary:

> Lord Buckingham and Captn. Badcock** called at one – the former told me
> in *Grand Secret* that Fremantle would be appointed one of the Lords of
> the Admiralty and have a seat in Parliament – this will be very comfortable
> and made me extremely happy.

---

* Capt. Sir Richard King, later to be Vice Adm. Sir Richard King Baronet KCB.
** Father of the midshipman who served with Fremantle on HMS *Neptune* at the Battle of Trafalgar. Capt. Badcock lived at Little Missenden Abbey, Buckinghamshire, and was a magistrate for the county.

However, the plans for Fremantle to be brought into the House of Commons via the constituency of Saltash were not going exactly as Buckingham hoped and Fremantle was forced to turn his attentions to another constituency, St Mawes. Again events conspired and eventually it was another member of the Temple-Grenville family who secured Fremantle's seat in Parliament. The Prime Minister, Lord Grenville, chose Fremantle as the most suitable Admiralty candidate to replace Sir Philip Stephens at Sandwich, then a safe seat in the gift of the Admiralty. Fremantle was finally returned as the Member of Parliament for Sandwich while still at sea and without opposition.

On 26 October 1806 Betsey was finally able to write in her diary:[4] 'Few joys can equal what I experienced on reading a Letter from Fremantle which he wrote at Sea in his way to Portsmouth where he wishes to meet me.'

He may indeed have wished to meet Betsey after being absent for nearly eighteen months but Fremantle was not about to let his political chances be blighted by a romantic reunion. While he had been at sea Grenville, in a bid to strengthen his political position, had petitioned the King to dissolve Parliament and go to the country to try to increase his majority. In theory, this should have caused Fremantle no concern whatsoever for his constituency and its voters did what the Admiralty told it to do. After all, had they not voted him in while he had still been at sea? Nevertheless, he chose to travel down to Sandwich to nurse his seat and to dine with the electors.* Having landed at Portsmouth on 26 October he departed for Sandwich immediately, leaving poor Betsey to arrive one day later to learn that her longed for husband had left. In the circumstances her comments in her diary that day seem mild in the extreme:[5] 'I felt rather tired and determined to see the Ship early tomorrow and return to Sunbury.'

Having reached London by Wednesday (29 October) and visiting her sister-in-law (Mrs W. Fremantle), Betsey found her errant husband had been back to London and again had travelled down to Sandwich, where the election was to take place the following Monday (3 November).**

---

* Not as strange as it seems given that there were, on average, fewer than twenty voters in this pocket borough. In 1885 the borough was disenfranchised for corruption in the Redistribution Act.

** At that time general elections were held over a matter of several weeks, as local, returning officers fixed the poll in their constituency on a date convenient to them. The 1806 General Election was held between 29 October and mid December.

It was not until Wednesday, 5 November that the couple were finally reunited in London and even then Fremantle insisted on going into his new office at the Admiralty for a day's work. Shortly after, they rented a house in Sackville Street, just off Piccadilly, and Fremantle began his duties at the Admiralty working from 10 a.m. until 6 p.m. Betsey enjoyed London and soon had their house comfortable with some of Thomas's furniture from HMS *Neptune* pressed into service as drawing room furniture. She had many friends in London, plus her brother-in-law, William, and his wife, Selina, so it was unlikely that she would have been starved of company while her husband was in the office.

Meanwhile, Grenville was fighting with an increasingly fractious opposition. His gamble of asking for dissolution and going to the country had not paid off and his majority, while theoretically increased by some 30 votes, was becoming difficult to guarantee. How much time Fremantle spent in the House of Commons is difficult to say as he is not recorded in Hansard as speaking in any debates. The big issue of Granville's second term was the abolition of slavery Bill, on which Fremantle had initially been true to his Whig roots, favouring abolition. Whether people at the Admiralty had spoken to him or not he is known to have weakened in his support when the Bill was introduced to Parliament on 7 May 1806.

A clue as to his change of attitude may be found in a speech made by his old commander-in-chief, Earl St Vincent, when Lord Granville introduced the measure into the House of Lords for its first reading:[6]

He deprecated the measure, which if passed, would, he was satisfied have the effect of transferring British capital to other countries, which would not be disposed to abandon such a productive branch of trade. As to the humanity, so much contended for, it would be well if noble Lords reflected upon this question, whether humanity really was consulted by abolition. If it were, their arguments would be well founded; but from his own experience he was enabled to state, that the West India Islands were Paradise itself to the negroes, compared with their native country. Knowing this, which, upon inquiry, it was in the power of any noble Lord to ascertain, he was surprised at the proposition before the House.

These views were essentially the same arguments used by the East India Company and had undoubtedly found a ready ear in the Admiralty. For many years the company had been a source of trained sailors for the

Royal Navy and it was not surprising to find both Earl St Vincent and Fremantle being nervous of what they perceived to be a handing over of an advantage to their enemies. Despite the organised opposition to the measure from vested interest, Granville was successful in steering the Bill through to enactment on 25 March 1807. The act did not ban the practice of slavery throughout the British Empire but banned the trade in human beings, making it illegal to carry enslaved persons in British ships.

Despite his absence from the hurly burly of debate in the House of Commons, Fremantle appeared to enjoy his time at the Admiralty. How true this would have been had the tenure been longer is open to conjecture but he was lucky to serve under Tom Grenville as First Lord. Grenville was a bachelor who seemed to have inherited most of the charm in the Grenville family despite being, at first appearances, shy and cold, especially to strangers. He was certainly no great parliamentarian, being a cold and dispassionate public speaker and unlikely to win over uncommitted supporters, but he was committed to the job and, while in office, made great efforts to carry it out properly and ensure the navy was well provided for.

The problem that beset every First Lord was how to avoid getting bogged down in the minutiae of day-to-day naval officer appointments. With all sea captains being free to take on as many midshipmen as they liked, the service was always over-provided with young officers and all commissions had to go through the First Lord of the Admiralty. In the 116 days he served as First Lord, Tom Granville made a staggering 889 appointments, an average of nearly eight a day.[7]

Despite this workload he did manage to carry out some strategic adjustments, stripping out some of the larger ships of the line from the Channel Fleet, he replaced them with newer frigates and greatly strengthened the Baltic Fleet to protect Britain's valuable trade with the Scandinavian and Russian states. This was a time when Napoleon's Continental system of economic blockade was at its height and all ships available were needed for Britain to retaliate in kind and blockade France's trade. On the whole, although their time in office was short, both Tom Grenville and Fremantle could be reasonably happy with their tenure at the Admiralty.

The same, however, could not be said of his brother, Lord Grenville. In a letter to his brother, the Marquess of Buckingham, he wrote:[8]

'I want one great and essential quality for my station. I am not competent to the management of men. I never was so naturally, and toil and anxiety more and more unfit me for it.'

It was a sad but truthful epitaph to Grenville's 'ministry of all talents'. Harassed by a resurgent opposition and with Grenville himself unable to hold things together, the administration fell apart most obviously over the eternally thorny question of Catholic emancipation. With King George sticking rigidly to his increasingly out of step position, Grenville had no other choice than to tender his resignation. He was to be replaced by the Tories, led by the Duke of Portland.

At the general election, Buckingham sought to keep Fremantle in the House of Commons but he had many other interests and family members to place, including his many nephews, and he could therefore only offer him a seat with his brother at Saltash. However, the Buckingham name did not wield the same kind of power in Cornwall as it did in Buckinghamshire and the Saltash community were beginning to show an unwelcome independence of mind such that Thomas never made it back to Parliament. After the election, on 24 May 1807, he wrote to his brother, William, telling him of a recent conversation he had with Lord Buckingham:[9]

I am afraid I was not as communicative to him as I have always been in the habit of, but I certainly then felt, what I still do, that under all the circumstances of electioneering business, and his express promise to me in writing, before I came home, that he had secured me a seat in Parliament, without its costing me a shilling, I have reason to be dissatisfied. This is not a subject on which it would be prudent to quarrel with one who has always been so much my friend, but it shows how much he appreciates the zeal with which I have always attended to him, and his preference of those, who to my judgement ought not to have it. I am beginning to enjoy my place and my farm, and hope I shall not have occasion to leave home these six months.

William also appeared hurt by failure to assure Thomas a seat in Parliament and, being less dependent than Thomas on the largesse of the marquess, wrote to him saying:[10] 'You may easily imagine that this unexpected state of affairs has been a cruel and most unhappy break up to the society and intercourse and domestic enjoyment of my family. I lament it most seriously.'

Betsey was far more phlegmatic and wrote in her diary in the last week of April[11] that her husband had been having a quiet holiday and that he would probably be far happier without the work at the Admiralty to tie him down. In truth, the family had not been that harshly treated for one of Tom Grenville's parting tasks prior to leaving government had been to appoint Fremantle as captain of the royal yacht *William and Mary*. This was a sinecure involving no extra duties but an addition to his salary of £500 p.a., which would enable him to take up the role of farmer and country squire for the foreseeable future. In February 1809 Fremantle was Buckingham's reserve choice for a parliamentary vacancy at St Mawes, but the gentleman who had been offered first refusal on the seat accepted and so his political career effectively faded away.

The Fremantles again settled down to their bucolic existence in Swanbourne, interrupted on 30 August 1807 by the birth of a son, William Robert, Betsey's seventh child in her ten years of marriage! Thomas, as usual, took on the role of head of the extended family by trying to sort out the complicated love lives of Betsey's sisters. Their Christmas visit to Stowe House was particularly grand, even by the extravagant standards of Buckingham, when he included among the guests King Louis XVIII of France plus a fair sprinkling of his immediate family and French nobility. At this stage of the proceedings he, of course, had no monarchical duties to detain him as Napoleon was firmly entrenched on what he regarded as his throne.

It was during his first year of semi-retirement (1807) that Fremantle collected the monies for and oversaw the construction of a monument to Lord Nelson erected above Portsmouth. There had been an earlier attempt to build a memorial and more than £4,000 had been raised and the monies entrusted to Nelson's prize agent, Alexander Davison. A design had been drawn up by John Thomas Groves of the Board of Works and had been exhibited at the Royal Academy in 1807. Unfortunately the money collected had disappeared. Fremantle took on the project and was successful in raising another £5,000[12] to ensure the project was carried out. The Nelson Monument is still standing to this day. It is situated on Portsdown Hill, about 2 miles north of Portsmouth harbour, overlooking the sea, and is 120ft tall and constructed of granite.

Despite this project and the successful marriage of Betsey's troublesome sister Harriet, there must have been a certain amount of boredom for Fremantle. Thanks to his long and frequent absences from Swanbourne, both the estate and the tenants were Betsey's projects. She had managed them and despite his frequent advice in letters from various parts of the Mediterranean, Fremantle could not have been blind to the fact that she was a competent woman, and did not really need him in order to run the estates efficiently. He was not to remain a farmer for long, for during his leave his name had still followed the relentless path up the seniority list of post-captains and on 31 July 1810 he finally reached the top of the list and was promoted to rear admiral and recalled to naval duties.

9

LIFE AS AN ADMIRAL, 1810–1814

It was not until the middle of August 1810 that Adm. Fremantle travelled down to Portsmouth. He had several appointments to carry out in Portsmouth and London before he sailed for the Mediterranean to take up his commission under Adm. Sir Charles Cotton, Bart. For the first time he was not alone for he took with him a midshipman, his son, Charles. He was just 10 years old. They sailed to the Mediterranean on the frigate HMS *Fortune*[1] to join Cotton on the continuing blockade of Toulon. Fremantle was to hoist his admiral's flag on HMS *Ville de Paris*, a three-decked, first-rate vessel of 110 guns. There is little doubt that Capt. Henry Vansittart,* the commander of HMS *Fortune*, would have breathed a sigh of relief as Fremantle left his vessel and boarded his flagship. It was never a popular duty ferrying admirals around, especially within the confined space of a frigate, as he would have had to give up his cabin to Fremantle and mess with his fellow officers in the wardroom.

Things had changed dramatically on the international front while Fremantle had been in Swanbourne. For the first time, Britain had sent a significant military detachment to fight Napoleon on main-

---

* Capt. Henry Vansittart was, coincidentally, first cousin to Nicholas Vansittart, who had accompanied Parker, Fremantle and Nelson to the Baltic as a diplomat to negotiate with the Danes prior to the Battle of Copenhagen.

land Europe. No longer was the war to be a naval and financial fight only, now Britain was truly going to war. In August 1808 a young lieutenant-general, Sir Arthur Wellesley, had landed at the head of the British forces in Portugal. Although overruled by Sir Hew Dalrymple who signed what many people viewed as a shameful armistice known as the Convention of Sintra, Wellesley had done enough to demonstrate that a Napoleonic army was not unbeatable. Subsequently the army, under Sir John Moore, had been forced to beat an ignominious retreat but, in April 1809, Wellesley again returned to the Iberian Peninsula to command the British and Portuguese forces. Many Spaniards had by now realised that their previous alliance with Napoleon was a farce and were ready to fight French forces, who they perceived as occupying their country. Their guerrilla forces, which were to harry the French throughout their occupation of the Iberian Peninsula, became a potent weapon in ensuring that the French troops could never relax their guard for a second.

By the time Fremantle put to sea Sir Arthur Wellesley, now Viscount Wellington, had withdrawn back to the defensive lines around Lisbon known as the Lines of Torres Vedras and there he was to stay until the besieging French army was forced to withdraw due to lack of supplies. In marked contrast, Wellington was resupplied constantly from the sea, which was made possible by the Royal Navy's control of the seas around Spain and Portugal.

The invasion force that landed in Portugal was to play a significant role in the future downfall of Napoleon for, disregarded by the Emperor who had his sights on Russia by this stage, it was to become an ulcer in the side of France that gradually but remorselessly drained the spirit and the virility out of France. This campaign, coupled with the tragedy of the invasion of Russia, would eventually lead the allies to Paris and the abdication of Emperor Napoleon Bonaparte. Of course, all this would have been unknown to Fremantle but the theme of military activity against Napoleon on Continental Europe, supported by Royal Navy power at sea with the two acting in concert, were to play a major part in his professional life from now on. For the immediate future, to the British and other European forces engaged, Napoleon looked as secure on land as he had ever done.

HMS *Fortune* had caught up with the fleet off Cap de sa Mola (western tip of Majorca) but, having taken over his flagship, Fremantle was almost immediately detached from the main squadron and sent to Port Mahon in Minorca, from where he wrote to brother, William, on 12 October 1810:[2]

> Cotton's reception of me has not been so kind as I had every reason to expect. I have not had much time to make much observation upon the line of conduct he is pursuing, every person I have conversed with condemns him with his mode of conducting the fleet – there is an outward appearance of this difference of opinion, but it appears to me that Hood is very much influenced by Hallowell, who has certainly a mean opinion of the abilities of our chief. I confess I see much to blame on both sides, and am determined to keep out of all cavil, indeed since I have been here I hope I have not made the thing worse, as well all yesterday dined with Hood in great harmony.

Already, Fremantle was up to his old tricks of finding fault with his commanding officer. In further letters he noted that the fleet was badly maintained and that there was a shortage of spares despite the fact the unending grind of the constant blockade made this inevitable to a degree. Cotton, an admiral with a distinguished fighting record, was perhaps wary of stripping out ships from the blockading force for maintenance but Fremantle was not slow to notice these deficiencies and, what is more, bring them to the admiral's attention. On 30 October he wrote to Betsey:[3]

> We are without a nail, a foot of plank or a fathom of rope spare in case of accidents – besides which our people want clothing for this time of the year. I have been obliged to write officially to Cotton on the subject, and I am not without apprehension that the line I am pursuing will occasion him uneasiness, because to him as Commander-in-Chief much blame must attach for the Neglect and degradation into which the ship has fallen. As you may imagine I am very anxious to keep fair with all the world particularly with the Commander-in-Chief, but certainly not at the expense of my reputation.

Further letters followed to William pointing out the inadequacies of Sir Charles Cotton and detailing why it was that he could not get on with his commander-in-chief:[4]

Cotton is a very strange man, there is no possibility of keeping him to any <u>serious conversation</u> relative to our situation, in the middle of what anybody else would consider as the most interesting subject and to him particularly, he flies off to make some remark about a cow or a horse or something as trivial. Whether this dislike to talk on business proceeds from jealousy, ignorance or stupidity I cannot determine.

Unknown to Fremantle, as he dispatched this latest diatribe on the shortcomings of his admiral, Betsey was faced with a trial far worse than a shortage of maintenance spares. Her sixth child, Louisa, had died of scarlet fever aged just 5 years. In the early nineteenth century child deaths were far from rare but nothing could assuage the grief felt by such a loving mother as Betsey. She wrote in her diary:

The dear little Angel expired at nine o'clock on Monday morning 29th Octr … her agonies were great from that day to the moment of her death. My affliction almost overpowers me, at the loss of such a darling and lovely Child, but on account of my Baby* I am obliged to exert myself in this severe trial.

Fremantle received the news of Louisa's death on 16 November and two days later he wrote back to Betsey:[5]

My dearest and best of women,
How am I to begin a letter to you in answer to the very melancholy one I received two days ago, naming the death of our poor Louisa? The anxiety I feel about you, as well as distress of mind from our severe loss, has made me at times feel like poor Marianne** in a state of stupor, this you will readily believe has not been alleviated by the death of Teresa, or the consideration of the impropriety of your sister's conduct. In short at no period of life have I ever received accounts from home so agonising.

It may be difficult to forgive Fremantle's apparent coldness in juxtaposing his grief at the death of their child right next to a complaint about

---

*   Betsey had just given birth to the last child she was to bear, Stephen Grenville, born on 30 August 1810. He was her ninth child.

** Fremantle's younger sister.

the grieving Betsey's wayward sister. However, Fremantle was not at ease when expressing strong emotions in writing and it is quite possible that Betsey herself had mentioned her sister in her letter, which she often composed over several days. His letters had never expressed the simple joy or deep felt loss that seemed to come so naturally to someone such as his great friend, Nelson, but his lack of feeling in his letters is in marked contrast to the reality of his character. As Betsey's diary makes abundantly clear, he was always a loving, affectionate father not scared to show his love to his children. He would have undoubtedly grieved deeply for his daughter. It is probable he was all too aware that as the captain of a large warship he was not in a position to succumb to his emotions and that the luxury of prolonged mourning for a lost child was simply not possible.

Whatever his true feelings, for the next few months he at least had the luxury of being kept busy. His ship had been detached from the main fleet and sent to Port Mahon, where he was to take control of the port that was the main resupply depot for the fleet. It was the chief Royal Navy base and the best deep-water port in the western Mediterranean. His chief worry was the French forces on the Spanish mainland that were pushing westwards from the south of France into Catalonia, from where he was nervous that they could mount a quick strike against Minorca and deprive Britain of this vital facility. As he wrote in letters to William, there were no soldiers of any worth on the island and he had pointed this out to Adm. Cotton. as he helpfully informed William:[6] 'I have by letter strongly urged Cotton to the importance of this place but I don't think he takes up anything with *animus*, although he seems obliged for my suggestions.'

It is almost possible to feel certain sympathy with Cotton as he tried to deal with his difficult and forceful junior. However, the low opinion Fremantle had of Sir Charles Cotton was shared by others. In a letter from Tom Grenville to his brother, Lord Buckingham, he mentioned the difficulties that he experienced as First Lord of the Admiralty with some of the older admirals, including Cotton. He wrote:[7]

My chief present difficulty is about Cotton, whose *claims* are hourly growing by serving in the Channel Fleet to reach the command of it, for which he is, entirely unfit ... How can I weed the list of Admirals? It is a list of incurables.

On 1 March 1811 Fremantle was again full of bile against his command-ing officer. Ever sensitive to any perceived slight, he wrote to William, complaining of not being given an independent squadron:[8]

> The removal of Pickmore from the San Josef to hoist his flag on the Temeraire again will place me fourth in command, and make my situa-tion most dreadfully tiresome. Cotton has behaved most shabbily to me having promised me he would take the first opportunity of detaching me, and now he does not mean to do so, and has offered it to Pickmore. The man is jealous of his shadow.

Some weeks later, in mid March, Fremantle transferred his flag to HMS *Rodney*, a seventy-four-gun two-decker, much smaller than the first-rate HMS *Ville de Paris*. He did so to preserve his 'independence' at Port Mahon by avoiding having to sail to Toulon on blockade duty where the larger first-rate vessel was required.

This time, however, he received better news in reply from William who, as always, had his contacts in the Admiralty. He was therefore able to inform his disgruntled brother that he would not have to work under Sir Charles Cotton for long as he was to be appointed commander-in-chief of the Channel Fleet and would be replaced in the Mediterranean by Adm. Sir Edward Pellew.

Despite all this grumbling and politicking RAdm. Fremantle seemed to be enjoying himself as commander of the naval station in Port Mahon. He had the place running efficiently, with refits taking place on a regular basis and supplies being sent out to the fleet off Toulon as and when required but, with things running so smoothly, it did not take Fremantle long to cause more friction with Cotton.

The Spanish navy contingent based in Port Mahon had, with British encouragement, busied themselves in bringing out their supplies of stores from Cartagena to prevent them from falling into French hands. One such cargo of good quality Baltic-sourced timber was to provoke the next disagreement between Fremantle and Cotton. The Spanish detachment in Port Mahon was practically destitute and, in a bid to boost their funds, the senior Spanish officer offered the timber to Fremantle, who immediately bought it for use by the Royal Navy. Fremantle's arguments were firstly that the timber was good quality and would be needed by the navy and secondly, as the British were putting pressure on the Spaniards to get everything of strategic value out of Cartagena before the French seized it, they had a moral duty to aid the Spaniards by buying the timber. Thirdly, the timber had been purchased at a reasonable market rate.

Cotton obviously took a contrary view and when he learned of the transaction wrote to Fremantle stating that it was only the fact that the deed had already been done: [9]

> could induce me to sanction a proceeding which already been refused us by the Government of Spain, upon the application of His Majesty's Minister at Cadiz to purchase the Stores in the Arsenal at Carthagena for British purposes.

Presumably Fremantle had not been informed of this fact but the dispute seemed to have rumbled on for some time as the two officers exchanged letters about the exact cost of the timber.

Despite this incident Fremantle, with the port running well, had plenty of time to enjoy himself and his diary at the time shows plenty of opportunities for balls, soirées and evenings at the theatre. Mahon society was by no means bereft of 'stars' with members of the Bourbon family and other Spanish aristocratic families prominent. There were also cryptic references to visits to ladies' houses and sitting with amiable females 'cozing' until the early hours of the morning.* Despite his enjoyment of the social life in Mahon,** as had been shown during the evacuation of Leghorn when he was a young frigate captain, he was a man who got things done. While it had been suggested he was not at his best in bureaucratic jobs, when required to do something of that nature he invariably buckled down. His one concern was still the possible threat to the island from the French forces on the southern coast of mainland Spain and he continued to pester Cotton and local army contacts to get them to reinforce his garrison.

By late June 1811 the town of Tarragona had fallen to the French and, even before the news reached Port Mahon, Fremantle was writing to William to set out, once again, his fears of a French invasion: [10]

---

*   *To coze*, an archaic term meaning to chat.

** At the time, Mahon society included representatives of the deposed French royalty, the Bourbons, whom Fremantle was familiar with, having been introduced at Stowe.

I am officially informed 1000 British troops have sailed from Gibraltar for the relief of Tarragona and that Campo Verde's army at Ajuilina amounts to 12,000 men. I have hopes the town may hold out, I believe I have told you the importance I attach to Tarragona, if the port is taken these Islands may be carried at any time, besides that upon that event must depend the fate of Catalonia.

In fact, the main French effort was being aimed at Wellington's forces that were just about to begin the long march back into Spain from his defensive position around Lisbon. From now on, the French would be forced more and more on to the defensive and had neither the time nor resources to spend on difficult amphibious assaults on Spanish islands.

On 10 July 1811 Adm. Sir Edward Pellew arrived to take command in the Mediterranean. He brought with him a new British minister to the Court of Naples at Palermo, Maj.-Gen. Lord William Bentinck, who was accompanied by his wife.

Pellew was reputedly slightly nervous of Fremantle and made efforts early on to win him over knowing that he could be a trifle awkward if he did not take to someone. In addition there were, of course, his connections in Parliament and the Admiralty. Few junior admirals had the political connections that Fremantle had so Pellew rightly judged it was worth making the effort. In any case, he was naturally gregarious and well known to keep an excellent table on his flagship as well as having more than a passing interest in the local ladies. All attributes that would naturally endear him to Fremantle.

After one of their first meetings Pellew wrote to Fremantle:[11]

> Sincere thanks for the good you have done my head and pleasure you have given my heart by your open and kind confidence ... I know I have a hard task but you may also believe that I will not stay the week in Command when I lose the confidence of those I serve with ... I do trust that <u>you</u> among many I esteem will not hide my faults from me.

Pellew hoisted his flag on HMS *Hibernia* and immediately made a favourable impression on Fremantle by inviting him on to the ship and spending the whole day discussing Mediterranean affairs.

Less than a week later he visited Fremantle and inspected the arrangements made at Port Mahon. Shortly after the visit Pellew reported to the secretary at the Admiralty:[12]

On arriving at Minorca, I have found Rear-Admiral Fremantle, in charge of the port duties, and everything under his authority in such excellent order, that I have not interfered in any manner with his arrangements.

Pellew also carried two further bits of good news for Fremantle in that he arranged for the garrison at the port to be strengthened with British troops and he proposed to offer him an independent command of the Adriatic Squadron to be based at Palermo in Sicily.* This independent command would also include all areas to the east of Sicily plus Tunis. As Fremantle's new flagship he offered him HMS *Milford*, a new seventy-four-gun third-rate battleship that had only been launched in April 1809.

Keeping the port in good running order was not, however, the only service that Fremantle arranged for Pellew for, on leaving the port, Pellew wrote to Fremantle:[13]

My Dear Fremantle will I am sure be satisfied that I feel my obligation for his care and kindness in the arrangement for this little personage ... I have no doubt but I shall be highly pleased with such a friend and I trust she will have no cause to complain of the doubloons whatever else may be wanting. I would rather know her wishes than go wrong as it really is no object for me. Secrecy is all we both want. Can I know what house ... Have it arranged as well as you can.

Shortly after this coy, private note Pellew followed up with orders to Admiral Thomas Fremantle dated 1 August 1811 that stated:[14]

---

* King Ferdinand of Naples and Sicily had been driven out of Naples by the invasion of the French army. Although he had been reinstalled on his throne for a short while by the intervention of Nelson, he was now once again in exile from the mainland and had based the monarchy in Sicily for the previous five years. A British army contingent and British subsidies prevented the island falling into French hands. However, the situation was made complicated by Queen Carolina, who reputedly hated her English benefactors almost as much as the French. In 1811 the court of Neopolitans, who had arrived on Sicily with the King and Queen, were hated by the islanders. Sir William Bentinck, who had been appointed Minister Plenipotentiary to the court, had the unenviable task of trying to reform the autocratic administration, as well as acting as commander-in-chief of British forces in the Mediterranean.

You are hereby required to hoist your flag in HMS *Milford* with the following vessels under your command *Victorious, Thames, Cephalus, Pilot, Herald* (all for service at Sicily) You are required to go to Sicily and liaise harmoniously with Sir Wm. Bentinck, His Majesty's representative to the court of Palermo.

On hearing that Fremantle was to relieve him, the previous squadron commander, Adm. Charles Boyles, wrote to welcome him to his new post:[15]

I understand from Sir Edwd. Pellew that as soon as Sir Richard Keats joins him you are to come and relieve me here. I assure you I have found it by no means unpleasant service, excepting rather too much political business for me, who am not fond of dabbling in diplomatic concerns, be assured it is dirty work.

It was not the only warning that Fremantle was to receive for, having told his brother of his independent command, he received a reply from William on 15 August 1811:[16]

I have only one piece of advice to give you and I do most earnestly and seriously, which is to be on your constant and increasing guard against the abominable intrigues and artifice of the women in that most nefarious and corrupt court.

With these warnings ringing in his head, Fremantle sailed for Palermo on 22 August and on arrival immediately wrote to Lord Buckingham, well aware that the letter would be shared with his brother. In it he lets the marquess know his arrangements:[17] 'In the mean time I am here with only the Milford, I shall live on shore to know everything that is going on.'

William had always been wary of his brother getting involved with Continental politics and/or women, and Palermo was full of both. The knowledge of Nelson's problems in Italy was all too fresh in William's mind, as were the weaknesses of his brother. On 22 October 1811 William's advice to avoid Palermo at all costs became more strident[18] and in his next letter he made it clear that he feared for his elder brother's reputation and his ability to resist the fairer sex:[19]

I own I should not in your case have settled myself on shore at Palermo, I do not think, with you, that it adds to your consequence or in any way assists your operations, your communication with Lord Wm Bentinck could as well be carried on from on board. You will save all the expense of which you complain, and you would avoid much of the risk, attached to your situation, arising from falsehood and misrepresentation. The same situation, almost ruined, indeed for the time did ruin the character of Nelson, and paralysed all the energy and zeal and ability which distinguished him in every other situation. I would have you look at the Coast of Calabria and see what the French are about, look also at the Adriatic, see what can be done there, in short anything but lead a Courtier's life or a shore life at Palermo.

However, William's advice had always fallen upon deaf ears if Thomas felt that it may hamper his enjoyment of life and he continued blithely to take a full part in Palermo nightlife. On 11 September he wrote a long letter, letting William know that he was not living beyond his means (always a concern of William's) and demonstrated to him that he knew how to steer clear of politics and thus remain unsullied and impartial:[20]

Nothing material has transpired since last I wrote, I continue to hear all parties, and belong to *none* which I conceive is the best line I can draw in my situation, and this I think leads more to be sought after, than following the example of some of our Country-men who are very unguarded in their conversation, which has only the bad effect of irritating the Court against the Nation.

During Fremantle's early stay in Palermo, Maj.-Gen. Lord William Bentinck returned to Britain in order to seek a fresh mandate from his political masters, particularly as to how much he should and should not interfere in internal Sicilian affairs. Fremantle by now stayed regularly with Lady William Bentinck, finding her company congenial albeit, so far as one is able to tell, the relationship was based purely on friendship. When Bentinck himself returned with his powers firmly endorsed by the British government he did so against a background of intrigue mostly emanating from Queen Caroline who, it was rumoured, was plotting with Murat to bring the French into Sicily. Privately, Fremantle considered her deranged.

Early in 1812, William wrote again to his brother to warn him of the dangers of getting involved with foreign affairs and scandals. In a long reply, mostly setting out the current political scene in Palermo, Fremantle finished with a touch of exasperation:[21]

> I think the tongue of scandal has not reached me, and I receive your advice on the subject, still three sides of paper on it is rather more than is quite palatable, but I know the honest and good motives that guide you.

In April Fremantle took Lord and Lady Bentinck on a voyage during which they took in Malta, where the lord left the party to return to Palermo and his official duties. Fremantle's party, including Lady Bentinck, carried on the voyage to Tunis where Fremantle led in negotiations with the Bey of Tunis to get 380 captive Sicilians released. His shore party, which went ashore to meet the Bey, included Lady Bentinck dressed as a Royal Marine. Fremantle describes her in his diary:[22] 'I was attended by 50 Officers and Gentlemen from the Ships and Lady William with a pair of loose *pantaloons* and a Great Coat that reached low down.'

He also drew up a formal truce between Tunis and Sicily to remain in force while Sicily was allied to Britain, all of which he told William gleefully had met with the full approval of Lord Bentinck. Encouraged by his success he suggested to Adm. Pellew that, with the judicious use of a little naval force, he could no doubt bring the Dey of Algiers to order as all of the Mediterranean African coast (then known as the Barbary Coast) was important to Britain from a trading point of view as well as assuring free passage for British merchant vessels through the narrow straits of Gibraltar.

In a passage that was hardly designed to endear him to his commander-in-chief he wrote:[23]

> We have not, I think kept up our relation with the Barbary States so much as we ought to have done, particularly during the time Lord Collingwood commanded the Fleet in the Mediterranean, we should constantly send Ships into their Ports to see our treaties are respected.

Pellew, however, was not of a mind to let Fremantle have his head in such negotiations and wrote to Lord Bentinck:[24]

Between ourselves I think Fremantle's opinion that we should resort to strong measures is wrong. And I always considered we were so on the occasion of Lord Nelsons treating with the Dey some years ago when we attempted to force upon him the admission of our Merchantmen from Malta. I have written to Fremantle and I think he has managed so well at Tunis that it is truly an object for him to try the effect of his persuasion on the Dey. As the prospect opens for our operations in Spain the importance of getting supplies from Barbary increases, and I am now sending our agent over on the offer made to our Consul of corn now laying there in Greek prizes – and I shall try hard to get a promise of the Surplus corn of the approaching harvest from Bona.

The refusal to let Fremantle have his head in an approach to the Dey of Algiers nearly brought the two men into open conflict but Pellew showed his mettle and calmly brought Fremantle into line with a soothing letter:[25]

I agree with you that it is a disgrace – not only to us but to Europe – to submit to these fellows, but the remedy is worse than the disease ... If we fall out with the Dey now we throw away all the supplies of Tartus at a moment our harvests are failing in England.*

Fremantle consoled himself with his usual letter to William from Palermo dated 20 May 1812:[26]

My Truce and Treaties with Tunis were very much approved of by all parties. I am prepared for a mission to Algiers for the same purpose but Sir Ed. Pellew does not seem inclined to force these barbarians into terms and I am quite persuaded we shall do nothing without threat. I have sent two vessels with my opinions and only wait his ultimatum. (I take some credit for myself for having projected and carried on the business without receiving <u>any instructions</u> except from papers in the office, and certainly a person more indolent than I might have missed the opportunity).

---

* It is an ironic coincidence that in 1816, when the Dey of Algiers was accused of breaking the treaty outlawing slavery, it was Pellew who commanded the fleet which, on 26 August, sailed into Algiers and bombarded the Algerian fleet for nine hours, setting fire to the fleet and parts of the city and thus, by force, bringing the Dey of Algiers into line with his treaty obligations.

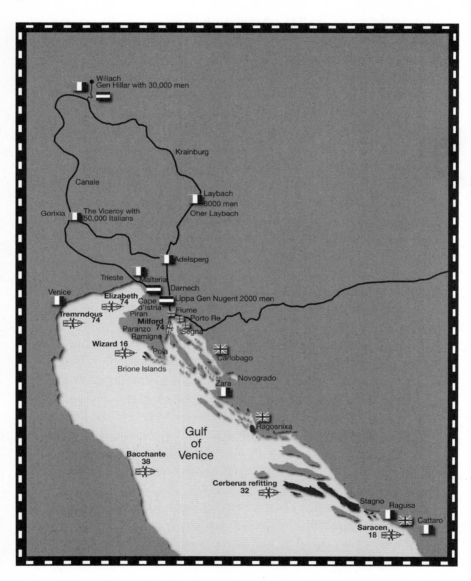

Fremantle's squadron in the Adriatic.

Fremantle did not have long to brood over what he perceived as Pellew's weakness. In June, reports were received by Lord Bentinck that the states bordering the Adriatic were rising in insurrection against the French occupiers. Previously, the states had been mostly under Austrian control with some nominally independent but, after the latest of Napoleon's defeats of Austria at the Battle of Wagram, the Emperor had required the Austrians to sign the Treaty of Schönbrunn, forcing them to cede to France Fiume, Istria and Trieste, and parts of Croatia. With France already in control of the Kingdom of Naples, the Papal States, Venice and Corfu, the control of the states on the eastern seaboard of the Adriatic gave it a virtual monopoly of the area.

News that the Adriatic states were taking advantage of Emperor Napoleon's troubles in Russia and Spain to assert their independence was welcome to the British. Lord Bentinck, in the second of his dual roles as commander-in-chief of the Mediterranean land forces, wrote to Fremantle in a letter of 8 June 1812 marked 'secret':[27]

By the accompanying extract of a letter from Lt. Colonel Robertson at Lissa, you will perceive that the Montenegrins are in actual insurrection against the French.

You are already acquainted with the spirit of disaffection to the French Government, prevailing in the provinces on the eastern side of the Adriatic lately ceded to France, with the warlike character of those people, with the demands made for our assistance, and with the communication that has been kept up with them. Always looking forward with certainty, that Italy universally discontented would assert her independence, it has appeared to me most desirable that no partial rising should take place until one general effort can be made by all the nations engaged in the same cause.

But as this insurrection has unfortunately broken out; and the apparent certain occurrence of War between Russia and France may probably produce a similar effect in Italy,* and thus give accidently to this transaction the desired coincidence, I have determined to give to the Montenegrins every assistance that the limited Force in the Ionian Islands will afford. If the Dalmatians should be successful it is impossible to calculate the

---

* Napoleon's invasion of Russia began with his Grande Armée crossing the Niemen River into Russia on 24 June, just sixteen days after Bentinck's letter.

extent to which this insurrection may go, or the important diversion that may be made in both of Russia and Spain.

As it has been already in your contemplation to go to the Adriatic, I must beg leave urgently to represent to you my opinion that the early execution of this intention may be attended with the most important advantages. The presence of a British Admiral of such high reputation would be far more serviceable to the cause, than the aid of even a much larger military force. The application also of the small number we can afford under the direction of your Judgement and enterprise could not fail to give very great annoyance to the enemy, and to establish that unity of operations from the want of which similar undertakings have generally failed.

Bentinck had worded his letter brilliantly to massage Fremantle's ego and he set out immediately for the Adriatic on 13 June, having sent Adm. Pellew a copy of Bentinck's letter as he currently had no direct orders from Pellew to sail there. In the event, Pellew saw the sense of collaborating with Bentinck and had already ordered Fremantle to co-operate fully with Bentinck, so he could hardly complain that Fremantle had exceeded his orders. Besides, he was probably somewhat relieved to temporarily rid himself of the potentially troublesome Fremantle.

When Fremantle arrived in the Adriatic he found the reports of a universal uprising to be somewhat premature thanks to Austria being forced into another unwelcome alliance with France. Britain had troops based in Zakynthos (then known as Zante) in the Ionian Islands at the southern end of the Adriatic, plus a small naval establishment on the island of Lissa (modern-day Vis, just off the coast of Croatia near Split). It was at Lissa that Fremantle made his headquarters and it was there he received the unwelcome news from Bentinck that he was to give up his ground troops, who were to be sent to Spain, and that he should on no account engage in any activities fomenting insurrection, thanks to the Franco-Austrian alliance.

Fremantle busied himself that summer in building up what he con-sidered a suitable naval establishment at Lissa, which, in turn, received Pellew's support. In September he reported to Betsey that he had built himself a house at Lissa. Later that month he wrote complaining of the lack of decent society and instead was amusing himself in fitting out his house, which he proudly reported as the most comfortable on the island.

As was often the case, the parsimonious clerks at the Admiralty were aghast at building a naval facility in what they considered to be close proximity to the naval establishment at Malta and wrote via Pellew:[28]

> I am commanded by My Lords Commissioners of the Admiralty to acquaint you that they do not approve any further expense being incurred in the establishment of a Yard at Lissa, and that they cannot think an Establishment to be at all necessary so near to Malta.

Pellew continued to support Fremantle, explaining to the Admiralty that Fremantle had been hurt by their note and that his motives for trying to build up the facility at Lissa were motivated solely by concern for the Royal Navy and that no extra expense had incurred. Later, plague broke out in Malta making it temporarily unsuitable for naval operations, which probably caused Fremantle a certain degree of quiet satisfaction.

At this stage of the proceedings Fremantle had three line-of-battle ships, HMS *Milford*, HMS *Victorious* and HMS *Eagle*. All were seventy-four-gun vessels and, in addition, his fleet was strengthened by the frigates HMS *Bacchante*, *Apollo* and *Orlando*. With this force he was able to blockade Venice and Corfu while keeping his flagship at Lissa. The blockades were important as Napoleon's strategy was to use the ports, particularly Venice, to build new warships and thus establish a superiority over the Royal Navy in the Adriatic. Gradually, however, as the extent of the disaster that was overtaking Napoleon's Grande Armée in Russia became apparent, the situation in the Adriatic began to change.

Russia made the first move when an old acquaintance of Fremantle, Adm. Chichagov,* proposed a plan whereby Russian forces would march across the Balkans to attack the eastern Adriatic states, thereby creating a diversion that would help to prevent Napoleon reinforcing his Russian invasion force. To do so they hastily concluded a peace with the Ottoman Empire in order to advance on the Adriatic. It was, however, a plan that was stillborn.

Adm. Chichagov wrote to Lord Bentinck to explain that British money was required if the Russian army was to march on the Adriatic coast. Bentinck firmly rejected his proposal, explaining that all his resources

---

* Fremantle had previously come across Chichagov while serving in the Baltic on HMS *Ganges*.

were being used on the Spanish mainland and that the most he could offer was some ammunition and medical supplies. The Russians had further difficulties in their planning when it became apparent that the Turkish rulers were not so amenable about letting a Russian army march across their territory as Chichagov had first imagined. Fremantle was informed subsequently that the Russians were encamped at Bucharest and later he heard Chichagov was back in Russia helping the Russian forces harry Napoleon's army as it retreated from Moscow.

Despite the absence of the Russians, things were beginning to move in the Adriatic and by 22 December Fremantle's small squadron was beginning to make itself felt with attacks on St Cataldo in the heel of Italy and subsequently, early in the new year, Fremantle drove French forces out of the two islands closest to Lissa (Corzola and Lagosta). By May 1813 the British were sufficiently confident to mount attacks on the mainland when Capt. William Hoste, in one of the frigates HMS *Bacchante*, seized the coastal port of Karlebago and Cdr Harper, in the sloop HMS *Saracen*, seized Zupana, an island off Ragusa.*

By the summer of 1813 events on the international scene were beginning to have an effect on the Adriatic. Austria had now left the forced alliance with France and had joined, yet again, what became known as the sixth coalition, which ultimately consisted of the UK, Austria, Prussia, Russia, Portugal, Spain, Sweden and a number of other smaller German states. Yet again, the majority of Europe had risen up against Emperor Napoleon and this time the French had nothing like the army that previous coalitions had faced. Only some 30,000 veterans had crossed the river out of the Russian winter and although Napoleon would rebuild his army, resistance within France to the annual drafts was beginning to grow.

The immediate effect on the Adriatic was that Fremantle was to be joined by Austrian ground troops. These were led by Gen. Laval Nugent von Westmeath, an Austrian general who had been born in Ireland at Ballynacor, the son of Count Michael Anton Nugent von Westmeath, Governor of Prague. He joined the Austrian army in 1793, became colonel in 1807 and Chief of Staff of the Army Corps of Archduke Johann of Austria in 1809. Despite his exotic beginnings he proved to be a steadfast ally trusted by Austrians and British alike.

---

* Some of the modern names of these Croatian and Slovenian places are as follows: Lissa – Vis, Corzola – Korčula, Lagosta – Lastovo, Zupana – Šipan, Ragusa – Dubrovnik, Fiume – Rijeka, Carlobago or Karlobago – Senj.

Fremantle was equally determined to prove a valuable ally to Nugent; the two men got on well and co-operated in the capture and occupation of Fiume. It was at the end of October, however, that the joint British navy and Austrian land forces came together to best effect. In order to overcome the French forces ensconced in Trieste citadel, heavy artillery was required. Nugent had none but Fremantle responded in a way that even his great hero, Nelson, could not have bettered. He landed some of HMS *Melford*'s heavy guns, dragged them into position and formed batteries that he personally supervised as they battered the French forces into submission.

A mark of the mutual respect between the two men was illustrated by their respective post-battle dispatches. Nugent sent his to the British Foreign Secretary, Lord Castlereagh. In it he paid handsome tribute to the efforts of the British navy and to Fremantle in particular:[29]

The labour of all these works was incredible owing to the softness of the ground occasioned by the continual rains, and the fire of the Enemy, and nothing but the extraordinary exertions of the Men and the perfect harmony which prevailed could overcome the difficulties. The Officers, Seamen and Marines of the British Squadron particularly exerted them-selves and were animated by the presence of the Admiral who himself superintended the works and directed the Batteries ... . The fall of the Castle of Trieste closes one most important part of our operations and gives us possession of the Coast from Dalmatia to the top of the Adriatic with all the roads that lead from thence. The whole of these operations prove how by the mutual assistance of the Army and Navy a very superior force will be overcome ... .

As to the siege of the Castle of Trieste your Lordship will perceive by the above that the greater part of the Credit must be given to Admiral Fremantle and the Navy and it is my duty to acknowledge it.

Fremantle, for his part, paid equally handsome tribute to his ally, Nugent:

General Nugent has deservedly all the merit of having liberated these Provinces in the space of two Months with so small a force. The action to take Trieste was the last direct action in which Fremantle was to play an active role. From this point on the baton passed to the younger generation such as William Hoste.*

The siege of Trieste was a fitting swansong to Fremantle's fighting career. It showed all the hallmarks of his greatest mentor, Horatio Nelson, who was probably the Georgian navy's greatest exponent of amphibious operations. Fremantle had overcome all the difficulties of getting guns ashore, he had established excellent relationships with his army colleagues and, crucially, when it came to the fighting, he had been right there in the front line exhorting his men and overseeing their work. Nelson would have looked down with pride and approval on his protégé's conduct.

By the end of 1813 Thomas was able to write to William reporting the liberation of the whole of the Adriatic and, while the Admiralty appeared to be unimpressed or at least indifferent, the Austrians were far more appreciative of his efforts and awarded him the cross of a commander of the order of Maria Theresa. Subsequently, Fremantle received permission from the Prince Regent to wear the decoration. Some months prior to the end of the campaign Fremantle wrote to the Admiralty asking to be relieved of his command and to come back to England. With the campaign picking up in intensity he had tried to rescind his request so it came as a rude shock to him when, in March 1814, Adm. Sir John Gore was ordered out to the Adriatic to take over his command. Gore arrived on 2 March 1814 and four days later, during his handover period, Thomas wrote to William:[30]

The 2nd of this month Sir John Gore arrived here in the Revenge with orders for me to go home, the matter and manner are both offensive and originate from the Admiralty Board, who have taken every means to mortify me, however I console myself in knowing I stand on high ground and if they do not reward me I hope to live and speak my mind freely.

---

* Captain William Hoste was very much a Nelson protégé, having served under his command both as a midshipman and a lieutenant. He was with both Nelson and Fremantle at Toulon and Tenerife (where he did not get ashore) and with Nelson at the Battles of Cape St Vincent and the Nile. Perhaps his most distinguished action, however, was in the Adriatic, just off Lissa, in March 1811 when he took on and defeated a combined French and Italian fleet of almost double his size, taking two French ships captive in the process.

Fremantle sailed with Capt. Charles Rowley in HMS *Eagle* and arrived back in Portsmouth, from where he wrote to the Admiralty to inform them of his homecoming. His comments to his brother concerning the Admiralty's attitude were proved correct when, in reply, he was admonished for not having informed them of his departure from his station and for not enclosing his admiral's journal and weekly accounts.

While there is little doubt that Fremantle had been the beneficiary of the eighteenth- and nineteenth-century system of patronage and had been well served by his contacts through the Grenville family, the system worked both ways and inevitably there were paybacks for his political contacts. Since his absence on Mediterranean duties his great mentor, the 1st Marquess of Buckingham, had died and had been succeeded by his eldest son, Richard Temple-Nugent-Brydges-Chandos-Grenville, who became the 2nd Marquess of Buckingham.* The 2nd marquess was universally disliked and his size led to him being nicknamed the Fat Duke. Fremantle never established the same rapport that he had done with his father; perhaps the fact that the marquess was eleven years younger meant there was a less deferential meeting of minds.

The second factor to count against Fremantle was that Britain was now firmly Tory. Lord Liverpool had formed a strong and talented administration that would last for fifteen years. He had appointed Robert Dundas, 2nd Viscount Melville, as his First Lord of the Admiralty, where he was to remain for the duration of Liverpool's administration. It would not have taken long for Fremantle, the ex-Whig MP, to see which way the wind was now blowing. There was a third reason not to hope for too much by way of gifts from the Admiralty as, by the time Thomas arrived back at Portsmouth, Napoleon was defeated and peace was declared.

While Fremantle had been serving in the Adriatic, William had been politicking on his behalf in order to get him an award. He had written to Lord Melville on 12 December, a few months prior to Thomas's return:[31]

I am sure your Lordship will excuse me for taking the liberty of writing to you on the subject of my brother, but I should be wanting that confidence he has reposed in me if I did not make known to your Lordship that the

---

* In 1822 he was made Duke of Buckingham and Chandos.

anxious object of his ambition has been the Red Ribband.* I will not presume to say whether the active and successful services in which he has lately been engaged may entitle him to any mark of the Prince Regent's Favour, but should it be so, I have only to assure your Lordship that this would be a mark the most gratifying to him and one which he would at all times feel he owed to your Lordships personal Favour and Kindness.

Fremantle admitted in his diary that he was nervous of going home, of how he would find the family and the estates and how the Admiralty viewed his work in the Adriatic.[32] He was reassured when Sir Edward Pellew showed him a private letter from Lord Melville that was complimentary about his work, albeit his official correspondence with the Admiralty remained on frosty terms.

---

* The insignia of a Knighthood of the Order of the Bath. William did not limit his lobbying on behalf of his brother to British honours, however, for he successfully lobbied Metternich at the Conference of Vienna, resulting in an Austrian baronetcy being awarded to Thomas.

10

DEATH OF AN ADMIRAL, 1814–1819

After France's defeat in Russia and the continual haemorrhaging of his army in Spain, Napoleon was, for the first time in his life, forced on to the defensive. Tsar Alexander, together with the Prussians, had marched their armies across Europe so that by March 1814 they were preparing themselves for the knockout blow. In early April Napoleon's marshals informed him that they had no plans to fight a civil war and neither did they wish to see Paris suffer the same fate as had befallen Moscow. Napoleon had at last run out of options and on 13 April 1814 he signed the treaty document, ratifying his abdication and claim to the French and Italian thrones. The Allies installed him instead as ruler of the derisory kingdom of the island of Elba. He was to be escorted to the island just off the coast of Tuscany by Col Sir Neil Campbell. Fittingly, it was in a Royal Navy vessel on which the Emperor was taken to Elba and he arrived at Portoferraio on 3 May.

Fremantle's homecoming coincided with peace breaking out in Europe. In contrast with the previous 'phoney' peace, this time it really did seem to the coalition members that they had won and could look forward to a prolonged period of calm and a restoration of the old order. The European economies needed peace and stability for war had been expensive to all of the combatants and especially so to Great Britain and France.

The treaty was signed at the end of May 1814 and, as far as the former belligerents were concerned, it was to bring the war to a permanent end. Various treaties and armistices had been signed during the past twenty years but they had never been considered a permanent end to war, merely a temporary cessation while armies gathered their breath or regrouped for further fighting. With the Bourbon monarchy reinstated and Emperor Napoleon exiled to Elba it seemed reasonable to expect something better and a restoration of the status quo that had existed prior to 1792.

The victorious coalition had no wish to punish France too heavily. After all, they were restoring someone they considered the rightful heir to the French throne and there seemed no sense in leaving his kingdom destitute. All they wished was for France to withdraw to her 1792 borders and for some of the colonies that she had seized during the Napoleonic era to be given up to the victors. Separate peace treaties had to be signed with each of the coalition members but paramount from the Allies point of view was an overall final settlement that the Treaty of Paris delegated to an international congress, at which all parties would be represented, and which would be convened in Vienna in September of 1814.

While these significant international events were taking place, Fremantle was reacquainting himself with Swanbourne life, inspecting the farms and his land that Betsey had so carefully tended during his long absences at sea. He was also getting to know the younger members of his family. Stephen, who was barely 4 years old and whom Betsey described as 'fixing his great eyes on his father',[1] was in awe of this stranger who had entered his world and Cecilia, his youngest daughter who was 1 year older than Stephen, was becoming Fremantle's favourite rapidly. Unfortunately, Betsey was feeling feverish and was in great pain with a severely rheumatic hand, requiring her to have her arm in a sling. It would not be long, however, before her normal robust constitution reasserted itself and she was up, taking the children on trips to London.

Fremantle, when not inspecting Betsey's estate arrangements, was visiting neighbours and one of the first visits was to Stowe to meet Richard Temple, the 2nd Marquess of Buckingham. After his visit Thomas wrote to his brother:[2]

> The house seems much improved and there is infinitely more splendour than in former times ... Lord Buckingham was very kind to me, but there

is much difference between him and his father, however I hope to like him better.

In January 1815 Thomas finally got his award for which both he and his brother had been working. However, it was not everything he had hoped for as the Prince Regent had just expanded the Order of the Bath to cater for the ending of the Napoleonic Wars and to ensure that senior military officers, who had significantly contributed during the war, could receive membership to this Order of Knights. The Order was to consist of three classes: Knights Grand Cross, Knights Commander and Companions. Fremantle's award as Knight Commander of the Order of the Bath, in the second category, was decidedly not the Knight Grand Cross for which he had hoped.*

Suddenly, in December 1814, the family was thrown into mourning when Betsey's youngest sister, Justina, died aged just 28. Further tragedy followed for the Wynne sisters when Eugenia's husband, Robert Campbell, also died, leaving her both a widow and an expectant mother. But even these traumatic events were to be overshadowed rapidly by international events.

On 15 September 1814 the Great Powers arrived in Vienna. As they began their talks the newly enthroned Louis XVIII began his reign with a series of bungled and clumsy administrative measures that would shortly result in French citizens looking back fondly to Napoleon's time. Indeed, by February 1815 when Napoleon's former secretary, Fleury de Chaboulon, visited his old master in Elba, he was able to tell him that France was ripe for his return. On 16 February Sir Neil Campbell left Elba to visit his doctor on the Italian mainland and Napoleon seized his opportunity. On the night of Sunday, 26 February, he left on the French vessel *L'Inconstant*, which he had painted to look like a Royal Navy vessel. On Wednesday, 1 March he landed back on French soil just outside the town of Antibes. As Napoleon made his triumphant way northwards to Paris, the Congress of Vienna was thrown into an uproar by the news and immediately took steps to form the seventh coalition in which Austria, Prussia and Britain pledged 150,000 men each for an army to crush the newly resurgent Napoleon once and for all.

---

* Three years later, in March 1818, Fremantle was to achieve his ambition and to receive the Knight Grand Cross simultaneously with his notification that he had been appointed to succeed Sir Charles Penrose as commander-in-chief of the Mediterranean Fleet.

In Swanbourne the breakdown of peace was followed by a recall to arms for Fremantle. He was offered the command of the Cape of Good Hope, or Commander-in-Chief Channel Islands, or second in command in the Mediterranean Fleet. Wisely, he chose the Channel Islands and in May 1815 moved to St Helier in Jersey, where he rented a property just outside the city. His 'fleet' consisted of two frigates and two sloops and, with no taxing duties to encumber his social life, he was joined by Betsey and the children so they could rent out their Swanbourne home. Unknown to Fremantle, he was never to see Buckinghamshire again.

Prior to the news of the Allies' victory at Waterloo Fremantle co-operated with a French aristocrat, the Duc D'Aumont, who with a small band and Fremantle's provision of sea transport arranged for his own foolhardy invasion of France via Arromanches. The Frenchman was lucky in that the news of the victory and armistice arrived in time to prevent the annihilation of his small band.

On 25 June 1815 the news from Waterloo reached Jersey and soon after that Napoleon had formally abdicated for the second time, Fremantle followed the French duc with his own foray into France. He used one of his vessels to transport him over to St Malo to see for himself the state of France. To justify his excursion, he wrote to the Admiralty to give a situation report on occupied France:[3]

I have the honour of acquainting you for the information of the Lords Commissioners of the Admiralty that I returned today from St Maloes having embarked in this ship for that place on Tuesday.

I found the Governor General very ill disposed towards us, he is a complete Bonapartist with very rough and bad manners, as also a great drunkard. There were no military in the town except the National Guards whose behaviour to us was generally offensive, on our first landing the gates of the town were shut and it was even an intention to fire upon the Kings Ships – on our entering the town the cries of Vive Le Roi was confined to the Women and Children, and occasionally we heard *Vive les plus forts*.

During the time I was in Brittany I went up the river to Dinan, where the inhabitants are much in dread of the Chasseurs who have threatened to plunder the town, they are equally disaffected with St Maloes, and nothing is more unsettled than that part of France I have lately visited.

Following the victory at Waterloo and with Napoleon Bonaparte exiled thousands of miles from Europe in St Helena, the British began to demobilise both troops and naval forces. Fremantle, who still had tenants in his home in Swanbourne, decided to ask for a year's leave of absence from the navy and planned to take the family over to Europe where he intended to rent a place in Italy. On 27 August 1815 Betsey records in her diary:[4] 'We are making our arrangements for leaving this instant we have answers from the Admiralty and shall go in the Wye to St Malo.'

Probably not coincidently, HMS *Wye* was skippered by Fremantle's old colleague, Capt. Andrew Green, who had been Fremantle's lieutenant at both Copenhagen and Trafalgar. On Monday, 4 September he embarked the Fremantle entourage of father, mother, the four daughters plus two sons and sailed to St Malo, where they hired carriages before setting off for Paris. When they arrived in the French capital they found the city awash with occupying military forces. Among them was Fremantle's nephew, Lt Col John Fremantle, who was one of the Duke of Wellington's aides. Betsey seemed to settle back into the itinerant life of the Continental wanderer so quickly that it is difficult to believe it was nearly twenty years and the birth of nine children since she had last travelled through France and Italy. She took the children back to places she had visited as a child: to the Louvre and to the museums and monuments of Paris, even including a trip to the catacombs under the Paris streets. They soon moved on, through occupied France, down to Switzerland, then onwards to Italy and Milan. Here they stopped for some six months and Fremantle wrote back to William:[5] 'For myself I am tolerably well but have such low spirits that I could cry like a child.'

It is hard not to sympathise with Fremantle in his self-imposed exile in Italy, for he was not in his element. There must have been so little for this active and powerful man to do. Betsey was busy with the children and cultural visits, while all too often Fremantle appeared to be alone with his thoughts. He tried to console himself with the thought they were living more cheaply in Italy than back in Britain but he was too much of a *bon viveur* to get much pleasure from such economies.

In the early spring of 1816 the family moved on again to Venice, where Fremantle was able to inspect some of the naval installations that he had been blockading just two years earlier. Despite the occasional brief item of interest such as Venice's port there was still the same spirit of ennui in his letters home. In May he wrote:[6] 'The Weather begins to get warm and most of the English who have wintered in Italy are on their return home.'

Betsey, however, had fallen in love again with Italian life and acted once again as if she were a young girl, meeting the great and the good of Venetian society including the great Italian sculptor Antonio Canova and Napoleon's brother and sister, Lucien and Pauline.

There was to be no return home for Fremantle. In August he moved on again, this time to Florence, where he rented the Palazzo Pucci and lived in some considerable opulence. Tutors were hired for the girls and a semi-permanent existence seemed to take over with Fremantle resigned to the fact that he could not afford the British lifestyle and that he would probably have to remain abroad.

He had not been forgotten by the Admiralty, however, for in March 1818 he was offered the plum position of commander-in-chief of the Mediterranean Fleet, taking over from Sir Charles Penrose.* The Admiralty seemed now to be falling over itself to accommodate Fremantle and told him he was quite in order to stay in Florence until offered the ship of his choice, with the almost new eighty-gun warship HMS *Rochfort* being fitted out in Portsmouth ready to embark for the Mediterranean. He was also given Capt. Andrew Green as his flag captain and the ship would be sailed to Leghorn to pick up its new commander-in-chief.

On 4 March 1819 Fremantle and his family, having travelled to Leghorn, embarked on HMS *Rochfort*. He described the scene in his letter to William:[7]

> The Rochfort anchored here yesterday ... and from all I have heard and seen I have every reason to be happy with the Ship and the appointments ... Today I sat down to dinner with my six Children, which I enjoyed much, and I have every reason to be satisfied with the behaviour and appearance of them all. Harry is a fine animated fellow and amused us much with his accounts of his voyages in the East Indies and America ...
>
> My present intention is to go from hence to Naples where I shall land my family and then proceed to Malta to arrange the Concerns of that

---

* By this stage the Marquess of Buckingham had changed his allegiance and was now a Tory supporter of Liverpool's government. He was therefore in a position to lobby effectively on behalf of Fremantle. Indeed, one critic attributed his appointment as commander-in-chief of the Mediterranean to Buckingham's 'rat tailed influence'.

Island. Maitland is at present at Corfu, and proposes I hear passing the summer in Italy …*

I have received a very civil letter from Lord Melville and have taken every opportunity of serving his Son who is a Mid on board the Ganymede. My Wife desires me to thank you for the diamond Tiara etc. which are very much approved, and the Star of the Order of St Ferdinand is beautiful,** and on the score of honours I may rest satisfied for the remainder of my life.

HMS *Rochfort* sailed almost immediately to Naples, where Fremantle installed Betsey and the children in a comfortable apartment. During this spell in Naples the King of Naples's granddaughter, Princess Maria Cristina, was married by proxy to her cousin King Ferdinand VII of Spain. Many of the crowned heads of Europe attended the ceremonies and the Emperor of Austria and Prince Metternich were entertained on board HMS *Rochfort* in suitably lavish style in order to outdo an American squadron that was also anchored off Naples for the occasion.

Fremantle's next few months were spent in a suitably leisurely fashion cruising around the Mediterranean seeing some of the sights that previously, when at war, had eluded him. He was proud to tell William in one of his letters that they had observed, within the space of three weeks, Vesuvius, Stromboli and Mount Etna, all of which were in various degrees of eruption. His one worry was the future of his sons in the navy. In particular, he was keen to see Charles made a lieutenant so that he could do all he could to assist his career.***

In late summer he revisited the Barbary Coast states. Since Pellew's bombardment of Algiers 1816 they had gradually resorted to their old habits of piracy and slavery and, following a congress at Aix-la-Chapelle in 1818, France (now back in the international fold) and Britain were deputed to visit the rulers and remind them of their international responsibilities. For the first time in his career Fremantle sailed in company with a French admiral to meet the Beys of Algiers, Tunis and Tripoli in order to remind them of the treaties. Assurances were duly given by all of the rulers and, just as quickly, forgotten.

---

* Sir Thomas Maitland, Governor of Malta.

** The Grand Cross of Ferdinand, a present from the King of Naples.

*** In fact, Charles rejoined HMS *Rochfort* as a midshipman just before the death of his father and was not commissioned as a lieutenant until 9 April 1820.

To Fremantle it seemed that however high in the navy hierarchy he rose, William continued to worry and to lecture him on his financial position until, on 25 July 1819, he finally rebelled against his younger brother's strictures:[8]

> You use me unkindly by worrying me continually with a reiteration on the score of economy, I have already explained so fully on that subject that I beg you in charity to drop it in future, the theme from habit is familiar to you, but I cannot adapt myself to it, so pray a truce.

William seems to have taken this to heart, for his copy of the letter is endorsed, 'Answd Aug 30th declining all further charges of his Money Transactions.' However, it did not produce a split between the brothers for on 6 December, just two weeks before his death, Fremantle wrote a further letter on the theme of personal finance and this time there seems almost a gentle teasing of his brother as he wrote:[9]

> Nothing can be pleasanter than the way we are living, certainly in the very best Society with every comfort imaginable, and I repeat to you notwithstanding all you may hear of the Splendour in which we live, I have not exceeded my personal pay except in 100 pound since I have taken the command ... I dread returning to England with the small means I possess, but patience, I trust to my good fortune which as yet has never forsaken me.
>
> ... The King has just sent me an immense Wild boar that was shot yesterday. You cant imagine how snug the ship lies at Baija, Naples Bay is too open to keep the Squadron there, but in the Summer Season. If you should see the Duke of Clarence you may mention that I am quite satisfied by his Sons who are improving daily* – he writes to me occasionally ... Last night there was a magnificent ball at the Spanish Ambassadors, the heat of the rooms always prevents me from sleeping. I am thank God in tolerable health, but trifles irritate me more than they used. I hope I am on good terms with the Admiralty for we have little intercourse, a proof all goes right.

---

* The illegitimate sons of the Duke of Clarence and the actress Dorothy Jordan. The duke was later crowned King William IV, his two elder brothers having pre-deceased him and both dying without leaving male heirs.

This was to be the last letter William was to receive from his brother for the next letter from HMS *Rochfort*, which was written by Fremantle's secretary, Henry Monro, was to tell William that his brother was dead.

HMS *Rochfort* was wintering in and around Naples during December. Fremantle, now promoted to vice admiral, was engaged most days in boring administrative duties that fall to a commander-in-chief with endless reports, correspondence and returns to be completed for the Admiralty. He spent a great deal of his time ashore in the apartment with Betsey and the children. On Saturday, 18 December he decided to stay in with his daughter, Emma, while Betsey, Augusta and Capt. Green attended one of the numerous social occasions. When they returned to the apartment Fremantle appeared to have retired for the night and Betsey went to bed unaware that anything was amiss. She was woken the next morning by her husband's secretary, Henry Munro, with the news that the admiral was unwell and had spent a troubled night.

Betsey hurried to her husband's bedroom to find him talking in his sleep and incoherent and immediately two doctors were sent for, Reilly and Griffith. Their treatment was to bleed him, give him a hot bath of rum and salt water and apply 'blisters' or hot poultices. Despite, or perhaps because of, this treatment Fremantle never again regained consciousness. Betsey had been sent from the room by the doctors and, as far as she was concerned, the situation was under control but unknown to her he must have slipped into a coma and at 10 p.m. he died.

For the first time in her life Betsey was unable to write her usual diaries and it was not until New Year's Day in 1820 that she felt able to return to her writing:[10]

Since the sudden, awful and most heavy loss I sustained I have been involved in too much sorrow and misery to attempt giving any account of an event so calamitous in its consequences, and for which I was so little prepared. A year which had begun with every prospect of happiness has ended with a misfortune which must weigh heavy upon us, but I must submit to the will of providence and bear my heavy affliction with Christian fortitude … he expired at ten o' clock without a groan or struggle – without a warning of his approaching end – and we are left to deplore his fate and the full weight of our Loss – I was not with him at the dreadful moment. I did not apprehend any immediate danger and the Doctors wished me out of the way – I scarcely know how I bore the blow,

Poor Charles was sent for and arrived in the night, his feelings can be easily conceived, he had left his father quite well on Saturday and found him a corpse on Sunday night.

Thus, at the age of 54, Fremantle's life ended. It can only be described as an ironic end for this man of action. He had lived amongst danger and violent death since the age of 12 and had led an extraordinary, charmed existence. Many of his contempories had been killed in battle, their lives cut short by enemy action, but for Fremantle there was to be no glorious end and, although he was given full military honours at his death, there is now no marked grave for this hero of Trafalgar. Urban sprawl in Naples has swallowed up any gravestone; the only remaining memorial is a carved stone inlaid in Valletta harbour. Betsey lived on for a further thirty-eight years and died at the age of 79 in the south of France.

11

THE MAN, THE LEGACY
AND SWANBOURNE

If Thomas Fremantle was one of the Georgian navy's greatest sea captains it must also be acknowledged that he never quite had the opportunities to touch the same heights as an admiral. From the occasional hints he gave in his letters home it is possible that he was at his happiest as a ship's captain rather than the more 'hands off' role expected of a flag officer. Whatever his personal views, if Fremantle did not make as great a mark as an admiral as he had as a captain it must have been, at least, partially due to having less opportunity to distinguish himself.

When promoted to rear admiral in July 1810 he had just nine years of life left. Of those nine years he spent five of them ashore, either in Swanbourne or travelling around Europe. The other pertinent factor to consider was that when he was promoted to vice admiral and commander-in-chief of the Mediterranean Fleet, peace was declared throughout Europe and the threat of Napoleon was removed to the outer distances of the southern Atlantic.

With the threat removed, the role of admiral became largely ceremonial and administrative, flying the flag, dealing with foreign dignitaries and the seemingly endless inflow of letters and instructions from the Admiralty. The opportunity to shine in battle disappeared and with it the chance to emulate his predecessors such as Nelson, Hood and Jervis. It would be almost 100 years after the death of Fremantle before a Royal Navy fleet once again sailed into battle to fight an enemy fleet.*

Like so many men, Fremantle divided his life into work and home. Indeed, in the case of navy officers, any other course was frankly impossible but in his case the two interacted sufficiently for there to be common threads and there seems to be little doubt that the success of his marriage and close emotional partnership with Betsey made his navy career easier for him to manage. Together with her brother-in-law, William, her close friendship with the Marquess of Buckingham's family kept alive the beneficial influence that the marquess exercised on Fremantle's career and her expert managing of the family estates in Swanbourne gave him little room to worry on that score.

Fremantle was lucky in several respects but it would be doing him a disservice to pretend that his career was successful solely as a result of luck or indeed, of undue influence. His luck was partially timing, in that his career coincided with a period of almost continuous hostilities in Europe and therefore, a period of naval expansion. It was partially as a result of buying a house so close to and becoming part of the 'Buckingham' circle and, partially the luck that all eighteenth-century naval officers needed in staying alive in the incredibly violent and arbitrary world in which he operated. Many talented officers never made it out of their twenties or thirties and therefore never had the opportunities to distinguish themselves as Fremantle did.

All successful careers need elements of luck: being in the right place at the right time, being noticed by a benevolent senior officer or avoiding the shot and shell of battle, not to mention the diseases of the tropics. What counts is how good fortune is turned into success and in this respect Fremantle usually excelled. He was a magnificent seaman with quite uncanny control over the complex world of the heavy, three-masted, square-rigged ships. When so much was dependent on tides, winds and currents, Fremantle proved to be the master of all these elements. No one captain of the age deserves the appellation of 'master mariner' more than Thomas Fremantle. Time and again, when under the greatest pressure and when faced with the most immediate dangers,

---

* In October 1827 a Royal Navy fleet went into battle at Navarino Bay against a fleet from the Ottoman Empire. This, however, was not an exclusively British affair but part of a tripartite force of the UK, Russia and France.

Fremantle managed to manoeuvre his ship with consummate skill to ensure he always gained whatever advantage was available by positioning his vessel at the precise point to inflict the greatest damage while protecting his own ship from being struck by the enemy.

These skills did not just happen, they came from a close and diligent study of his profession, and it was not just in ship handling for he showed the same attention to detail when it came to the equally difficult but vital task of managing up to 750 crew on a battleship, often when away from Britain for months at a time. Managing the large and multinational group of men who made up the crew of a typical British man-of-war was no easy task. Over-reliance on harsh corporal punishment only worked so far and Fremantle was very aware of this fact. Some of the men would have been taken from a life of criminality, others press-ganged or otherwise conned into a life at sea. Whatever their origins, they needed to be welded into a crew who worked together, accepted orders without question and, in the case of able seamen, be intelligent and skilled enough to anticipate what was required and could reef and break out the heavy sails of a warship almost by instinct and as the weather conditions required. This welding together of a crew from such unpromising material could not be done by the threat of physical punishment alone, other factors were needed.

While working in the Admiralty, Fremantle began to turn his mind to the problems of man management, discipline at sea and how the same kind of professional pride that motivated the officer class could be reproduced amongst the non-commissioned ranks. His thoughts were gathered together in two small notebooks, much altered, with deletions, additions and obviously, from the multiplicity of inks used, written over a period of time. They represented his thoughts, experiences and ideals built up from nearly thirty years of seagoing duties.[1]

The opening paragraph read as follows:

In consideration of the very different systems of discipline observed on board His Majesty's ships of war induced me to set out my ideas in paper and although I have not the vanity to imagine that what I have written is worthy of much consideration, still they may from professional practice be someday useful. The following which is the conclusion of a very scarce little piece, inscribed to King Charles I by Thomas Heywood I copy from that interesting publication of Mr Charnock on marine constitutions, it is dated in the Year 1637, and shows that at that period Courts Martial were held on board His Majesty's Ships of War.

Fremantle then moved on to his main idea, which he believed would eradicate some of the inconsistencies of discipline on warships and be more acceptable and transparent to the crews who were subject to the vagaries of the system.

In volume one he elaborated on a system that he wished to see instituted on all His Majesty's warships and which he believed would make the system fairer, be less expensive to administer but, most importantly, would be seen by the men, including the defendant, as being fair. In short, he recognised and articulated that principle of justice that the law should not just be fair but should be seen to be fair. His idea was that all offences where sufficiently petty not to warrant a fleet court martial should be tried by a court of inquiry on board the offender's own vessel by the officers in command of the ship. It was rather like the army system of regimental court martials. He borrowed from the newest navy in the world at that time;

> The United States of America have mostly followed the rules and regulations now in use onboard the King's Ships, but they have wisely adopted Courts Martial on board their ships for small offences. There can be no sort of objection as to the eligibility of the officers to give a just and honest sentence; all officers in the Navy are protestants, and must have served six years before they are qualified to receive a commission, consequently they may without any reflection on the Army, be supposed to have as much experience or more than officers of the same rank, – and why not a ship be considered a garrison?

During his time on board HMS *Ganges* from 1802 to 1803, Fremantle had trialled the type of system that he proposed in his memorandum. Instead of him arbitrarily deciding what punishment should be given he asked the officers to set up mini courts of inquiry in a public place on the ship, usually the gun room, and establish what the facts were and guilt and innocence before punishment was imposed by the captain, if required. He ensured that written records were kept and a fair legal trial system adopted. Because people could see justice being done there would be less gossip around the wardroom table that, via the servants, would often get to the crew and could cause discontent.

Volume two began with his reasons for wishing to change the system and demonstrate fairness:[2]

Although what is contained in the following paper will probably not meet with many advocates among the officers of the Royal Navy who are naturally tenacious of any innovation, of the discipline of the Ships of War, still the subject is so important to my mind that that I shall not be deterred from offering any opinions which are founded on observation as well as the most mature and serious reflection. Every officer must be gratified at knowing precisely the extent of his powers, and the certainty of being supported in the first legal exercise of his authority, as the law and custom of the service stands it is indefinite and the Captain of a man of war is liable to a civil process in Westminster Hall and answerable to Censure by the Admiralty Board or his Commander in chief for following the Custom of the Service in violations of an act of Parliament.

He acknowledged that seamen were more aware of their rights than had previously been the case and were insistent on them being honoured. He therefore argued that a more transparent system would do away with the pernicious habit of men writing anonymous letters to the commander of a fleet complaining of their officers.[*] He added in another ink (therefore presumably added afterwards) that such a system would do away with the source of their complaints.

He was pleased that the Admiralty had discontinued the barbaric practice of 'running the gauntlet' on ships and he used the example to argue why the customs of the navy need to be changed as times and attitudes to authority changed.[**] He pointed out that in his time the practice of running the gauntlet had resulted in the death of some men.

---

[*] Fremantle had been the subject of at least two such letters and probably felt strongly on this subject!

[**] In the Royal Navy, running the gauntlet was used as a punishment for relatively minor offences, such as theft of another sailor's possessions. The condemned rating was pushed between two rows of his fellow seamen and was prevented from rushing by the master-at-arms with a cutlass, at the same time being encouraged forwards by a petty officer. His fellow crew members were equipped with lengths of rope that were plaited into knots known as 'knittles'. These were effectively smaller versions of the cat o' nine tails. The condemned man was often given a dozen lashes from the cat o' nine tails beforehand, so that blows received while running the gauntlet would aggravate the lacerations on his back. This punishment was abolished by order of the British Admiralty in 1806.

The recent trial of the Mate of an Indies man will show more clearly than I have words to express the necessity of abolishing a practice more offensive to the foremast men than any others.

Finally, Fremantle moved on to the social and welfare reasons for treating the men more fairly. He wished to see the petty officer class lifted up and given the same pride in their profession as was enjoyed by the officers. To bring this about he suggested they be allowed more home leave to see their families, which he believed was the reason so many British seamen served with foreign privateers, even those of the enemy. He stressed the importance of petty officers and felt they should wear a badge of distinction rather as sergeants and corporals did in the army. He was insistent that they should not, on any account, be allowed to be struck or be dis-rated except by sentence of a fleet court martial and, in the event of peace, they should be given preference by being placed 'in the Ordinary' or being kept on the ships if so disposed and being adequately provided for after a number of years' service.

In short, Fremantle's ideas were by no means radical but were a practical set of reforms that were all designed to improve the conditions in the navy, improve professionalism and the ability to retain and motivate the workforce. They were ideas that flowed naturally from the earlier ideas instituted by Anson some forty-five years earlier and although the proposals were not adopted during his lifetime, within thirty years of his death all had been adopted by the navy.

While he was a captain his reputation was as a tough disciplinarian but an unbiased study of his record shows he was not as quick to flog as is commonly supposed. His record is that of a fair man, modest by the standards of the time. Capt. Thomas Hardy was notoriously strict in his discipline and had far more sailors flogged than Fremantle ever did. The mutiny that Fremantle experienced on HMS *Inconstant* was a strange affair but was by no means unique. At that stage in the Royal Navy's history there were many such minor uprisings, which culminated in the major mutinies at Spithead and the Nore. These mutinies, however, were rarely about flogging but were more about unfairness, pay and conditions. The publicity and revolutionary ideals that travelled over from France were everywhere in British life and the navy was not immune to the febrile atmosphere.

Fremantle dealt with his crisis of command on HMS *Inconstant* quickly and fairly and it was a tribute to his qualities that, when he called on that same crew just weeks later for extra efforts in the fight against the *Ça Ira*, they responded so magnificently that he was able to plead for, and receive, a pardon for the five ring leaders of the discontent. Together with his Memoranda on Discipline, these acts show a man with a keen sense of practicality and fairness. The views expressed in his draft memoranda were not those of an unthinking petty tyrant who ruled his ship with a rod of iron. Rather, they were the thoughts of someone who had observed life on board a ship carefully and thus was aware of the things that rankled with the crew, and importantly had kept up to date with changing attitudes and aspirations of those he commanded. While he was only too aware of the innate conservatism from his fellow naval officers he still made a cogent argument for change in the hope that it would improve standards in his beloved navy. However, it would be wrong to leave any summary of Fremantle at that point. It is impossible not to look at the other side of the coin, which was his attitude to his senior officers and to authority.

As the evidence shows, he was a fair commanding officer and one who took his crew's interests seriously but, in stark contrast his own attitude to authority, often left a little to be desired. His problems began after his spell under the command of Adm. Nelson at Bastia, Cádiz, Tenerife and Copenhagen. His relationship and regard for Nelson were such that unfortunately all senior officers seemed to fall short in comparison. There is no doubt that after the serious wound he sustained in the assault on Santa Cruz he experienced a great deal of pain for some years. However, this surely does not provide an excuse for his conduct with Adm. Cochrane, where he was rightly forced into a public apology. Was it simply a case that he had become 'too big for his boots' or was it a case of dislike between two individuals driving the junior to acts of childish rebellion? Did his proximity to the Grenville family and the people with political power give him an inflated sense of his own importance? Whatever the reason, or combination of reasons, it was undoubtedly the least attractive part of his personality, especially during his latter years, and did little to enhance his reputation with his professional colleagues.

In his mature years the public face of Fremantle could sometimes be dominated by his irascible nature, bouts of ill humour and the occasional descent into despondency, but behind this public face was a loving husband, a kind and caring father and a man with a keen sense of right and wrong. In most situations, with perhaps some persuasion, his sense of fair play would reassert itself. His predecessor as commander-in-chief of the Mediterranean Fleet, Adm. Sir Charles Penrose, recalled Fremantle near the end of his life talking about Lord Exmouth (Admiral Pellew):[3]

> I know you admire and are a particular friend of Lord Exmouth and therefore, as I am known to dislike him personally very much, I would not mention him could I not say truly that when he had command of the fleet the Admiralty could go to sleep without care. And the noble devotion and skill he took to his station at Algiers would alone immortalise his name.

Sir Charles commented: 'This does honour to both parties' and amply demonstrates that Fremantle was able to see merit in his senior officers when pushed. If there was an overriding reason that caused Fremantle's tetchy relationship with authority it must have been rooted in his own complex and close relationship with Admiral Lord Nelson. It was very much a relationship of hero and acolyte but this relationship was probably mirrored in at least nine or ten other close friends that Nelson had in his 'band of brothers' and did not seem to have caused the same problems with the others. Having made this point, however, it would be wrong not to acknowledge the fact that Fremantle's falling out with senior officers was by no means unique. In a service where a captain's word was law and where big egos were commonplace, tantrums, arguments and long-running feuds were everyday facets of navy life.

Despite the drawbacks of Fremantle's intense response to Nelson's leadership, he certainly learned a great deal from him. Fremantle's campaign in the Adriatic from late 1812 to 1814 was a brilliant exhibition of Nelson-inspired tactics. The amphibious nature of much of the campaign with sailors fighting equally well on land and sea, the close co-operation Fremantle had with the army, use of ships' cannons as shore-based artillery and the reliance on the good sense and the initiative of junior captains, was exactly how his great hero would have conducted the campaign.

Following the death of Nelson, Fremantle seemed to believe that no one else was fit to take the admiral's place. Whether he thought that he was the natural successor, or whether he was looking for a replacement in the succession of senior officers who followed and was disappointed, is hard to say. Whatever the truth, it seemed difficult for him to adjust to naval life after Nelson's death. With the ending of the Napoleonic regime differing skills were required. Nelson was never the reforming admiral, working through the corridors of power in Whitehall, as Anson had done. His natural métier was the heat and hell of a sea battle and as Fremantle reached the latter stages of his career that aspect of his hero's genius became increasingly irrelevant.

Nevertheless, whatever Fremantle's strengths and weaknesses it was obvious to all, including the Admiralty, that the former far outweighed the latter. When William Fremantle wrote to the First Lord of the Admiralty after his brother's death to solicit his help in looking after the prospects of his nephews Charles and Henry, he received the following reply from Lord Melville:[4]

> It will be most satisfactory to me, though it will be a melancholy satisfaction, whenever an opportunity shall be afforded to me of advancing your nephews in their professional career ... In perusing last night the list of Flag Officers, I could not help feeling how large a blank the loss of your brother has left in the efficient portion of them.

If Fremantle's contribution had only been his naval service it would have been an impressive CV but it was not his only mark on life for in his marriage, and his stewardship of the village in which he lived, he was to make two further contributions that would far outlive his own abbreviated life.

When Fremantle purchased a house in Swanbourne he could little have dreamed that more than 200 years later his descendants would still be living in the same place and that they would still be taking the same interest in the inhabitants of Swanbourne as he and Betsey had all those years ago.

Since the purchase of the original house by Sir Thomas in 1798, successive members of the family have added to the family holdings. Additional farms, tenants and a new family house have all been added to the estate such that by the start of the twentieth century a great deal of Swanbourne and its environs were in the family's ownership.

This pastoral care for Swanbourne was not to be Fremantle's only contribution to the future. Of greater national importance was the contribution made by the dynasty he founded. Of course, it would be nonsensical to record the achievements of his progeny as being directly attributable to Thomas Fremantle, neither is it intended that this book should be the story of the Fremantle dynasty. If it were to be so it would be twice its current length. Nevertheless, the spirit and example of Thomas as the patriarch of the family, and how this affected his descendants, is surely a part of this remarkable man's life.

To date, there have been eight other Fremantles, all descended directly from Thomas, who have commanded a Royal Navy warship, of which four (including Thomas) rose to be admirals and all of whom were made Knights Grand Cross of the Order of the Bath (GCB).* However, the list of credits does not end there, for politics, the army, the Church, the arts and the sporting field have all benefitted from contributions made by the Fremantle family.

Betsey and Thomas Fremantle were blessed with a fruitful marriage. In all they had nine children, albeit their daughter Louisa died aged just 5. There were five sons, Thomas Francis, Charles Howe, Henry Hyde, William Robert and Stephen Grenville. Together these boys and their offspring were to ensure that the Fremantle family were to carry on and make a huge contribution, not just to Buckinghamshire life but to the nation as a whole.

Their eldest son, also called Thomas Francis, was arguably the least influenced by his father, who had been absent for so many of his formative years. The chief male influence over Thomas was his uncle, William. It should therefore be no surprise that, after being educated at Eton and Oxford, he would choose politics as his career. Some two years after the death of his father the King created him a baronet in recognition of his father's service. He also held the honorary title of a Baron of the Austrian Empire, inherited from his father, neither of which prevented him taking up a seat in the House of Commons, which he did in 1826 when he inherited the seat for Buckingham from his uncle, William.

Two years before becoming an MP he married Louisa Elizabeth Nugent. In a scene reminiscent of his father's matrimonial preliminaries, he was initially refused by her father, Sir George Nugent, unless

---

* The eight other members of the family are Adm. Sir Charles Howe Fremantle, Capt. Stephen Fremantle, Adm. Sir Edmund Fremantle, Adm. Sir Sydney Fremantle, Capt. Charles Fremantle, Cdr Edmond S.D. Fremantle, Cdr John Tapling Cottesloe (the current Lord Cottesloe) and Cdr Charles Fremantle.

his family contributed more. Eventually the matter was settled and the couple were married on 24 November 1824. It proved to be a marriage every bit as successful as that of his parents, producing five sons and six daughters. The size of the family and the recognition that they were moving up in society encouraged Thomas to build a new house for the family known as Swanbourne House, a far grander establishment than his father's house, known to all as the Old House, and one that was to cause his mother some disquiet as she considered it far too expensive.*

Thomas's political career proved successful for he soon moved up from the backbenches to play a prominent role in Sir Robert Peel's government. His first ministerial post was as Financial Secretary to the Treasury, a post he held between 1834 and 1835. He subsequently served as Parliamentary Secretary to the Treasury between 1841 and 1844, before being promoted to the full Cabinet as Secretary at War between 1844 and 1845 and as Chief Secretary for Ireland between 1845 and 1846. He became a Privy Counsellor in 1844 but finally left the House of Commons in 1846 to be appointed firstly as deputy chairman and subsequently as chairman of the Board of Customs, where he served between 1846 and 1874. Following his retirement from the Board of Customs he was elevated to the peerage in recognition of his services as Baron Cottesloe of Swanbourne and Hardwick in the County of Buckingham.

Lord Cottesloe's wife, Louisa, died in August 1875 but her husband lived on for another fifteen years, dying in December 1890, at the grand age of 92. He was succeeded in his titles by his eldest son, who had also been christened Thomas Francis.

Thomas Francis (the second Baron Cottesloe) was born on 30 January 1830 and like his father he initially built himself a career in politics. He entered Parliament via his father's old constituency, Buckingham, where he replaced the ennobled Benjamin Disraeli, and held the seat for nine years. He had already married by the time he became an MP, to Lady Augusta Henrietta Scott, daughter of Lord Eldon. He never rose to the political heights scaled by his father, apparently putting a lot of his energies into business rather than politics. He became a director of the London, Brighton and South Coast Railway in January 1868 and from 1896 until his retirement in February 1908 he served as chairman of the board.

---

* Swanbourne House still stands and is now a co-educational prep school.

By the time he retired from his active business role his wife had already died, but Thomas was to live on for another twelve years, finally dying aged 88 in 1918.

The third Baron Cottesloe was again christened Thomas Francis and inherited the title aged 56. He had a lifelong devotion to the armed forces and as well as commanding the Territorial Army he was also an honorary colonel of the Buckinghamshire battalion of the Oxfordshire Light Infantry. He was an expert rifle shot, publishing books on the subject and serving on the War Office Small Arms Committee. As a marksman he was good enough to represent his country for twenty-seven years and was the captain of the English team from 1920 until his death in July 1956. He also competed in the 1,000-yard free rifle shooting at the 1908 summer Olympics held in London.*

Tragically, his eldest son, Thomas Francis Halford Fremantle, was killed during the First World War on 17 October 1915. He served in France with 'C' Company of the 5th Battalion of the Oxford and Bucks Light Infantry and had joined the regiment direct from Eton College. He had been serving for just over a year before he was killed.

It was therefore a break with tradition, in more ways than one, when the third Lord Cottesloe was succeeded by his second son. For the first time the title was to be held by someone not called Thomas; more significantly, John Walgrave Halford Fremantle was the first one of the family to make a major contribution to the arts rather than the military or political facets of the British nation. He was educated at Eton and Trinity College, Cambridge, where he rowed twice in the Boat Race, in 1921 and 1922, both times in a winning Cambridge eight.

Later in life, from 1960 to 1965, Lord Cottesloe served as chairman of the Arts Council of Great Britain. Taking over from Sir Kenneth Clarke, he piloted through the controversial South Bank Centre and the Cottesloe Theatre was named in his honour.** Following his death in 1994 he was succeeded by his eldest son, the Hon. John Tapling Fremantle, the current and fifth Baron Cottesloe.

Curiously, although there have been many Fremantles who have been naval officers since Sir Thomas, it was not until the fifth Baron Cottesloe

---

* He finished sixteenth in the individual event but Britain still managed to win the gold and bronze medals.

** The Cottesloe Theatre was recently renamed the Dorfman Theatre.

joined the navy in 1945 that one of the eldest sons and inheritors of the title had pursued a career in the senior service. He joined the navy direct from Eton and, having passed out top of his year's intake from Eaton Hall in Chester,* his first commission as an acting sub-lieutenant was to HMS *Concord* in the navy's Far East station. It was on this ship that Acting Sub-Lt the Hon. John Fremantle was to play a role in an event that was to go down in British naval history.[5]

During a routine trip up the Yangste River, a Royal Navy frigate, HMS *Amethyst*, had been fired upon by Chinese communist forces, which had caused considerable damage to the vessel and killed and wounded many of the crew. Among those killed was the ship's commanding officer, Lt Cdr Bernard Skinner. Thanks to the bridge receiving most of the hits from the nationalist artillery, the helmsman, who was badly wounded, lost control and the vessel went aground on a sandbank. There the vessel was stuck fast while international negotiations began to try to ensure the safe passage of the vessel out of the river. With the British rightly refusing to concede that they had a) fired first, and b) had not received permission from the Chinese government to sail up the Yangste, the situation looked to be a stalemate.

Eventually, HMS *Amethyst* was able to refloat herself and under the command of the naval attaché, Lt Cdr J. Kerans, she made her bid for freedom. On the night of 30 July 1949 she slipped her chains and, under cover of a Chinese merchant ship, which was also going downriver at that time, she began the 100-mile trip to the mouth of the river. HMS *Concord*, navigated by Sub-Lt Fremantle, sailed up river to Wusong and Baoshan where hostile artillery forts were known to exist to suppress the communist artillery and to offer assistance to HMS *Amethyst*.

To this day, Lord Cottesloe has perfect recall of that night, despite the sixty-six year gap. The perils of navigating up the river with its shifting sandbanks, listening to the echo sounder constantly to ensure there was sufficient water, was a feat of seamanship of which one instinctively feels his great-great-great-grandfather would have approved. At 5.30 a.m. on the morning of 31 July, HMS *Amethyst* was spotted by the lookouts on HMS *Concord* and the two vessels proceeded back down the river, sailing out of the mouth of the Yangste some two hours later.

---

* In 1943, Britannia Royal Naval College, Dartmouth, was bombed. It moved to Eaton Hall, Chester, where it continued to train regular officers for the Royal Navy until 1946.

Later in his career, and after promotion, Cdr Fremantle captained HMS *Palliser* during the first Cod War with Iceland. Again, in this curious anomaly of a non-shooting war, he was to demonstrate his seamanship as the larger British ships tried to interpose themselves between the small Icelandic fishery protection boats and the British trawlers fishing in waters off Iceland that the Icelandic government had declared as part of its exclusive economic zone and over which it claimed exclusive fishing rights. He left the navy in 1966 with the rank of commander, a fact still fondly recognised by the inhabitants of Swanbourne, who refer to their landlord as the 'Commander'.

To return to Adm. Sir Thomas Fremantle, however, it is perhaps worth exploring the claim made in the title. Was Fremantle really Nelson's 'right hand man' or were there others more worthy of such a title? Nelson's closest naval friends and the ones he was mostly associated with were probably Troubridge, Hardy, Berry, Collingwood and Fremantle. In addition to these five officers there were the Battle of the Nile captains, the original 'band of brothers' so dubbed by Nelson himself. Each had a claim to have occupied a close role in Nelson's professional life and, more importantly, were also emotionally close to him, but it is to one of the above named that the honour would surely be bestowed, if at all.

Thomas Troubridge was probably Nelson's first real friend in the navy. He served with him throughout his early years on the East Indian station. Troubridge's career eventually took him to the Admiralty where his personal antipathy to Emma Hamilton led Nelson to believe that Troubridge was conniving with the First Sea Lord in securing him postings that ensured his separation from her. Thus, the once close friendship broke down with acrimonious exchanges of correspondence. If anyone was to be honoured as Nelson's right hand then it was, almost certainly, not Troubridge.

Capt. Thomas Hardy served as Nelson's flag captain on several of Nelson's flagships including, most famously, HMS *Victory* where Hardy was at Nelson's side during his last minutes of life. Hardy's views on crew discipline probably precluded him from being a true soulmate of Nelson but there are several examples, despite their different approach to crew matters, where the two men appeared to be close even if one discounts the emotional last scenes of Nelson's life. What differentiated the two men and probably excluded Hardy from Nelson's closest circle was his taciturn nature and self-containment when compared to Nelson's more outgoing and emotional nature. While this made Hardy the ideal junior partner and foil to Nelson it did not bring the two men close and for this reason Hardy was probably not the closest confidante of Nelson.

Trafalgar was also notable for the part that Adm. Collingwood played, not just because he took over from his commanding officer after he was killed but also the extremely gallant part he played in leading the lee column into battle. Nevertheless, despite the kindly and friendly way that Nelson always dealt with Collingwood, there was always the feeling that the north countryman's natural taciturnity kept him from being a real friend to Nelson. Nelson liked men who would sit down with him over a dinner table and discuss naval subjects, offer suggestions, perhaps disagree with his admiral and offer counter-suggestions. This was not Collingwood's way and, although he was an extremely valued colleague, he was never a close, emotional friend.[6]

But surely Sir Edward Berry was deserving of the title? After all, had not Nelson introduced Berry to the King by describing him as his 'right hand man'. However, Berry was no great officer, lacking the intellect, initiative and seaman skills to make a really outstanding flag officer. What he did have in bucket loads was courage. He was always first when it came to meeting the enemy in hand-to-hand combat and there were few qualities that Nelson admired more in a man. Because of his shortcomings, however, there is always the suspicion that Nelson treated Berry as a favoured schoolboy and did not take him wholly seriously. Nevertheless, after Nelson was wounded at the Battle of the Nile it was Berry, as his flag captain, who looked after him and later Nelson wrote to him thanking him for his kindness and saying, 'I shall never forget your support for my mind.'[7]

It had been Berry, however, when serving as Nelson's flag captain on HMS *Vanguard*, who had nearly deposited both the admiral and his flagship on to the rocky and treacherous shore of Sardinia. Had it not been for the timely intervention of Capt. Ball on HMS *Alexander* taking them under tow, that would have been the probable outcome. There remained, however, a cheerful and almost paternal friendship between Nelson and Berry, albeit probably not a true meeting of minds.

Fremantle served with Nelson at Bastia, Tenerife (Santa Cruz), Copenhagen and Trafalgar. He had been as close and supportive of the charismatic admiral as any man could be. Indeed, this had been recognised by the other captains serving in the squadron at Santa Cruz where, because of the unique relationship between Fremantle and Nelson, they had deputed him to represent their views as to whether or not to continue the action. Again at Copenhagen, Fremantle was ordered to anchor next to Nelson and was called on to the flagship even before the firing had ceased. In the negotiations with the Danish authorities, which took place immediately after the battle, it was Fremantle who accompanied Nelson as he negotiated the ceasefire.

Perhaps equally as important were the lessons Fremantle learned from Nelson. When he had served as a junior frigate captain within Nelson's squadron operating around Corsica, Fremantle had shown early signs of immaturity by referring decisions to his squadron commander that he, with greater self-confidence, may well have taken himself. He soon learned the Nelson 'way' and in later years no Royal Navy captain, nor admiral, showed a greater degree of control of Nelson-type tactics and methods of waging war than did Fremantle. In the littoral warfare fought by Fremantle along the northern and eastern coasts of the Adriatic he showed all the hallmarks of his illustrious mentor.

Fremantle had as good a claim as any man to the title of Nelson's 'right hand' but was it a title that could justifiably be claimed by any single man? When Nelson was chosen by the Admiralty to command the Mediterranean Fleet, immediately prior to the Battle of Trafalgar, the newly appointed First Lord of the Admiralty, Lord Barham, offered him the captains of his choice. Nelson refused to change any of them on the grounds that they were all motivated by the same offensive spirit and as such he did not wish to choose between them. As a great leader of men Nelson knew only too well that he could not get too close to any one officer or group without weakening his command over them all.

Despite this, Nelson was mortal and like all men needed reassurance and people around him who fed his ego. This was Emma Hamilton's great strength and provides the main reason for her tight hold over his affections. But he also needed the reassurance and the support of his peers and it is in this role that Fremantle played so pivotally in his life. An example was provided by a letter Fremantle wrote to Nelson shortly before the Battle of Trafalgar in August 1805:[8]

You will on your arrival in England find everyone disposed to do you entire credit, and at no period according to my judgement did you ever stand higher in the estimation of the public, and indeed we are much in want of all the ability the country can find.

Nelson undoubtedly relied on such reassurance. In the claustrophobic world of an eighteenth-century warship and with the awesome pressures of wartime command he needed someone to converse with, someone he could discuss ideas with but, most of all, someone who boosted his self-esteem and valued his immense talents. In this respect Fremantle was the ideal friend; from the days of their first co-operation in the fighting around Corsica, Italy and the Baltic, before eventually reaching their climax in the waters off Cape Trafalgar, Fremantle was by his side playing the loyal aide's role to perfection.

However, it would be a mistake to see Fremantle as an adjunct of Nelson and by so doing suggest that without Nelson's career there would have been no Fremantle career. In an age of naval brilliance and British domination of the seas, when the pool of talented naval officers was second to none, Fremantle's brilliance and command of naval warfare still shone brightly. His total understanding of the subtleties of complex battle ships, their tactics and their crews, plus his enormous physical and moral courage, all combined to ensure him a place at the top table of the navy's brightest stars in his own right.

He was also a man with political clout and contacts, not just throughout the British corridors of power, but also around the Mediterranean. When he was appointed to the post of commander-in-chief of the Mediterranean Fleet he was uniquely qualified to take on the post and it would not have taken too great a leap of imagination, had his life been prolonged, to believe that he would have made an excellent First Lord of the Admiralty. His thoughts set down in his notebooks while he was working at the Admiralty show a reformer who would not have been scared to take on the vested interests, who he believed held back desirable reforms to the navy that he loved so much.

Judging what might have happened had Thomas Fremantle lived on is nugatory. There are surely sufficient accomplishments to place him among that pantheon of naval officers jostling for position just below Lord Nelson. Without these men the victories at the Nile, Cape St Vincent, Copenhagen and, most gloriously, at Trafalgar would have been impossible. There is no marked grave now in existence for Adm. Thomas Fremantle but his name and reputation are engraved irreducibly in the annals of Royal Naval history. That is surely sufficient memorial for any man.

NOTES

Chapter 1

1 *The War that Ended Peace*, Margaret MacMillan, Profile Books, 2014, p.104.
2 *Napoleon*, Georges Lefebvre, Folio Press, p.86.
3 *Iron Admirals: Naval Leadership in the Twentieth Century*, Ronald Andidora, Greenwood Publishing, 2000, p.3.
4 *The Navy as I Have Known It*, Admiral Sir Edmund Fremantle, Cassell & Co. Ltd, 1908, pp.458–9.
5 *The Trafalgar Companion*, Mark Adkin, Aurum Press Ltd, 2005, p.137.
6 *Empire of the Deep*, Ben Wilson, Weidenfeld & Nicolson, 2013, p.301.
7 *Britain Against Napoleon: The Organisation of Victory 1793–1815*, Roger Knight, Allen Lane, 2013, p.93.

Chapter 2

1 *A Fremantle Chronicle*, David R. Fremantle, published for private circulation by the Poets' and Painters' Press, 1983, p.10.
2 *Fremantle Chronicle*, Fremantle, p.13.
3 *Fremantle Chronicle*, Fremantle, p.14.
4 *The Wynne Diaries Vol. II*, edited by Anne Fremantle, Oxford University Press, 1940, p.233.
5 *The Admirals Fremantle*, Ann Parry, Chatto & Windus, 1971, p.11.
6 *Admirals Fremantle*, Parry, Part I (Foreword).
7 *Admirals Fremantle*, Parry, p.11.
8 *Nelson's Navy 1793–1815 (12th ed., Vol. 1)*, Brian Lavery, Conway Press, 1989.
9 *Personal Narrative of Events from 1799–1815*, Wm S. Lovell, with anecdotes published by Wm Allen & Co. of London in 1879 (Second edition), pp.4–5.
10 Doc Ref 89/85/206 folio 590 Martinho de Mello e Castro to R. Walpole, Doc Ref SP89/85/211 Folio 590 Martinho de Mello e Castro to R. Walpole, Folio 603 R. Walpole to Ares de Sá e Mello ref 89/85/205 Folio 588 R. Walpole to Viscount Weymouth, National Archives, Kew.
11 CNN News, 13 January 2013.

12 *Thrilling Narratives of Mutiny, Murder and Piracy*, Hurst & Co. of New York, 1870.
13 D-FR 151/37, TFF Service Record, Centre for Buckinghamshire Studies.
14 *Nelson's Navy, The Ships, Men and Organisation*, Brian Lavery, Conway Publishing, 2012, p.96.
15 *Nelson's Navy*, Lavery, p.93.
16 ADM6/22/534 Officers service records, National Archives, Kew.
17 D/FR/151/37, TFF Service Record, Centre for Buckinghamshire Studies.

Chapter 3

1 D-FR general naval papers used by Ann Parry for *The Admirals Fremantle*, Centre for Buckinghamshire Studies.
2 *Ibid.*
3 *Ibid.*
4 *Ibid.*
5 D/FR/151/37, TFF Service Record, Centre for Buckinghamshire Studies.
6 D-FR general naval papers used by Parry for *Admirals Fremantle*.

Chapter 4

1 The Logbook of HMS Tartar ADM/52/3104, The Caird Library, National Maritime Museum.
2 *The Dispatches and Letters of Lord Nelson* (Vol. II), edited by Sir Nicholas Harris Nicolas, Chatham Publishing, 1997, p.349.
3 Nelson to Udny AGC/18/3, Caird Library, National Maritime Museum, 24 February 1794.
4 *Dispatches and Letters* (Vol. II), Nicolas (ed.), pp.357–8.
5 Sir Gilbert Elliot's Journal, ELL/162, Caird Library, National Maritime Museum.
6 Letter from Hood to D'Aubant, dated 24 March 1794, Hoo/9, Caird Library, National Maritime Museum.
7 *Admirals Fremantle*, Parry, pp.29–31.
8 *The Wynne Diaries*, edited by Ann Fremantle, Oxford University Press, 1937, p.252.
9 Letter to William Fremantle, dated 1 July 1795, *The Admirals Fremantle*, Ann Parry, Chatto & Windus, 1971, p.32.
10 Letter from Pollard to Nelson enclosing financial accounts, dated 7/1/1797, Ref. CRK/10, Caird Library, National Maritime Museum.
11 Court Martial papers 1795, January–June, National Archives.
12 FRE/02, Centre for Buckinghamshire Studies.
13 Letter of 24 March 1795, *The Admirals Fremantle*, Ann Parry, Chatto & Windus, 1971, p.36.
14 'Vice Admiral Hotham's Dispatch', *Dispatches and Letters* (Vol. II), Nicolas (ed.), p.13 (footnote).
15 *Dispatches and Letters* (Vol. II), Nicolas (ed.), pp.12–13.
16 Ref D/FR/235/1 Folio 50, Centre for Buckinghamshire Studies.
17 D/FR/33/11, letter from Hotham to Fremantle, Centre for Buckinghamshire Studies.

Notes

Chapter 5

1 *Admirals Fremantle*, Parry, p.37.
2 *Admirals Fremantle*, Parry, p.38.
3 Log of HMS *Inconstant* 26 August 1795, Ref FRE/3, Caird Library, National Maritime Museum.
4 Order Book D/FR 235/1 Folio 74, Centre for Buckinghamshire Studies.
5 'Nelson's dispatch of 27/8/95 to Admiral Hotham', *Dispatches and Letters* (Vol. II), Nicolas (ed.), p.73.
6 *Empire of the Deep: The Rise and Fall of the British Navy*, Ben Wilson, Weidenfeld & Nicholson, 2013, p.395.
7 *London Gazette*, dated Saturday, 28 May–Tuesday, 31 May, 1796, p.528.
8 *The Wynne Diaries: The Adventures of Two Sisters in Napoleonic Europe*, edited by Anne Fremantle, Oxford University Press, 1952, Preface.
9 Ref. D/FR/235/ 1 Folio 40, Centre for Buckinghamshire Studies.
10 *London Gazette*, Number 13924, Saturday, 20 August–Tuesday, 23 August 1796, pp.802–3.
11 *London Gazette*, Number 13924, Saturday, 20 August–Tuesday, 23 August 1796, p.802.
12 *Dispatches and Letters* (Vol. II), Nicolas (ed.), pp.195–6.
13 *The Wynne Diaries Vol. II 1794–1798*, edited by Anne Fremantle, Oxford University Press, 1937, p.97.
14 *Wynne Diaries Vol. II*, Fremantle (ed.), p.98.
15 *Admirals Fremantle*, Parry, pp.41–2.
16 *Wynne Diaries Vol. II*, Fremantle (ed.), p.222.
17 *Nelson: A Dream of Glory*, John Sugden, Jonathon Cape, 2004, p.637.
18 *Admirals Fremantle*, Parry, pp.42–3.
19 D/FR/235/1 Folio 47, Centre for Buckinghamshire Studies.
20 *Admirals Fremantle*, Parry, p.43.
21 *Admirals Fremantle*, Parry, p.45.
22 Ref. ADM 1/395, Letters from the C-in-C Mediterranean, 1796, National Archives Kew.
23 *Wynne Diaries Vol. II*, Fremantle (ed.), p.126.
24 *Admirals Fremantle*, Parry, p.47.
25 *Wynne Diaries Vol. II*, Fremantle (ed.), p.146.
26 Letter from TFF to WF, dated 2 March 1797, *The Admirals Fremantle*, Ann Parry, Chatto & Windus, 1971, p.47.
27 *Dispatches and Letters* (Vol. II), Nicolas (ed.), p.384.
28 *Nelson*, Sugden, p.741.
29 *Wynne Diaries Vol. III*, Fremantle (ed.), p.282.
30 *Dispatches and Letters* (Vol. II), Nicolas (ed.), pp.403–5.
31 *Wynne Diaries Vol. II*, Fremantle (ed.), p.183.
32 *1797: Nelson's Year of Destiny*, Colin White, Royal Naval Museum Publications, 2001, p.10.
33 *1797*, White, p.100.
34 *1797*, White, p.109.
35 *1797*, White, p.101.
36 *1797: Nelson's Year of Destiny*, Colin White, Sutton Publishing, 1998, p.109.

37 *Wynne Diaries Vol. II*, Fremantle (ed.), pp.184–5.
38 National Maritime Museum, Caird Library, MON/1/7 Monsarrat Collection – Vol. I, letter from Nelson to Sir Andrew Snape Hamond, controller of the Navy, Bath, 8 September 1797.
39 *Wynne Diaries Vol. II*, Fremantle (ed.), p.185.
40 National Maritime Museum, Caird Library, MON/1/7 Monsarrat Collection – Vol. I, letter from Nelson to Sir Andrew Snape Hamond, controller of the Navy, Bath, 8 September 1797.
41 *Letters and Dispatches*, Harris Nicolas (ed.), p.435.
42 Journal of Surgeon HMS *Theseus*, Ref. ADM 101/123/2, National Archives, Kew.
43 *Ibid.*
44 *Wynne Diaries Vol. II*, Fremantle (ed.), p.189.
45 Letter from Marquess of Buckingham to W.H. Fremantle, dated October 1797, Ref. D-FR/46/7 Folio 1, Centre for Buckinghamshire Studies.
46 *Ibid.*
47 *Wynne Diaries Vol. II*, Fremantle (ed.), p.191.
48 *Wynne Diaries Vol. II*, Fremantle (ed.), p.191.
49 *The Wynne Diaries Vol. III 1798–1820*, edited by Anne Fremantle, Oxford University Press, 1940, p.1.
50 *Wynne Diaries Vol. III*, Fremantle (ed.), p.10.
51 *Wynne Diaries Vol. III*, Fremantle (ed.), p.13.

Chapter 6

1   D/FR33/11 Fremantle papers, Centre for Buckinghamshire Studies.
2   *Britannia's Realm: A History of the British Merchant Navy*, Richard Woodman, The History Press, p.193.
3   *The Battle of Copenhagen*, pamphlet written by Nicholas Tracy for The 1805 Club, dated 2003, p.3.
4   *Wynne Diaries Vol. III*, Fremantle (ed.), p.20.
5   *Wynne Diaries Vol. III*, Fremantle (ed.), pp.21–2.
6   *Swanbourne Enclosures 1762–63*, Swanbourne Village History Society, courtesy of Ken Harris.
7   Letters between Lt Rice and Capt. Fremantle, Ref. D-FR/31/5, Centre for Buckinghamshire Studies.
8   *Wynne Diaries Vol. III*, Fremantle (ed.), p.28.
9   *The Dispatches and Letters of Lord Nelson*, edited by Sir Nicholas Harris Nicolas, Chatham Publishing, 1998, pp.290–1.
10 *Dispatches and Letters*, Nicolas (ed.), p.291 (Notes).
11 *Wynne Diaries Vol. III*, Fremantle (ed.), p.29.
12 *Who's Who in Nelson's Navy*, Nicholas Tracy, Chatham Publishing, 2006, p.257.
13 *Admirals Fremantle*, Parry, pp.53–4.
14 *Dispatches and Letters*, Nicolas (ed.), pp.295–6.
15 *Wynne Diaries Vol. III*, Fremantle (ed.), p.37.
16 *Wynne Diaries Vol. III*, Fremantle (ed.), pp.45–7.
17 *Nelson's Band of Brothers*, Peter Hore, Seaforth Publishing in association with The 1805 Club, 2015, p.59.

18 *Dispatches and Letters* (Vol. IV), Nicolas (ed.).
19 *The Life of Nelson*, Robert Southey, Frederick Warne & Co., 1813, p.250.
20 *Life of Nelson*, Southey, p.250.
21 *Wynne Diaries Vol. III*, Fremantle (ed.), p.41.
22 *Dispatches and Letters* (Vol. IV), Nicolas (ed.), pp.315–6.
23 *Dispatches and Letters* (Vol. IV), Nicolas (ed.), p.316.
24 *Wynne Diaries Vol. III*, Fremantle (ed.), pp.42–4.
25 *Wynne Diaries Vol. III*, Fremantle (ed.), p.48.
26 Letter of 23 May 1801 from Fremantle to Nelson on the *Ganges* at Bornholm, Ref. CRK/5/folio 111, National Maritime Museum.
27 *Wynne Diaries Vol. III*, Fremantle (ed.), p.57.
28 *Admirals Fremantle*, Parry, p.37,
29 *Wynne Diaries Vol. III*, Fremantle (ed.), p.52.
30 *Wynne Diaries Vol. III*, Fremantle (ed.), p.63.
31 Letters from Lt Rice to Captain Fremantle, Ref. D/FR/31/5, Centre for Buckinghamshire Studies.
32 *Ibid.*
33 *Ibid.*
34 *Wynne Diaries Vol. III*, Fremantle (ed.), pp.82–3.
35 Letter from Fremantle to Nelson January 1804, Ref. CRK/5/112, Caird Library, National Maritime Museum.
36 *Dispatches and Letters* (Vol. V), Nicolas (ed.), p.341.
37 *Wynne Diaries Vol. III*, Fremantle (ed.), p.128.
38 *Wynne Diaries Vol. III*, Fremantle (ed.), p.117.
39 'Fremantle as an MP', paper by J.M. Collinge.
40 *Wynne Diaries Vol. III*, Fremantle (ed.), p.107.
41 *Wynne Diaries Vol. III*, Fremantle (ed.), p.133.
42 Letter from Adm. Cochrane to Admiralty, Ref. D-FR/31/15, dated 26 October 1804, Centre for Buckinghamshire Studies.
43 *Ibid.*
44 Letter from Admiralty to Captain T.F. Fremantle, dated 24 November 1804, Ref. D-FR/31/15, Centre for Buckinghamshire Studies.
45 *Wynne Diaries Vol. III*, Fremantle (ed.), p.148.
46 Website: http://www.historyofparliamentonline.org/volume/1790-1820/member/cochrane-%28afterwards-cochrane-johnstone-%29-hon-andrew-james-1767-1833.
47 *Wynne Diaries Vol. III*, Fremantle (ed.), p.150.

Chapter 7

1 *In the Hour of Victory*, Sam Willis, Atlantic Books, 2013, p.278.
2 *London Gazette*, Number 15858 [1365], 'Dispatch from Vice Admiral Collingwood', dated Wednesday, 6 November 1805, printed by Andrew Strahan.
3 'The Battle of Trafalgar', Sir Humphrey le Fleming Senhouse KCH CB, then acting Lieutenant on HMS *Conqueror*, *Macmillan Magazine*, Vol. LXXXI, https:www//openlibrary.org.
4 ADD/MSS/1374 account of the Battle of Trafalgar by Midshipman W.S. Badcock, West Sussex Records Office.

5 *Wynne Diaries Vol. III*, Fremantle (ed.), pp.221–2.
6 *Wynne Diaries Vol. III*, Fremantle (ed.), p.228.
7 D-FR transcripts of correspondence used by Ann Parry in writing *The Admirals Fremantle*, dated 1810–14, Centre for Buckinghamshire Studies.
8 MS 54/013, letter from Lieutenant George Hooper of HMS *Neptune* to Miss Sybilla Shanach, dated 31 October 1805, Ref. BG/7/H/9, Caird Library, National Maritime Museum.
9 *Wynne Diaries Vol. III*, Fremantle (ed.), p.239.

Chapter 8

1 *William Pitt the Younger*, William Hague, Harper Collins, 2004, p.582.
2 *Wynne Diaries Vol. III*, Fremantle (ed.), pp.289–90.
3 *Ibid.*
4 *Wynne Diaries Vol. III*, Fremantle (ed.), p.304.
5 *Wynne Diaries Vol. III*, Fremantle (ed.), p.305.
6 *Life and Correspondence of John, Earl of St Vincent, Vol. 2*, Edward Pelham Brenton, reprinted on demand in the USA, p.40.
7 *Britain Against Napoleon: The Organisation of Victory 1793–1815*, Roger Knight, Allan Lane, 2013, p.36.
8 *Lord Grenville 1759–1834*, Peter Jupp, Oxford University Press, 1985, p.412.
9 Letter from TFF to WHF, FRE/1, Centre for Buckinghamshire Studies.
10 *Wynne Diaries Vol. III*, Fremantle (ed.), p.311.
11 *Ibid.*
12 D/FR 32/7/22, Centre for Buckinghamshire Studies.

Chapter 9

1 ADM/50/139, Caird Library, National Maritime Museum.
2 Letter from Adm. T.F. Fremantle to Sir William Fremantle, Port Mahon, on board HMS *Ville de Paris*, dated 12 October 1810, Ref. FRE/1 and FRE/3 – Sundry Naval Correspondence, Sir Fremantle 1765–1819 – Caird Library, National Maritime Museum.
3 *Wynne Diaries Vol. III*, Fremantle (ed.), p.328.
4 D-FR/235/5, Correspondence from TFF, Centre for Buckinghamshire Studies.
5 *Wynne Diaries Vol. III*, Fremantle (ed.), p.329.
6 D-FR transcripts of correspondence used by Ann Parry in writing *The Admirals Fremantle*, dated 1810–14, Centre for Buckinghamshire Studies.
7 *Ibid.*
8 Letter from Adm. T.F. Fremantle to Sir William Fremantle, on board HMS *Ville de Paris* 1 March 1811, Ref. FRE/1 and FRE/3 – Sundry Naval Correspondence, Sir Fremantle 1765–1819 – Caird Library, National Maritime Museum.
9 D-FR transcripts of correspondence used by Ann Parry in writing *The Admirals Fremantle*, dated 1810–14, Centre for Buckinghamshire Studies.
10 *Ibid.*
11 Letter from Adm. Pellew to T.F. Fremantle, Ref. D-FR/235/4, dated 12 August 1811, Centre for Buckinghamshire Studies.
12 *Admirals Fremantle*, Parry, p.88.

13 Letter from Adm. Pellew to T.F. Fremantle, Ref. D-FR/235/4, dated 1811, Centre for Buckinghamshire Studies.

14 Orders from Adm. Edward Pellew to Adm T.F. Fremantle from HMS *Hibernia*, dated 1 August 1811, Ref. FRE/1 and FRE/3 – Sundry Naval Correspondence, Sir Fremantle 1765–1819 – Caird Library, National Maritime Museum.

15 D-FR transcripts of correspondence used by Ann Parry in writing *The Admirals Fremantle*, dated 1810–14, Centre for Buckinghamshire Studies.

16 Letter from William Fremantle to Fremantle, dated 15 August 1811, Ref. FRE/1 and FRE/3 – Sundry Naval Correspondence, Sir Fremantle 1765–1819 – Caird Library, National Maritime Museum.

17 D-FR transcripts of correspondence used by Ann Parry in writing *The Admirals Fremantle*, dated 1810–14, Centre for Buckinghamshire Studies.

18 Letter from W. Fremantle to T.F. Fremantle, dated 22 October 1811, Ref. FRE/1 and FRE/3 – Sundry Naval Correspondence, Sir Fremantle 1765–1819 – Caird Library, National Maritime Museum.

19 Letter from W. Fremantle to T.F. Fremantle, dated 30 October 1811, Ref. FRE/1 and FRE/3 – Sundry Naval Correspondence, Sir Fremantle 1765–1819 – Caird Library, National Maritime Museum.

20 Letter from Adm. T.F. Fremantle to Sir William Fremantle, from Palermo, dated 11 September 1811, Ref. FRE/1 and FRE/3 – Sundry Naval Correspondence, Sir Fremantle 1765–1819 – Caird Library, National Maritime Museum.

21 Letter from Adm. T.F. Fremantle to Sir William Fremantle, from Palermo, dated 6 April 1812, Ref. FRE/1 and FRE/3 – Sundry Naval Correspondence, Sir Fremantle 1765–1819 – Caird Library, National Maritime Museum.

22 *Wynne Diaries Vol. III*, Fremantle (ed.), p.354.

23 Letter from Adm. T.F. Fremantle to Sir William Fremantle, from Palermo, dated 8 April 1812, Ref. FRE/1 and FRE/3 – Sundry Naval Correspondence, Sir Fremantle 1765–1819 – Caird Library, National Maritime Museum.

24 *Admirals Fremantle*, Parry, p.100.

25 Letter from Pellew to Fremantle 29 May 1812, D-FR 39/1, Centre for Buckinghamshire Studies.

26 Letter from Adm. T.F. Fremantle to Sir William Fremantle, from Palermo, dated 20 May 1812, Ref. FRE/1 and FRE/3 – Sundry Naval Correspondence, Sir Fremantle 1765–1819 – Caird Library, National Maritime Museum.

27 D-FR transcripts of correspondence used by Ann Parry in writing *The Admirals Fremantle*, dated 1810–14, Centre for Buckinghamshire Studies.

28 *Ibid*.

29 *Ibid*.

30 *Ibid*.

31 *Ibid*.

32 *Wynne Diaries Vol. III*, Fremantle (ed.), p.370.

Chapter 10

1 *Wynne Diaries Vol. III*, Fremantle (ed.), p.372.

2 D-FR transcripts of correspondence used by Ann Parry in writing *The Admirals Fremantle*, dated 1810–14, Centre for Buckinghamshire Studies.

3 *Ibid*.

4 *Wynne Diaries Vol. III*, Fremantle (ed.), p.379.
5 *Admirals Fremantle*, Parry, p.131.
6 *Ibid.*
7 *Admirals Fremantle*, Parry, p.132.
8 *Admirals Fremantle*, Parry, p.134.
9 *Admirals Fremantle*, Parry, p.135.
10 *Wynne Diaries Vol. III*, Fremantle (ed.), p.392.

Chapter 11

1 Memoranda on discipline Vol. I, Ref. FRE/06, Caird Library, National Maritime Museum.
2 Memoranda on discipline Vol. I, Ref. FRE/07,Caird Library, National Maritime Museum.
3 Ref. RNM 500/88/57 Folio 153, Caird Library, National Maritime Museum.
4 *Admirals Fremantle*, Parry, p.139.
5 Lord Cottesloe's personal memories, as recorded by the author on 8 July 2015.
6 *Nelson, The Sword of Albion*, John Sugden, The Bodley Head Publishing Co., 2012, p.779.
7 'Letter from Nelson to Berry, dated 10 December 1798', *Dispatches and Letters Vol. III*, Harris Nicolas (ed.), p.192.
8 Letter from Fremantle to Nelson, dated 15 August 1805, Ref. CRK/6, Caird Library, National Maritime Museum.

BIBLIOGRAPHY

Adams, E.D. (1904). *The Influence of Grenville on Pitt's Foreign Policy 1787–1798.* Washington: Carnegie Institute of Washington.

Adkin, M. (2005). *The Trafalgar Companion.* London: Aurum Press.

Adkins, R. & Adkins, L. (2006). *The War for All the Oceans.* London: Little, Brown Book Group.

Adkins, R. (2004). *Trafalgar: The Biography of a Battle.* London: Little, Brown Book Group.

Allen, J. (1841). *Memoir of the Life and Services of Admiral Sir William Hargood.* Greenwich: Henry S. Richardson.

Allen, M. (1999). *Travellers' Tales.* London: Castlereagh Press.

Anonymous (1890). *Thrilling Narratives of Mutiny, Murder and Piracy.* New York: Hurst & Co.

Bennett, G. (2002). *Nelson the Commander.* London: Penguin Books.

Bew, J. (2011). *Castlereagh, Enlightenment, War and Tyranny.* London: Quercus.

Bradford, E. (1977). *Nelson: The Essential Hero.* London: Macmillan Ltd.

Brenton, E.P. (1838). *Life and Correspondence of John, Earl of St Vincent, G.C.B., Admiral of the Fleet, &c., &c. &c., vols I & II.* London: Henry Colburn.

Buckland, K. (1999). *The Miller Papers.* The 1805 Club.

Chandler, D. (1966). *The Campaigns of Napoleon.* London: Macmillan & Co.

Clayton, T.A. (2004). *Trafalgar: The Men, the Battle, the Storm.* London: Hodder and Stoughton.

Clowes, W.L. (1996). *The Royal Navy: A History from the Earliest Times to 1900* (Vol. 3). London: Chatham Publishing.

Clowes, W. L. (1997). *The Royal Navy: A History from the Earliest Times to 1900* (Vol. 4). London: Chatham Publishing.

Coleman, T. (2001). *Nelson: The Man and the Legend.* London: Bloomsbury.

Colson, B. (2011). *Napoleon on War.* Oxford: Oxford University Press.

Constantine, D. (2001). *Fields of Fire: A Life of Sir Wm. Hamilton.* London: Weidenfeld & Nicolson.

Corbett, J.S. (1907). *England in the Seven Years' War.* London: Longman, Green and Co.

Crane, D. (2009). *Men of War.* London: Harper Collins Publishing.

Davies, D. (1996). *Nelson's Navy: English Fighting Ships 1793–1815.* Mechanicsburg, USA: Stackpole Books.

Feldbaek, O. (2002). *The Battle of Copenhagen 1801.* Barnsley: Leo Cooper.

Fitchett, W.H. (2011). *Nelson and his Captains.* London: Paean Books.

Fraser, E. (2012). *The Enemy at Trafalgar.* London: Leonaur.

Fremantle, A. (1937). *The Wynne Diaries – Vol I–III* (1st ed. vol. 2, E. Fremantle ed.) London: Oxford University Press.

Fremantle, A.F. (1933). *Trafalgar.* Manchester: Peter Davies Ltd.

Fremantle, C.H. (1979). *Diary and Letters of Admiral Sir C. H. Fremantle G.C.B.* Fremantle: Fremantle Arts Centre Press.

Fremantle, D.R. (1983). *A Fremantle Chronicle.* London: Poets' and Painters' Press.

Fremantle, E.R. (1908). *The Navy as I have Known It.* London: Cassell & Co Ltd.

Fremantle, S.R. (1949). *My Naval Career.* London: Hutchinson.

Fremantle, T.F. (1782, Jan.). Miscellaneous papers. Admiralty: Service Records, Registers, Returns and Certificates. Commission and Warrant Book. Described at item level. Thomas Francis Fremantle, Lieutenant.

Fremont-Barnes, G. (2010). *Napoleon Bonaparte.* Oxford: Osprey Publishing.

Gardiner, R. (1999). *Warships of the Napoleonic Era* (Vol. 1). Barnsley: Seaforth Publishing.

Glover, G. (2012). *Wellington's Voice.* London: Frontline Books.

Guimera, P.A. (1999). *Nelson and Tenerife.* The 1805 Club.

Hague, W. (2004). *William Pitt the Younger.* London: Harper Collins Publishing.

Hague, W. (2007). *William Wilberforce: The Life of the Great Anti-slave Trade Campaigner.* London: Harper Collins.

Halloran (1905). 'In the Days of Trafalgar'. *English Illustrated Magazine Vol. 34,* pp.18–23.

Harland, J. (1984). *Seamanship in the Age of Sail 1600–1860.* Naval Institute Press.

Haythornthwaite, P.J. (1990). *The Napoleonic Source Book.* London: Guild Publishing.

Heathcote, T. (2005). *Nelson's Trafalgar Captains & their Battles.* Barnsley: Pen & Sword.

Hore, P. (2015). *Nelson's Band of Brothers.* Barnsley: Seaforth Publishing.

Howarth, D. (1969). *Trafalgar: The Nelson Touch.* London: World Books.

James, M.W. (2002). *The Naval History of Great Britain Vols I–VI.* London: Conway Maritime Press.

Jupp, P. (1985). *Lord Grenville 1759–1834.* Oxford: Oxford University Press.

Knight, R. (2013). *Britain against Napoleon: The Organisation of Victory.* London: Allen Lane Publishing.

Knight, R. (2005). *The Pursuit of Victory: The Life and Achievement of Horatio Nelson.* London: Penguin Books.

Konstam, A. (2011). *Horatio Nelson: Leadership, Strategy and Conflict.* Oxford: Osprey Publishing.

Lambert, A. (2004). *Nelson: Britannia's God of War.* London: Faber & Faber.

Lavery, B. (1989). *Nelson's Navy 1793–1815* (12th ed., vol. 1). London: Conway Press.

Lee, C. (2005). *Nelson and Napoleon.* London: Headline Book Publishing.

Lefebvre, G. (2009). *Napoleon.* London: The Folio Press.

Lefebvre, G. (1930). *The French Revolution.* Paris: Presses Universitaires de France.

Lewis-Jones, H. (2013). *Trafalgar Chronicle 2013.* London: The 1805 Club.

Lovell, W.S. (2003). *From Trafalgar to Chesapeake*. Annapolis, Maryland USA: Naval Institute Press.

Lovell, W.S. (1879). *Personal Narrative of Events from 1799–1815*. London: Wm Allen & Co.

Millard, C. (1895, June). 'The Narrative of Midshipman William Salter of HMS *Monarch*'. *Macmillan Magazine*, pp.80–93.

Nicolas, Sir Nicholas Harris (ed.) (1845). *The Dispatches and Letters of Lord Nelson Vols I–VII*. London: Henry Colburn.

Nicolson, A. (2006). *Men of Honour: The Making of the English Hero*. London: Harper Collins Publishing.

Parry, A. (1971). *The Admirals Fremantle 1788–1920*. London: Chatto & Windus.

Pearce, E. (2010). *Pitt the Elder*. London: Bodley Head.

Pocock, T. (1987). *Horatio Nelson*. London: Cassell Publishers.

Pope, D. (1959). *England Expects*. London: Weidenfeld & Nicolson.

Pope, D. (1981). *Life in Nelson's Navy*. London: Chatham Publishing.

Pope, D. (1972). *The Great Gamble: Nelson at Copenhagen*. London: Weidenfeld & Nicolson.

Roberts, A. (2014). *Napoleon the Great* (1st ed., vol. 1). London: Allen Lane, an imprint of Penguin Books.

Robinson, W. (1836). *Jack Nastyface*. New York: Naval Institute Press.

Rodger, N. (2004). *The Command of the Ocean*. London: Allen Lane.

Rose, J.H. (1922). *Lord Hood and the Defence of Toulon*. London: Cambridge University Press.

Schama, S. (2005). *Rough Crossings: Britain, the Slaves and the American Revolution*. London: BBC Books.

Schom, A. (1990). *Trafalgar: Countdown to Battle 1803–1805*. London: Michael Joseph Ltd.

Southey, R. (1813). *The life of Nelson*. London: Frederick Warne & Co.

Spilsbury, F. (1807). *Account of a Voyage to the Western Coast of Africa; Performed by His Majesty's Sloop Favourite, in the Year 1805*. London: Richard Phillips.

Starkey, D. (2006). *Monarchy*. London: Harper Press.

Sugden, J. (2004). *Nelson: A Dream of Glory* (vol. 1). London: Jonathon Cape.

Sugden, J. (2012). *Nelson: The Sword of Albion* (1st ed., vol. 2, W. Sulkin ed.) London: The Bodley Head.

Taylor, S. (2012). *Commander*. London: Faber & Faber.

Tracy, N. (1996). *Nelson's Battles: The Triumph of British Seapower*. Barnsley: Seaforth Publishing.

Tracy, N. (2003). *The Battle of Copenhagen 2 April 1801*. Nottingham: The 1805 Club.

Tracy, N. (2006). *Who's Who in Nelson's Navy*. London: Chatham Publishing.

Vincent, E. (2003). *Nelson: Love and Fame*. New Haven: Yale University Press.

Warner, O. (1987). *A Portrait of Lord Nelson*. London: Penguin Books.

Warner, O. (1966). *Trafalgar*. London: Macmillan.

Warwick, P. (2005). *Voices from the Battle of Trafalgar*. Cincinnati, Ohio, USA: David and Charles.

Wetherell, J. (2008). *Wetherell of HMS Hussar*. London: Leonaur.

White, C. (2005). *The Trafagar Captains: Their Lives and Memorials*. London: Chatham Publishing.

White, C. (2005). *Nelson: The Admiral*. Stroud: Sutton Publishing.

White, C. (1998). *Nelson's Year of Destiny 1797*. Oxford: Oxford University Press.

White, C. (2002). *The Nelson Encyclopaedia*. London: Chatham Publishing.

Wilson, B. (2013). *Empire of the Deep: The Rise and Fall of the British Navy*. London: Weidenfeld & Nicolson.

Winfield, R. (2005). *British Warships in the Age of Sail 1793–1817*. London: Seaforth Publishing.

Woodman, R. (2009). *Britannia's Realm: A History of the British Merchant Navy Vol II*. Stroud: The History Press.

Woodman, R. (2001). *The Sea Warriors Fighting Captains and Frigate Warfare in the Age of Nelson*. Barnsley: Seaforth Publishing.

Wynne, E. (1937). *The Wynne Diaries Vol. II 1794–1798*. London: Oxford University Press.

Wynne, E. (1940). *The Wynne Diaries Vol. III 1798–1820*. Oxford: Oxford University Press.

INDEX

Index